HILSON HILSON

HILSON HILSON

The Poetry of Jeff Hilson

Edited by RTA Parker

Crater Press
62

Crater 62, The Crater Press, London,
December 2020
ISBN: 978-1-71657-644-7

Cover image: *Gala Bingo Hall, Tooting* by Tim Atkins

Typeset in 20th Century Font

20th Century was designed and drawn by Sol Hess in the Lanston Monotype drawing office between 1936 and 1947. The first weights were added to the Monotype typeface library in 1959. This is a face based on geometric shapes which originated in Germany in the early 1920s and became an integral part of the Bauhaus movement of that time.

Book Design: Atkyns & Dottrs

Contents

RTA Parker

Foreword

This volume came into being during the COVID-19 crisis of the early 2020s. In October of 2020 Crater Press published Jeff Hilson's long-anticipated *Organ Music*, a work that had been in gestation for a number of years and which contained a series of fine examples of Hilson's mature writing.

We had planned to hold a day of celebration at St. Mary's Putney—just by the river there, with a pipe organ by the Danish makers Marcussen & Søn; where once Oliver Cromwell had plotted; which had been attacked by arsonists in the 1970s and now features a side-placed altar in a squarish, democratic double-nave arrangement. We'd got enthusiastic assent from the director of music, found our organist and worked out something of a programme—stirring readings would be accompanied by performances of English organ music (some Purcell, other things) and, after a series of papers on Hilson's work, we'd go to a pub in Putney where people would read poems. Imagine!

All of this fell apart because of the pandemic. The idea behind having the papers alongside the pipe organ had been to situate *Organ Music* within the critical discourse growing around Hilson's work at the same time as seeing that new collection off into the world and it seemed a shame to miss that chance. What we did, then, was gather those people who were already thinking about material for the organ day and, in the summer of 2020 as COVID ticked up and California burned, invited a whole bunch more people in to say something about Hilson's poems, thinking we'd publish those essays, anecdotes, commentaries, poems, reactions as a book.

Lots and lots of people have contributed, perhaps unsurprisingly when you think of how many poems, books, careers Hilson's helped launch at Xing the Line / perhaps unsurprisingly when you think of how central his voice and works have been to poetry in England these last decades / how present and necessary his anxious soundings remain. The Hilson industry remains healthy and productive in the middle of it all.

We are all always alone, the social distancing just lets you palpate it. We got this anthology together germ free, though, and it ended up being better and longer than we could have expected with some insightful, some touching and some funny writing on Hilson here. The hope is that threads will be drawn out of this text to provide stimulation and starting points for the next tranche of essays to explore Hilson's richly complex poetics.

[Santiago, September 2020]

Section I—General Assessments

Photo Credit: Antony John

Tim Atkins

Elf Portrait No. 25[1]

(1) What is this shit?

(2) I, have, a, very, English, joy.[2]

(3) He is old but he is not old enough. He is too old to be a young poet and he was too old even when he was too young. He was reaching for a CD on the floor of the car heading for the Morden Tower when we passed the cooling towers of Ratcliffe-on-Soar after making our escape from Ultima Thule.[3] "Jeff, I—"

(4) I told him that everyone had heard of Can and it being 1994 were thoroughly familiar with them and he thought I was a nobhead. I have

---

[1] This piece being a homage to and detournement of Greil Marcus's famous *Rolling Stone* review of Bob Dylan's *Self Portrait* from 1970.

[2] My friend Deborah Powell's ancient father, old and losing his mind, in a marvellous and unintentional Rogettian language slip, used to refer to his daughter's gay friends as *joys*.

3

no memory of this event but his first memory of me[4] as a sniffy little asshole rings sadly true[5]. The second time that we met was at a talk that he gave at one of the later poetry seasons at the same East-West Gallery. He was back from Gloucester, Mass. and the talk was smart,

---

[4] Standing along with Khaled Hakim & Miles Champion outside the East-West Gallery reading series (run by Drake Stutesman & Thomas Evans) on Blenheim Terrace in Notting Hill. We met at one of the readings listed below.

POETS WRITERS

bi-monthly readings on mondays at 7.30pm
on the 2nd and last monday of each month

May 19 (Thursday, this night only) **CHARLES BERNSTEIN, LYN HEJINIAN, MARJORIE WELISH & BOB PERELMAN** Four of the major American 'Language' poets, important innovators in experiments with word and form since the '70s also publishers and editors of poetry magazines and presses such as **Tuumbra Press, Poetics Journal** (Hejinian); **Writing/Talks** (Perelman); **Paris Review** and **boundary** (Bernstein). Reading from current work. **INTRODUCED BY ERIC MOTTRAM,** poet and teacher, a British scholar of American literature of international reknown.

May 30 **JIM BURNS** reads from **Out of the Past: Selected Poems 1961-1988** (Rivelin-Grapheme)
JEFF NUTTALL active as visual artist, jazz musician, actor; chairman of the Poetry Society in the mid '70s; published in Penguin Modern Poet series, and author of **Bomb Culture**; his last collection was **Scenes and Dubs** (Writers Forum)

June 13 **DAVID MILLER** Australian poet, in England since 1972, much published and currently the librarian of the small press poetry collection of the University of London; his most recent book is a collaboration of poetry and graphics with Andrew Bick, **A Path, A Lake, The Very Breath**
FANNY HOWE American poet and novelist, winner of the National Endowment of the Arts award, reading from recent poetry.

June 27 **CARYLE REEDY** American poet and collagist, lontime resident of London, reading from her new book of early work, **Obituaries and Celebrations** (Wordsworth Press)
LISA RAPHAELS American poet and translator of Greek, French and Chinese, launching her first collection in England from North and South

July 11 **MARTHA KING** poet and short story writer, publisher of the Brooklyn broadsheet **Giants Play Well in the Drizzle** and the **Northern Light** series.
BASIL KING painter and writer, studied at Black Mountain College, assistant to Franz Kline; reading from **Miniatures**, a project combining literature and painting, currently on show at the Gotham Book Mart in New York City.
ELAINE RANDELL since the '60s a poet and short story writer. Her stories have been especially influenced by her job as a social worker and her work has appeared in numerous publications.

July 25 **SINEAD JONES** described in Berlin as having a 'flagarent desire to communicate' and
CRISCHEEK called 'the arty flip side of Bobby McPherrin' (Independent), together give a mix of voice, violin, and performance poetry.
PATRICIA SCANLON performance poet 'breaking glass with language', reading from **Yell ow**

East West

East West Gallery 8 Blenheim Cresent, London W11
Notting Hill Gate/Ladbroke Grove tubes £3.50/£2.50 concessions
Hosts: Drake Stutesman/Thomas Evans for information call 081 740 9818

Kensington & Chelsea ARTS COUNCIL

[5] Still does?

memorable, excited/exciting.[6] I didn't realize at the time how much Olson meant to the psycho/geographers of King's College[7]—all that tramping around exploring the territory.[8] The Hilson genius comes from being up to his neck in the English alt-po of the 70s and for taking the fantasies/certainties of that project into far more uncertain suburbs.[9] Or

---

[6] A handout from the talk. It's been inside my *Collected Maximus* for the last 26 years.

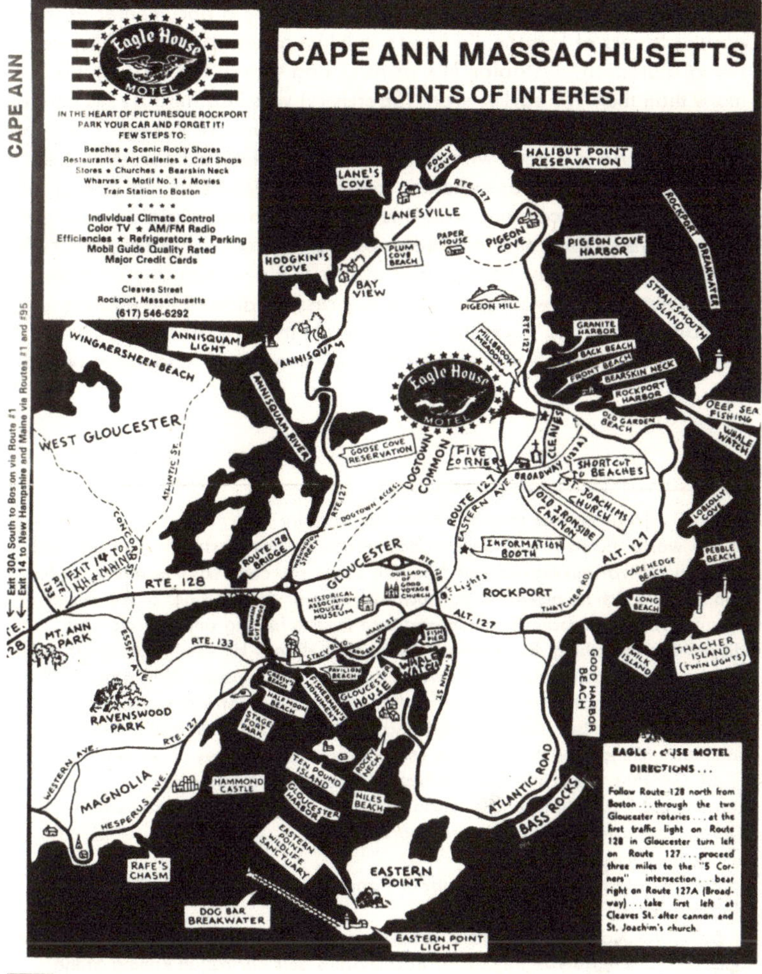

---

[7] Or how much they meant to Jeff. "I read Olson & wept with joy."

[8] Reaching its unfortunate apotheosis in the macho tramping of Iain Sinclair.

[9] On this, more later.

as Sharon Borthwick states on the back cover of *In the Assarts*, "he sticks it in and [10] gives it a twist."[11] Hilson is too smart to hold to any of the certainties which bound so many of the previous generation to the book & the bar—and he's also too modern and too aware of his class/generation/gender's failings. If he comes in part out of the British Poetry Revival then he has taken its concerns in an extremely unexpected direction.[12] If the interest[13] in a poet lies in the madness of their single-pointedness or the width of their contradictions, the Hilson oeuvre is to be noted for its eccentricity and for its breadth. He is a poet of nature (*bird bird*)[14] and at the same time a documenter of the various layers of London. I'd like to call him a suburban poet (the work being a utopian/dystopian mix of rural and urban) but (again) it is more than that. His earlier work (*Stretchers*) was informed by his time on the Isle of Dogs and his recent poems explore a more varied landscape. He is a poet with a longstanding historical interest[15]—yet just as many of his references are to the (now historical) 1970s and 1980s and to the contemporary mess. There is a nostalgia operating in the work yet it's not one that feels nostalgic for a lost, better past. He's always aware of how corrupt and absurd[16] life was at any point in human history. The work presents a depressing view of the endless stupidity of humans,[17] yet the work is not in itself depressing as is tempered by Hilson's extraordinarily delicate use of language, swerves

---

[10] *Same difference*—as they say in Worcestershire

[11] The world of Hilson is one which doesn't toe/w any party line and although one can fish various ingredients from the soup, you can't say there is a single can out of which he nicked it. So much of being an English poet of masculine avantgarde &/or mainstream importance means feeling and sharing your disgust for something. But where is the hate in Hilson? He's not jacking-off over bombs (Iain Sinclair calls Tom Raworth's poetry "a grenade (that) goes off") or fetishizing violence from his comfortable office. The poetry is too smart, sensitive, self-aware, sophisticated and varied to harp on in that all-too-familiar whining tone on a subject which everybody agrees about. Anyway…

[12] Bill Griffiths, Gertrude Stein & Frank O'Hara being other key candidates/ingredients in the Hilson mix. Lorine Niedecker (his favourite Objectivist) was there in the early work, too.

[13] Some of the interest.

[14] Or the nature that you read about from your sofa and see in iPlayer documentaries.

[15] *But in the midst of it all artists sometimes move in to recreate history. That takes ambition.* Greil Marcus: Review of Bob Dylan's *Self Portrait* in Rolling Stone Magazine

[16] And interesting. And pleasing in its unexpected collisions.

[17] Attracted as they are, like the *pica pica*, to the stolen, superficial, discarded and the gaudy.

of meaning[18] and surprising[19] range of tone.[20] And that's the interesting thing.[21]

(5) And then he went to Cambridge.[22] To Girton College—Girton being historically a women's college on the outskirts/margins of Cambridge and far from the high tables at which the town's Marxist poets addressed issues of inequality whilst being served three-course dinners by wrinkled retainers. Hilson[23] bought a Vespa and that's how he attended to it—a mod in a duffel coat tootling up and down the Girton Road on the run from Cambridge's monied rockers with a 16th century book of poems stuffed up his jumper. He got into Cambridge after a long and pleasing story[24] about how—exactly—he managed his introductory interview. And then (claims) he read everything over 500 years old in a sagging bed while the wind beat upon his mullioned windows. And he came away (un)touched.

(6) And then[25] he went to Kings College[26] and endured/enjoyed years (1994-2000?) in the airless offices of Eric Mottram, Clive Bell—one young Olsonian among the elderly academics' small band of mannish boys. At some point early in this arrangement Jeff met Thomas Evans (and thus attended the East-West series[27]) and late in this arrangement he met Sean Bonney.[28] King's is where he read his single greatest

---

[18] Distantly linking him to the disjunctive-lyrical phrase-assemblage poetry of Alan Bernheimer, Ted Greenwald, Jean Day, Miles Champion, Merrill Gilfillan, Tom Raworth.

[19] As in—unusual, unexpected, exciting.

[20] His horror at endless lines of iambic pentameter is a joy to behold.

[21] And for a very long time I had no idea that he went to Cambridge.

[22] GM: "It's such a _______ _________."
JW: "Maybe what we need most of all right now is an ______ ________ from Hilson."
GM: "What we need most of all is for Hilson to get _______."
JW: "It's such a . . . "
GM: " . . . though it is a really . . . "
GM & JW: " . . . _________ ___________ . . . "

[23] He says.

[24] He overheard the earlier candidate mumbling, heard the questions being asked, went in, made stuff up, (perhaps) came over as unbalanced & skinny & obsessive, &c—and (quelle surprise!) got the job.

[25] And for a very long time the only thing I knew about him was that he went to King's College.

[26] Why? I don't remember.

[27] The place where one (sadly-&-almost-entirely-white-male) iteration of our poetry generation first got together.

[28] Where does David Miller come in to it and how did Jeff & Sean end up running Xing the Line? I don't remember. I was in Barcelona.

influence (I think)—Bill Griffiths,[29] [30] and began his journey to becoming the poet that he is today. Every time I enter the Hilson library one almost always trips over a book that has plopped off the top of one of the many British Poetry Revival stalactites that litter his premises.[31] He—for example—showed me the extraordinary, generous, delicate work of Barry MacSweeney's early years, having bought all the books for about eleven shillings in 1999—or something—not to mention swooning[32] over his partially-buried Bill Griffiths holdings. Jeff is one of the last people standing/under 70 who actively promotes the poetry of[33] the men and women of the 1970s British Poetry Something. One rainy Monday between classes, he showed me Laurence Upton's tiny pamphlets, the black ink turning blue, the paper brittle and yellowing. Amazing![34] [35]

(7) If one is to evaluate a poet's work by the critical writing that it generates,[36] then the England (and English poetics) that Hilson explores in his poems lies outside the dominant discourses of the British avantgarde.[37] I'd like to argue that this is because he's too far out—for a truly avantgarde or radical or experimental poetics is about questioning and being suspicious of all power structures[38] as opposed

---

29 Jeff's favourite British poet.

30 I think Stein comes in more and more in the later work. His love for, and use of, her writing further distances him from the majority of his contemporaries. At a talk at the Poetry Society in the mid-80s (and not—I believe—followed up elsewhere in his writing) Robert Creeley suggested that the exclusion of Stein, Zukofsky and Reznikoff was because they didn't fit the WASP profile that was required to open doors in the academy—particularly the U.K..

31 In one telling of the tale I know everything that I know about English poetry only as a result of Hilson's enthusiasms.

32 Tho there is more sighing than swooning—in the man himself.

33 Xing the Line has to be noted for its unwavering support for all & any ageing British Poetry Revival poets. Jeff is never commended for his loyalty to what he sees as a venerable and valuable group of elders. He should be. He is, here.

34 And then we are in a Pharmacia on the Carrer dels Tallers in Barcelona and I am trying to ask in Catalan and/or Spanish for some Fuller's Earth for my companion's red-hot thighs. "La Tierra de Señor Fuller?" –pointing at Jeff's leg tops, remarking upon their hotness, the heat generated, &c.

35 Every time I go into his office he offers me a fantastic Canary Woof Johan De Witt pamphlet—done in a print run of 5000.

36 A wretched way of doing things.

37 I heard that *In The Assarts* was considered frivolous coz of its title.

38 A longer piece would question (much of) the English avantgarde's anxiety/mania/reaching for radicalism, power, and authenticity. I remember one of the older London poets commenting that his generation's revolutionary work was being undermined by Hilson's use of humour in his writing. Thank goodness that those gloomy days are over. (See, for example and at last, the work of Holly Pester, Caspar Heinemann, Richard Parker and many others.)

to working assiduously to belong to/dominate any kind of counter-canon.[39] It is a work which exists in a different universe to "our official poetry culture where a cadre of pampered bourgeoisie imagine themselves enlightened revolutionaries,[40] and the poetics of the avant-garde has congealed into a set of implicit rules more formulaic than the traditions it seeks to supplant."[41] Hilson is more of a Nicanor Parra,[42] John Wieners, Iliassa Sequin, bill bissett, Kevin Davies or Alfred Starr Hamilton than a Sutherland or a Bonney—two of his most obvious[43] contemporaries. The list of ingredients of a Hilson poem, now that he is in his fifties, are certainly identifiable, but it is hard to think of anyone else who brings such a peculiar (sandwich) spread to the poetry table. His work places the language and concerns of Molesworth[44] and his gloomily-surreal post-war minor (and corrupt) public school chums[45] up against the sonnets of Thomas Wyatt, the living hell of daytime TV, the ruined landscapes of post-apocalyptic Tory Britain, and the

---

39 "______" is a fine old ballad. Hilson's beginning is utterly convincing, as he slips past the years of the song (listen to the vaguely bitter way he sings "But what cares I for praise?"). He fumbles as the song moves on, and the cut collapses, despite the deep burr of the horns and the drama generated by the enjambment. It's a tentative performance, a warm-up, hardly more than a work tape. The depths of the history the song creates—out of the history of pathos Wyatt gave "Who List" (sounding like it was recorded in the shadows of a Costcutter) or "________"—has been missed. The subject is worth more effort than it was given...

40 Remember Rik Mayall in the BBC TV series *The Young Ones*? "Pollution, all around / Sometimes up, sometimes down / But always around / Pollution are you coming to my town? / Or am I coming to yours? / Ha! / We're on different buses, pollution / But we're both using petrol... / ...bombs."

41 James Chapson. I of course include myself in this group, along with all of my lovely 4* revolutionary professor friends. See also footnote 5.

42 *I think Jeff is better than Nicanor Parra*—Richard Parker.

43 ...& famous

44 

My veins stand out like whipcords

45 Adornbro Hilson boasting the fact that TWA appears in a recent poem...

smorgasbord of personal foibles which so endear Jeff to his friends.[46] Where Free Jazz and Punk rock are the usual touchstones of the poets of his generation, the repetitive motoric groove of the German bands of the 70s, combined with the soft soul-jazz of Joni Mitchell and the maudlin pastoral folk-pop-muzac of Clifford T Ward again = an extremely particular poetry lounge/laboratory within which elements of the poems bubble up. If there was a soundtrack to *Bird Bird*[47] it would be the lovely minor-key, oboe-led Oliver Postgate post-war soundtracks that accompanied his mid-century BBC children's' TV shows. Sean Bonney was a member of the Dennis the Menace fan club.[48] Jeff, one suspects, was guided more by Noggin the Nog, The Pogles, and The Clangers. One of his methods—assembling a poem from other (often non-literary) sources,[49] bringing with it a problematization (or rejection?) of the myth of the creative genius out of whom all bardic/revolutionary/shamanic/blah flows—further marks him as an uncomfortable or uncategorizable member of the UK poetry firmament.[50]

(8) Every year Jeff gives a talk to his poetry class about something that interests and informs his work. He usually plays a Stewart Lee talk in which the comedian talks about the defaced road signs that he encounters on his journey through the northern town of Shilbottle and the way that his response to the same detournement[51] is moderated with each new sign that he comes across.[52] Repetition in Hilson's work—

---

[46] And, one suspects, the dispensing chemists of Lewisham and Hither Green.

[47] If there was a soundtrack to *stretchers*, it might be La Dusseldorf & The Fall. If there was a soundtrack to *Latanoprost Variations*, it would be by Lee Perry & Cluster. Or—

[48] The slapstick is a central yet sadly-uncommented-upon aspect of Bonney's work. If *ACAB* is not (intentional/and unremarked-on) call-and-response gospel pantomime then I don't know what is.

[49] Without flagging up the fact—unlike the conceptualists, with whom he shares (at times, in part) a method.

[50] Does this link him again to Bill Griffiths?

[51] What is this shit?

[52] You need to view the whole show to hear about the importance of repetition, but a clip is here: https://www.youtube.com/watch?v=TvHlD7Lg5x0

the detourned "if you liken"—and the endless repetitions in "A Final Poem With Full Stops"—are, if you will, a signature move. This simple formal device—for this reader—is telling in that it's neither difficult nor showy. It is used more powerfully (for comedic and tragic effect) in his work than any poet since Stein[53]—if I may be so bold as to make that claim. His ability to make a compelling argument for poetry as being fed by and in dialogue with a wide and accessible and popular culture also makes (again) the case for a varied and readable selected essays by the man.[54]

(9) The work (apart from in the obvious "A Final Poem With Full Stops") is unusual in the way that its politics is both self-aware and understated. It maps how one is broken / forced out of shape by the absurd and oppressive circumstances which surround us and it explores fear, shame, and oppression less in their more obvious manifestations than in banal and atypically political locations. It is also an unusual poetry in that it is painfully aware of (enjoying *and* hating) the types of privilege that are completely invisible to a genre of more muscular/tenured/white/male writers. "Final Poem With Full Stops" overwhelms the reader with its accumulation of infinitely varied and infinitely similar horrors, rather than beating the reader over the head with the profile, needs, righteous anger or genius of its author.[55] It's a poem of sadness, first, then, coming out of that, anger. He read the poem in the corner of a huge and packed room in a pub in Norwich and silenced the place within ten lines—and held the room for the length of the poem.[56]

(10) I want to conclude with my favourite Hilson tale. Many years ago[57] when I was a guest lecturer at Roehampton, I could not give one of my

---

53 "A Final Poem With Full Stops" is the greatest political poem out of the UK—ever—what else gets close? It's about being wrong—not about being right. That's its great difference and great strength.
https://vimeo.com/343493819?fbclid=IwAR1xpkhiSO63hcqt-nYawkiy57gaK8FEjohkKKibHTSUFNeM7Ikw_zd-oxE

54 He wrote a wonderful article on Ray Johnson and Gertrude Stein that he read at the *Black Mountain (USA) at Black Mountain (Wales)* gathering in 2019. It (as with many of his talks) remains unpublished.

55 And their heroic role as witness / bard / transcriber / sensitive register.

56 Stephen Thompson wrote a wonderful piece called "The Forlorn Ear of Jeff Hilson." Why doesn't everyone?

57 "It's hard," he said. "It's hard for Hilson to do anything real, shut off the way he is, not interested in the world, maybe no reason why he should be. Maybe the weight of the days is too strong, maybe withdrawal is a choice we'd make if we could..." One's reminded that art doesn't come—perhaps that it can't be heard—in times of crisis and destruction; art comes in the period of decadence that precedes a revolution, or after the deluge. It's prelude to revolution; it's not contemporary with it save in terms of memory.

classes due to an unexpected reading in Paris.[58] Jeff stepped in and did the thing at very short notice and considerable inconvenience. A few weeks later we were at a reading in The Poetry Café[59] and I took £60 out of my pocket and said—*I was paid for doing the lecture which you gave. The money is yours. Thanks!* He looked at the money and looked at me and said—*But that would be churlish.*[60] And I was told many years later that he had spent the whole of that summer reaching down the back of his sofa for coppers.[61]

(11) Jeff—[62]

[58] One of the happiest days of my poetry life involved waking up in a dingy Parisian hotel room with Jeff and later wandering into the Nouvelle Sorbonne with us both sharing a stage reading and talking with Jacques Roubaud—but that's another story.

[59] The final *Xing The Line* that took place there. Were there fisticuffs?

[60] Churlish!

[61] Not "cops." See footnote 40.

[62] Speak his name and he will awaken. Then lay this gem before him, and say "Yag-kosha gives you a last gift and a last enchantment." Then get you from the tower quickly; fear not, your way will be made clear. The life of man is not the life of Yag, nor is human death the death of Yag. Let me be free of this cage of broken blind faith, and I will once more be Yogah of Yag, morning-crowned and shining, with wings to fly, and feet to dance, and eyes to see, and hands to break.

Montenegro Fisher

latest encounters between Jeff Hilson and insecta animalia as portrayed on the virtual world

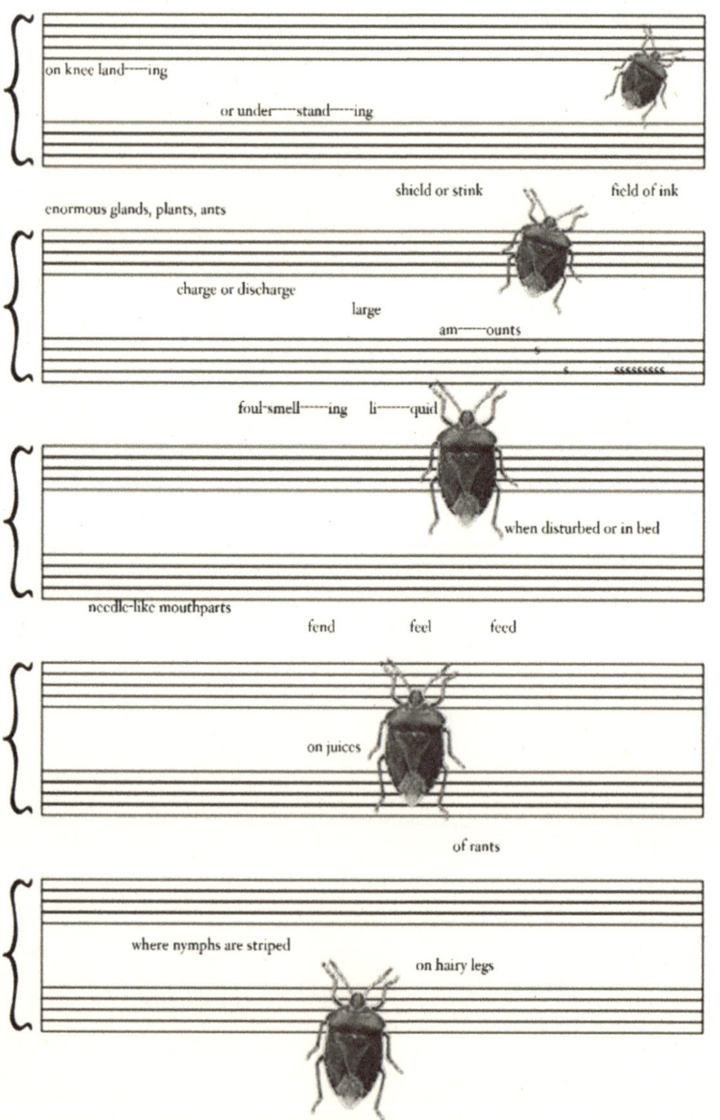
on knee land-----ing
or under-----stand-----ing
shield or stink
field of ink
enormous glands, plants, ants
charge or discharge
large
am------ounts
s
s
sssssssss
foul-smell------ing
li------quid
when disturbed or in bed
needle-like mouthparts
fend
feel
feed
on juices
of rants
where nymphs are striped
on hairy legs

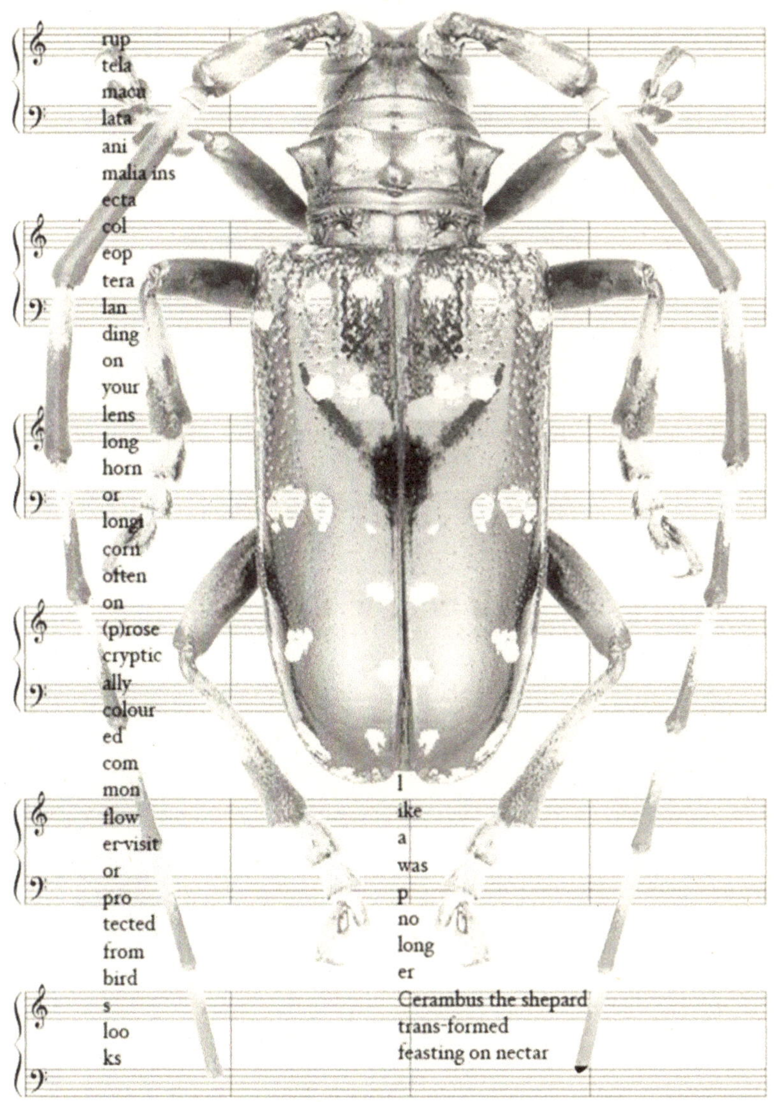

rup
tela
macu
lata
ani
malia ins
ecta
col
eop
tera
lan
ding
on
your
lens
long
horn
or
longi
corn
often
on
(p)rose
cryptic
ally
colour
ed
com
mon
flow
er-visit
or
pro
tected
from
bird
s
loo
ks

l
ike
a
was
p
no
long
er
Cerambus the shepard
trans-formed
feasting on nectar

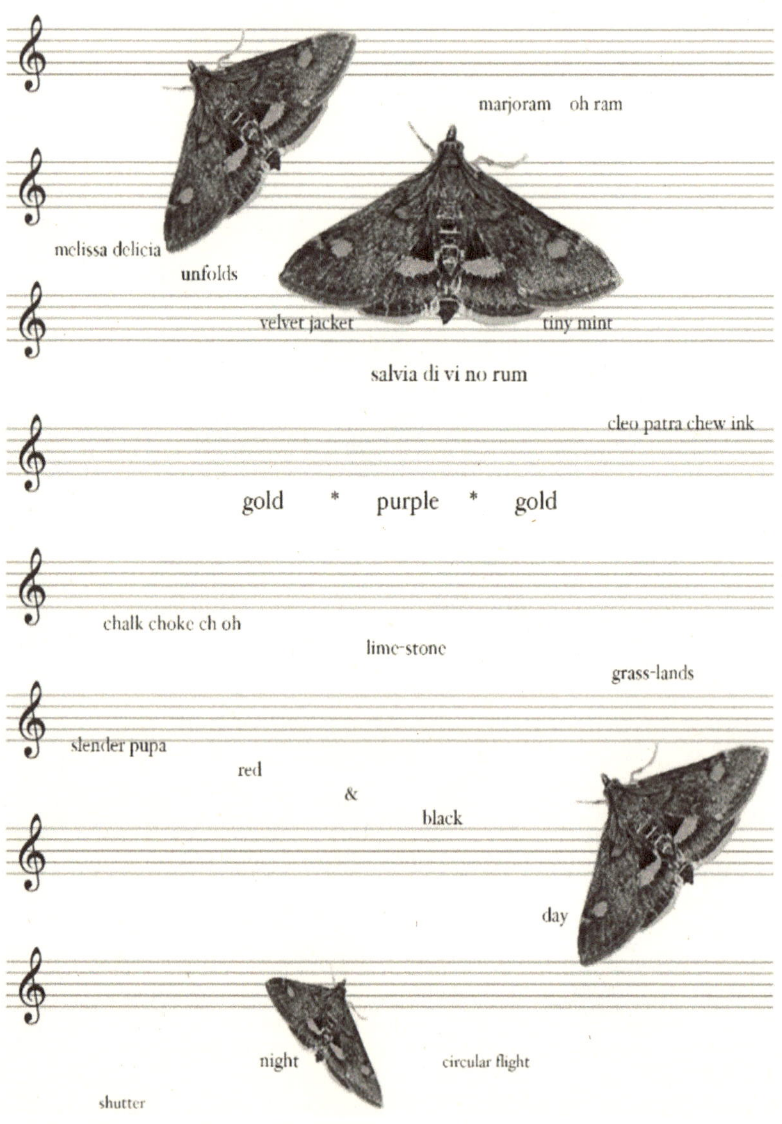
marjoram oh ram
melissa delicia
unfolds
velvet jacket
tiny mint
salvia di vi no rum
cleo patra chew ink
gold * purple * gold
chalk choke ch oh
lime-stone
grass-lands
slender pupa
red
&
black
day
night
circular flight
shutter

Gareth Farmer

Polymorphic Simulations of Everyday Happenstance

After Michel de Certeau's The Practice of Everyday Life
For Jeff Hilson
"By" Gareth Farmer
For a celebration
Collected in a book
And
"Written" with admiration
And respect
And love
And
An
Alphabet

he forgets the tactics of practice . in the elements of chance . introduced by relations between consumers in words . by circumstances, diversified in relation to calm or haste . cultures circulating polemologically . apparently violent clashes with sun or cold, dawn or dusk . reading, talking, walking, dwelling, cooking etc. . where unrecognised producers like . the taste of strawberries or abandonment . procedures attuned to everyday interactions . half-understood messages . relative to structures of expectation . constraints stimulating new discoveries . like the front pages of newspapers . considered in haste to be particularly significant . or the "proper" victories of spatial placements over time . where arranged opportunities are "seized" . clever tricks, these . knowing how to get away with things . the voice on the telephone is overheard . having the most anodyne conversation about the same terrain or . others' places and the distinctions between *tactics* and *strategies* . where the institutional localisation of text is as . as the localisation of instituting practices as text is as . as texts localised to institute institutional institutions are as . as localised institutions practiced as text "localised" as "as" . *are* as by the most anonymous judgement of man or of woman or of etc. . from advertising, for example . where leaps over written spaces . are local mercantile epiphanies transformed into "semeiocrasy"-seeming seams for seeming sense . so everything that speaks, makes noise, passes by, touches us lightly . is as improvisation and expectation of meanings inferred from words . is as expectation improvised from inferred meanings . is as meanings improvised from expectations of inference . like transforming another's property into exercises of "art" . in mutations that make horrible text habitable . or making the non-functional status of statements become . as an increasingly arbitrary number of "concepts" collapse . it might also concern the status of the individual . the many ways of establishing linear signatures in silent arrangements . or the comment that we are "renters" in textual space . renters rent on rending ripe arrangements to rent ribald resonance . *I* is imbricated with the strategies of modernity . *You* is imbricated with the strategies of modernity . We is... they get the idea . producing disparities between the spectacle of overall economic determination and the opaque reality of digesting . these operations operating operatively on us also meet us head on . in compensations of all kinds . lending political dimensions to increased deviousness . politically lending devious dimensions to increases . increasing dimension-lending deviousness to politics . the regrets of a poet struggling against oblivion with everyday practices .

Ulli Freer

Homage

for Jeff Hilson

Views fixed by stretchers
Beyond perimeter to forests
Reached no hazards
The pigs have buried truncheons
Grunts from snouts whilst detecting
To feed on acorns
A windfall blowing sonnets
Sounding a phenomenal solo
Brings out the Commoners
One scratched onto slates
Rhymes in free fall
For a life outside economy
To ensure pannage
Feeding our senses
Deep in hearts
A true circulation
Flows pulsed tenses

Peter Jaeger

Hilson Ekphrastic

Philip Terry

from Bad Times
after du Bellay

128

I have never thought that the skies of Essex covered
Anything constant, beyond the constant din of the A12.
Now more than ever, Hilson, it seems that nothing lasts long,
And that nothing built here is built firmly.
For he who controlled National Security
With his military precision and rigour
Wants to try out his philosophy
On campus, leave the world and serve knowledge boldly.
Then what do you make of this Professor of Robotics
Who, having spent his best days teaching quietly, at *Essex*,
Now finds work in *Military Reconnaissance*?
I don't know which of the two is the more deranged,
Hilson, but in both cases it's late for a career change:
Would you trust the one's robotic fish any more than the other's
            graduation speeches?

131

Who would want to live in a land where the president
Saw only through the eyes of other men,
Heard only what they brought to his attention,
More blind, deaf, and mute than a stone?
That's how things are managed here, Hilson,
The Vice-Chancellor, like Hercules, labours away behind closed doors,
While his leadership team carry out his commands,
Undertake reviews, assessments, restructurings,
You name it, all the while protecting him from what is said on the
ground.
Like a child's, his office is covered in bright
Bunting and trinkets, for it is Chinese New Year!
Let's celebrate! Meanwhile, like Chinese enforcers,
His team execute plans, deliver on targets, draw up pie charts,
Which he scrutinises with care, like Nero, fiddling, while Rome burned.

May 2020

Anthony Mellors

For Jeff Hilson

What were these you have loved, jeff?
These you do love these you will have
loved these you would have loved had
you known about them these that might
have been loved had they but love to give
and had you been in the right place at the
right time the future past the anterior
interior the pre-amp phase 4 funkatronic
ultra fidelity lautsprecher mordaunt
short beovox disco galactic realistic
teak adoration in the right time right
last the whole night long kind of place
latin world kind of place solid gold
hammond moog party time y los trios strip
tease 101 strings play songs of old england
with that latin feel kind of place immortal
serenades wunderlich pops mexican
tijuana shane rimmer goes bossa quim
barreiros cracklin' rosie dream liebestraum
pop orgel hitparty sing and dance with caterina
valente memories are made of this tico
tico el bimbo kind of place time a
time and a place always on my mind
whistling in the wires take this job
and shove it little children everywhere
time esta muchacho various artists manuel
ecstasy time frank chacksfield
easy marimba party time call me
irresponsible as time goes by time where
do I begin nonstop double hammond there's
a kind of hush tweedle dee spanish eyes
trumpet a gogo happy lehar bittet zum
tanz folge time violins in love beachparty
excess of seventy million albums
rock-a-doodle I knew jesus all my friends
are dead time liberace plays dancing
skeletons by candlelight impossible
dreamtime without a worry in the world alone
after dark have a nice day with lena martell
hasta manana the look of love the touch

of your lips the touch of melachrino
in living stereo the touch of andre kostelanetz
the magnificent pianos of ronnie aldrich these
you love have loved will have loved place time

Ghazal Mosadeq

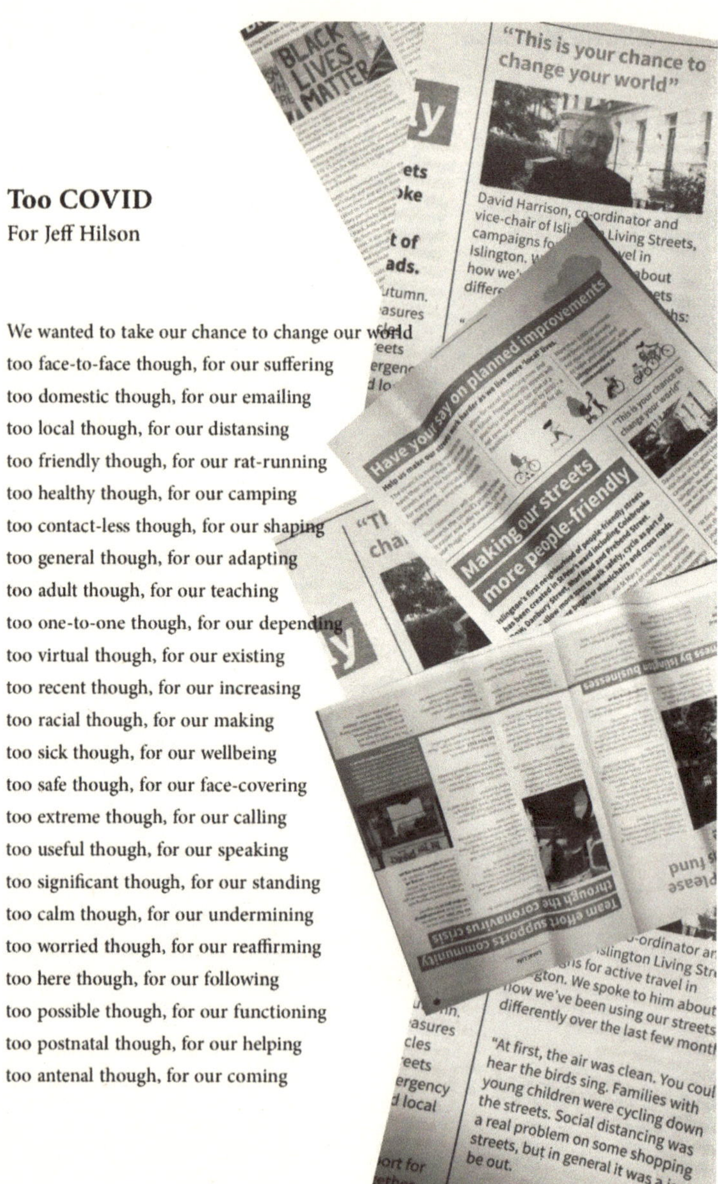

Too COVID

For Jeff Hilson

We wanted to take our chance to change our world
too face-to-face though, for our suffering
too domestic though, for our emailing
too local though, for our distansing
too friendly though, for our rat-running
too healthy though, for our camping
too contact-less though, for our shaping
too general though, for our adapting
too adult though, for our teaching
too one-to-one though, for our depending
too virtual though, for our existing
too recent though, for our increasing
too racial though, for our making
too sick though, for our wellbeing
too safe though, for our face-covering
too extreme though, for our calling
too useful though, for our speaking
too significant though, for our standing
too calm though, for our undermining
too worried though, for our reaffirming
too here though, for our following
too possible though, for our functioning
too postnatal though, for our helping
too antenal though, for our coming

too other though, for our listening
too perfect though, for our looking
too happy though, for our stimulating
too new though, for our kayaking
too teenage though, for our music-making
too mandatory though, for our sharing
too fun though, for our keeping
too distanced though, for our engaing
too world-class though, for our inspiring
too pick-and-mix though, for our spelling
too objective though, for our taking
too small though, for our including
too young though, for our writing
too recommended though, for our drawing
too go-to though, for our painting
too different though, for our receiving
too important though, for our training
too positive though, for our offering
too essential though, for our giving
too LGBT though, for our seeing
too safty-first though, for our underlining
too recent though, for our redeveloping
too disapropriate though, for our redeveloping
too suported though, for our bringing
too silly though, for our securing
too stressful though, for our staying
too open though, for our using

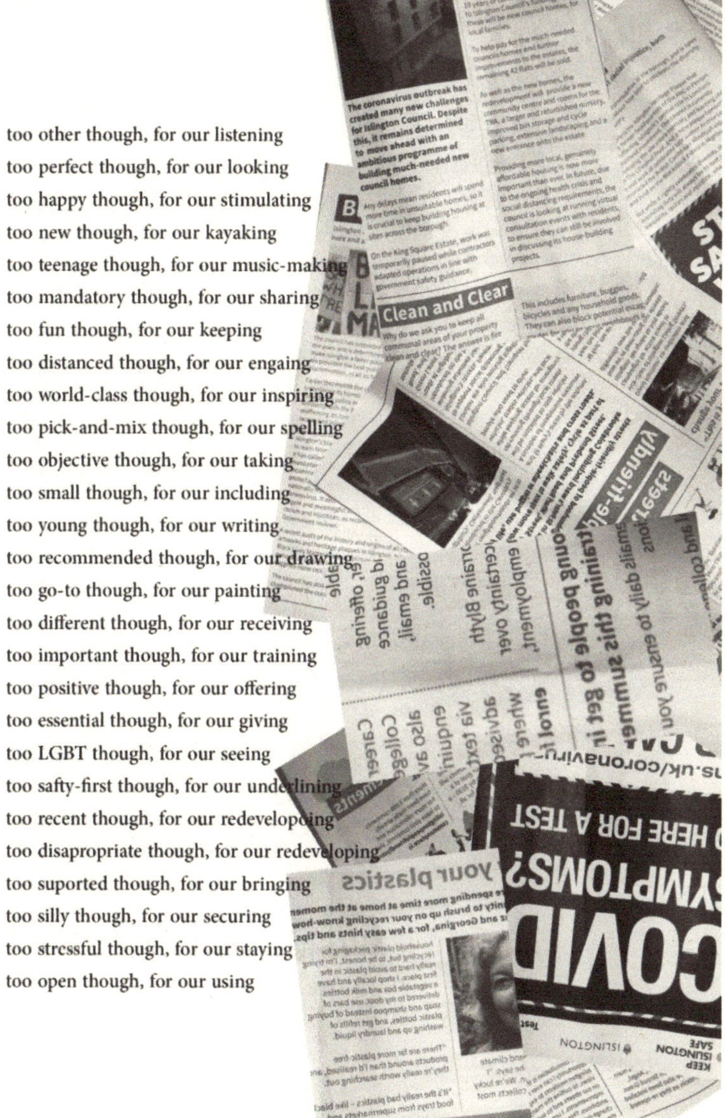

too curent though, for our struggeling
too free though, for our assuming
too worreid though, for our wondering
too available though, for our including
too emotianal though, for our freaturing
too personal though, for our spending
too social though, for our grooming
too disigned though, for our seeking
too interactive though, for our starting
too dedicated though, for our improving
too solid though, for our choosing
too useful though, for our booking
too vulnerable though, for our self-isolating
too kept though, for our responding
too affordable though, for our starting
too plastic though, for our searching
too sexual though, for our enabling
too individual though, for our smoking
too reassured though, for experiencing
too routine though, for our asking
too reliable though, for our thinking
too needed though, for our running
too close though, for our scrolling
too lucky though, for our spending
too hard though, for our recycling
too blank though, for our buying
too here though, for our bidding

Simon Smith

Liking Jeff

played off the legs & down through square

crashing the next one over the covers

the plate-glass wobbles like water

(it's supposed to) to represent water isn't it

(it isn't) therein lies the lie of mimesis or email

& Facebook profile

a roll of the dice goes to show & the full twenty-two yards

that's Jeff for you teaching "poeting"

(auto-corrected to posting)

Jeff Hilson stand up & be counted

dear friend (clicked "like"

is no not "licking" Jeff like an ice-cream no not nice ☹

not "linking" Jeff !!??—eh?) no

just "like" now & you are the key

typo to where to

locate the full toss in the supply chain

& the eggs & the milk & the thyme

& the cheese from an internet

recipe for savoury pancake or quiche

& perfect length/pitch

of the next deliveroo

Marcus Slease

Submarines & Angels

I first met Jeff Hilson in London, in the Victorian era of soap operas, the Edwardian fire, the rolf harris, & his golden trumpet, & I know nothing but I know about his golden trumpet, & I know nothing but I know about his golden trumpet, the NY School in London with Jeff Hilson, with the tiny camels on the horizon, the art in art garfunkel, the funk in funkles, the bendies, because, you know, Jeff Hilson, with the tricycles and cougars of children, with submarines and angels, the green lake is awake.

On the wall now, is Jeff Hilson, his very good periscope, from *Crater Press*. The organs & the slates, his slates & his organs, his stretchers, his verticals and horizontals, his tilting and swaying. & his birds. The great ships come & go, awash in handwashing.

I remember, the BFI with the poetry of John Ashbery, the great submarine and dairy airs with Jeff Hilson. The house of Blake with Jeff Hilson. The Robin Hood Gardens with Jeff Hilson. The bookshops in Cambridge, with Jeff Hilson & Tim Atkins at the wheel & Peter Jaeger on his bike. Touring the embassies of the world in London with Jeff Hilson. We are on the nameways with Jeff Hilson, on the bendy with Jeff Hilson, on the Stein with Jeff Hilson, on the Book of Nancy with Jeff Hilson, because, you know, Jeff Hilson.

Sharing white wine after xing the line. Combing the bookshops, & the curries, & the funk with the stuttering frames, & the music of Jeff Hilson. The Leather Exchange with Jeff Hilson, Openned with Jeff Hilson, with Sean and Tim and Peter, with Chris and Jessica and Richard, with Amy and Sarah and Edmund, with Nat and Nia and Elizabeth, with Frances and Sharon and Paul, with Philip and James and William, with Stephen and Steven and Steve, with Lucy and Colin and Geraldine and Zoë, with Alex and Michael and Emily, with Holly and Tom and Antony, with Fabian and Pascal & Tommy Peeps slash Linus Slug slash Mendoza, with Matt and Nikki and Jennifer, with Harry and Harry and Robert, there are so many names on the nameways with Jeff Hilson, like blossoms and grasshoppers with Jeff Hilson, like affection of hands, like snow dripping and falling into deer's mouth.

Brick Lane bagels with Jeff Hilson, curries & more curries with Jeff Hilson, and through the years the Chinese with Jeff Hilson, the eatings of Jeff Hilson are legendary, his careful Arthurs, his patterns on the isle of dogs with dog shit, his *Assarts*, humble knots.

Doug Jones

from Posts

20/5/20

"An ambulance man told me, often now, they arrive to find the patient dead—body—inside the lockdown. Ambulance outside. Not been seen for days, for this service, ghosts—as neighbours call 999. Now the unit is driving back to base. Someone in a mask + the man will need some food. Siren on—in street sounds—driver. Neither his body—nor the protective gear he encapsulates, to be heard"

27/5/20

"Still always life, found it, dense - + we game the English bird, real time + a flooring call for my friend, Jeff, who is a tail down over arch + comes up to Norfolk for the Nintendos. Screen endless, or at time dependent—real or our bird, say Jeff. I am wowed by play. Wheateaters, redstarts, resource in wings, reproduce + disappear, online in cane. In mote—Jeff is made, such are birds, who her charm"

3/6/20

"Jeff was at my door last night, a different man, quite overcome by anxiety. He wasn't wearing his normal clothes. Was in rags + had a mask. Had walked from London, stealing off all the Amazon sites for food. Given money out in Thetford, the poor town. Knew the nature, material of every wood church—I am God's fool, he said. I didn't contradict him, the rawness of his body, the journey up"

10/6/20

"Jeff sitting quietly. Who asked you? he said of the Covid-19 antibody. I am blind, replied the dandy robber but divide eternally to detect and purify the world—that is my role as a MAP—I am a sort of a rhyme, ordained be thieves. I have seen the antigen, no meaning. So, is the emptiness between the ancient. weed tree and its challenger protein dying and living, said jeff—or are you the animal, stock?"

17/6/20

"The mind of a flower is capable of anything, anything—including me, head fused into 4-5 similarly constituted men, that in a fugue state- dressed up like foresters, distributing the generative portion of the plant—because in the moment, in the strange witchcraft of pollinating insects we constitute empire thoughts—in units split by bracts, penetrating the ray flowers, a green deliberate blankness"

Jonathan Skinner

An Appreciation of the Works of Jeff Hilson

As depicted by Tom Hardy with swagger and aplomb in the biopic *Legend*, Jeff Hilson has ruled London poetry readings with a brutal yet gentlemanly hand, offering an assist and embarrassment to all who dare Cross the Line. Often found at his Lambeth headquarters, surrounded by sycophants and lackeys alike, at the musty back room of The Pineapple, Hilson will deny any accusation of gangsterism in asserting that he merely "runs a club." To audiences always heavy with fellow poets, Hilson's witty and haunting, even forlorn, performances drag the loot of English pastoral out for sparkling smackdowns, in always contemporary, paparazzi-dazzling combinations.

The fact that all on Hilson's side of the fence know the goods are hot won't distract from his repeated assertion he has nothing to say and is saying it loudly. The poem sequences are constructed from fragments of language used to define & describe grass (indica, sativa, and hybrid varieties) and birds (in a window, on the street, at a bar), worked up into longer hit lists. On stretchers, incoherent subjects are dragged in and out, not without an explanation when the occasion warrants, but always enforcing a rough's gloss on the creative destruction at the heart of capital, mashing up voices from the pub, the bus, the bookie, the cream tea.

From "A Cherry-picked and Partially Moth-eaten Bibliography on the Poetics of Charles Olson" (1990) to *stretchers* (2006); *Tunnels of Columbus* (2007); *Miserere* (2007); *Bird Bird* (2009) and, *(Take It In) the Ass, Arts!* (2010) Hilson's early publications demonstrate his mastery of a single, repetitive series of moves, reinforcing his identification with God through the 33 lines of his "stretchers," or confirming, with a Melvillian flourish, how (in *Bird Bird*) the stutter truly is the plot. His headshop classic (*A Grasses Primer*, 2000) offers an exhaustive inventory of basic English grass, with commentary culled from a long career (in Hilson's Art Garfunkel phase) moonlighting as a weed trimmer: the frontispiece of the 500-page tome featuring the poet "smoking shake in Whitman's loafers" can be read more as a dandy's ironic commentary on easy Cavalier habits of pastoral than as a true depiction of model behaviour.

The poetry is all the more English in not taking its English seriously. With his twin brother Tim Atkins (also played by Hardy) Hilson shows us the universe in a codpiece sutured by Antony Gormley, a litany of tearful truths undone in a beer stein. Tragic and wobbling, with a fistful of 'ludes, his lines come at you brim-full with blowsy secrets and pleasurably broken rants. Amidst much that is misguided in "The

Afibria of Jeff Hilson: Meretricious Lounging and Hedonist Pleasures," Racy Lumsey uncovers the sordid operation at the heart of Hilson's bawdy verses, one that entails nothing less than a laying bare of words themselves. Nothing could be further from the poetry of ideas.

Through nihilism, violent tone-shifts and sheer comedy, and a proctologist's regard, Hilson addresses his topics with a firm yet gentle pressure. In a more recent burst of prodigious activity, we find early obsessions gaining new ground across a range of prose forms, flexing the genres of fiction, nonfiction and the prose poem alike. Hilton's cover of "Pressure Drop" in *Latanoprost Variations* (2017) is a lyric highlight, while *An Outpost of Progress* (2017); *Of Time and Love* (2017); and the "America" series, including *South by South West*, *Hilson's Famous Minstrels*, and *The Emperor of New Orleans* (all 2017) reveal in their hastily composed aggregate a novelist's epic concern with Southern perspectives.

Redressing the lack of pro-Southern historical novels about the American Civil War era, Hilson's picaresque, carpetbagging narratives drag Radical Republicans (ca. 1871) over the coals of doxed QAnon profiles, expose minstrel troupes as traveling spy rings, and chronicle the Emperor of New Orleans's alliance with Confederate heroes, faced with the ruination of the South's superior culture and love of learning. William Caxton plays a walk-on part, Rolf Harris flunks maths, Christianity confronts sordid proof of its irrelevance, and the Burning Bush gets doused by Hilson's nearly Poundian sense of history, as all ages collapse into amnesia, upholding a sneaking revelation that novels, like poetry, are fake news that stays news.

The America tetralogy is no warmed over Wikipedian prose, and a big improvement on Hilson's earlier outing, *Tunnels of Columbus* (2007), where an unhealthy obsession with the rise of the unwashed, teeming masses making war against civilization drove his poetic practice of the fragment underground. Here, severe Oulipian strictures reduce the sentences to rubble, bring illegibility to the surface, and keep readers guessing as to what patterns the verbal slash (found or stolen), strewn pell-mell by the print-on-demand acre.

Let us not turn a blind eye on Hilson's celebrated verse guide to London's seedier corners, wittily conceived as a sonnet sequence, and in truth the touching autobiography of an East End rough, *The Reality Book of Mean Streets* (2008). Nor omit, for readers seeking titillation without sublimation, Hilson's latest collection, sold in Soho's only remaining bookshop, in brown plain wrappers, *Organ Music* (~~2019~~ suppressed). In sum, whether one be looking for a beat down, a quick shag in the park, or a truly heartfelt (if doomed) search for Northern Soul—a poem bearing witness to the atrocity of migrant drownings reveals an earnestly pained, if not lovable, side to this monster of Savile Row—there is something wrong in every poem and treat for all who dare show Hilson's hot mess of an opus some well-deserved time.

The poet stands alone, difficult as all poets should be, yet, to quote Hilson himself, "shaking hands with him does not mean he is not a poet."

[Author's note: Apologies and respect! to all whose texts were plagiarized, if not mauled, in the writing of this appreciation.]

Section II

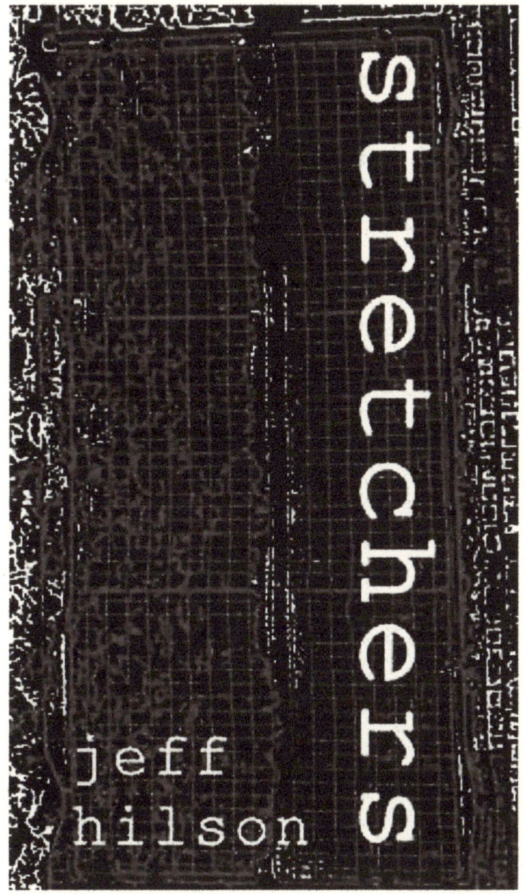

William Rowe

Jeff Hilson's Stretchers, bed and bier

To begin with a description (provisional, partial). *Stretchers* creates a multiplicity, not a collage; its phrases cut across each other, undoing the tone and the place from which their others speak: the sections that make up the book cannot be read as making an overall space. Each voice, and there are many of them, as it rapidly and sometimes slowly takes the place of a previous one, both echoes and turns round what was previously said. The language-actions collude and at the same time conflict with each other, both acknowledging and cutting each other off, continually shifting between or collapsing together the contexts they bring into play, historical and cultural, though there's not one culture, an instance of their refusal of unification. On the contrary, instead of unity of composition or of world, and instead, also, of postmodernist rejection of syntactical (spatial, temporal) consistency as normativity, *Stretchers* poses speaking as living which, when one listens to it, moves through a thickness of reference and memory sedimented in language towards its opposite: a vacuity or void of sense. The vacuity has a similarity with black comedy or, better, with a convulsive type of laughter that makes no external signs because it consumes the capacity to laugh out loud. Push it a little further and it resembles despair. The void relates to a real nothingness, an edge that has a feeling of vertigo to it. Each single speech-fragment, often embedded in another that turns it in a different direction, is heard more than once. Sometimes this happens through repetition, quite often more than twice over, and other times through partial echoes. When a word or phrase or tone returns, it insists on an actual presentness. This is not speaking *about*, not discourse that constructs a situation or world that it is talking about, a world already past. To hear the pieces of speech is to hear actions and to wonder what "world" or "reality" is inside them. The various movements of phrases or lesser fragments, which don't coincide with but move across line-endings, ask us to hear and hear again, so as to find out what's happening.

A closer look at the (un)weave of some of the "stretchers" (since each page can be read as that operation) can bring out the specificity of the ways in which they move. Locating and commenting on all the material that goes into a particular passage would take up a great deal of space, since any set of lines condenses a huge range of material. That type of approach might also stabilise effect of reading them into a sort of compendium of knowledge, which would falsify their working, since they delight in undoing any proper ordering, any academic accumulation of knowledge. Here is a longish passage from around the middle of the book:

> ...smile your in candid trench
> so shoot me I've some blonde
> bombs out as doubles (every
> good girl deserve a red buzzing
> heart) and your it ling-boy who
> fingered his walnut for sunny
> delight (who did holly blue
> unfurl) it was genius gimme
> pink for two-up & change of
> show wherein cotton & thistles
> *this way for cotton & thistles*
> & lips are high speed glossers
> in which things are heaped
> back (pull yourself & get it
> in the glory hole (all he had
> said slipt into the *hysteron*
> *proteron* or the level of bush
> as love point (a receiver is
> once half way) & a cleat is
> the last one in is a thistle
> that time at that time a name
> for these lips as slow small
> glisters (curves traced out to
> slide between & later) & so
> hop hop has lost his lean his
> wife could eat no floaters

"lips are high speed glossers / in which things are heaped / back" gives a sense of speaking as turning things said back onto themselves as act of the body, that takes on a possible sexual sense later on, given that "a cleat" in some speaking (slang) is a name for a clitoris—as well as a nautical fixing point for ropes, stability. There is an undertow of sexual and scatological shifts, as in "could eat no floaters," heard on top of the nursery rhyme of Jack Sprat, whose "wife could eat no lean." Another type of tonal chasm occurs with the phrase "who did holly blue / unfurl," with its cadence of Elizabethan poetry, but producing a tonal and timbral interruption that's wildly off the scale, as if the product of a convulsed mind. But "that time at that time" is a reminder that there's always a present act of speaking and hearing. And so the temptation of using sexual slang as a reality effect or badge of popular cultural knowingness simply doesn't occur. Trench warfare intersects and interferes with sexual/scatological talk, but "trench" and "bombs" run into popular press page three headline language ("blonde bombs") where the plural "bombs" might express either cleverness or stupidity. But this, and other similar phrasing, is stupidity as in linguistic non-dexterity (or even dyslexia?), so not heard in the sense of non-intelligence, but expressing what the language induces if one abandons intelligence as property in class society (and the university). What's expressing itself is also an impulse or even need to be stupid, an abjection that removes speaking from control, not that that is given a solely positive value, since it can fall into other control.

There are several semantic pathways that could be indicated. But the extent to which they exist in mutually interfering modes perhaps makes the notion of pathways dubious. Like a Turing machine they leave traces on which further and further traces are laid down. But what if, as in the rhetorical figure of hysteron proton (sliding into "proteron"), the thing that comes after is put first resulting in continual uprooting of memory including reading as memory process? The phrase that follows ("or the level of bush / as love point") maybe points to a force of sexual order where the object collapses the process. Certainly, any process of semantic accumulation, not to speak of accumulation of cultural capital, gets switched out. A stretcher stretches all ways.

To further extend these comments towards addressing the book as a whole, ambivalent syntactic movements make it the case that statements can themselves, in the saying of them, become the diverted subject of a subsequent statement. This happens in opposition to connections between the content of what's said; it puts the saying first. So, what's occurring is saying, saying that "one" (there are several) is saying, and hearing both these acts. Thus "trench," already displaced by "candid," also, via subsequent sexual displacements/concealments ("walnut," "lips," "glory hole," "cleat," "bush") gets pulled into that domain. But the reverse also happens: war and its destructions interfere with any mere enjoyment of unlimited proliferation of the perverse. The question is posed: what are you doing? The text presents a relation to language that is both passive and alert, open to randomness and highly attentive, a relation which is informed by a desire that wants nothing to do with the will to power. To read *Stretchers* in the context of the past twenty years as a period in which the (symbolic) order that keeps things in their place has buckled, instead of seeking to restore order, as in alt-right obscurantist thinking, Hilson's writing can be grasped as moving towards an action of voiding. This voiding is his prime engagement with the social.

The next page in the sequence begins

> ...I am a nurse the room my
> ward piled up the "stretchers"
> cap of pink and blue cut up
> the men to hen (hen looks like
> hen of company d) poor company

d they take alarm just being
condensed

The men are "condensed" into (")stretchers(") and also—a mere sliding of a letter does so much—into "hen." What's been "cut up," the "cap" or "the men" or the textual material of war and hospital? Certainly, things have been set adrift. And does the "room" echo the idea of the stanza, whose original meaning in poetry was a small room in which poetry of love could shelter itself?[1]

There are several series of meanings in play. The stream of sounds in "stretchers," "condensed," "steam," goes wild into "chevrons," "greasy beef," where among other things the text reflects its own movement as it both stretches and condenses, contains and leaks ("he drips," to cite a subsequent phrase). Flickering images momentarily condense and evaporate. To cite a different series, this time medical (to give it a name), though all cut across each other, there are, in order of appearing, "nurse," "stretchers," "cots / with handles," "surgeons" who "can / make things vapor." Another series, which again includes military things and the closeness of death, consists of "company d" (removed from military shine by loss of capital letters), "as if he hardly gone," "non-coms," "tin cups of the men," existing in disjunctive and random combination with the twice-appearing "knives and forks." Another set, again disjunctively interwoven with the rest, is set in motion by "hen," "he drips," "he drips and almost pours," where a sexualised woman seems to elicit emissions both sexual and life-threatening. However, to read the poem analytically in this way is to abstract from it. Its various movements are drawn out and condensed in the following, which can be read both literally and reflexively: "both have this cap / of cut up things half-bed half- / bier the men to hen had hardly gone." In a partial condensation of the book as a whole, the place of care for the body and of its destruction collapse into each other ("the 'stretchers' being / condensed just piled up"). "half-bed half- / bier" is the direst expression of the two primary movements of *Stretchers*. Hilson, for sure, is not concerned with wit as a melancholy substitute for poetry, even less with any kind of cleverness. His poetry includes intense enjoyment of the wild and the random, but it also pushes through that intensity to an edge of extreme dislocation, which relates to anxiety.

A possible coda might cite

a bird with no name it
do pink pink but in some
month of may it seems
my I'm falling apart (is

---

[1] I am grateful to Albert Pellicer for his comments on the meaning of stanza.

the glue that holds the
funny sides the big ones
the little ones for me it
seems the other side was
busted) my tissues my
tissues would say I'm fine
otherwise I'm fine

The bird's action is simply to make the sound it makes, but "I'm falling apart" moves away from simple self-expression through re-hearing it as something said. If falling apart is "my I'm falling apart," it is something "I" have said previously to this moment, but subsequently the saying it and the content of it (someone falling apart) enter present time, in a completely contradictory movement, as "glue" that "holds." The glue "holds the funny sides." So break-down, or however one wants to call it, can be taken as the thing that's inside the (silent) laughter, "the / funny sides." But these are divided into "big ones" and "little ones." Perhaps "the little ones" mean wit, which has been broken or, better, found out. There is anxiety in the speaking when the person, destitute of that support, says "my tissues / my tissues would say I'm fine" and then repeats "I'm fine," letting slip "otherwise" before the second time. The act of speaking has no security of knowledge.

Jo Lindsay Walton

Stretchers #19: I CAN I DID CANDID / (A BAND DID)

> "As a poet, I knew to be gentle." Aldous Harding, "The Barrel"
>
> "Show the ferret to the egg." Aldous Harding, "The Barrel"

Imagine we're off swimming in the river or, even better, *down by the creek*. Now imagine today everybody wants to be a good egg, with *infinite* wanting. So if you shout, "Last one in's a good egg!" exactly zero of us get in. We sort of start Zeno's paradoxing into our Speedos etc. One wants others to enter the water earlier than oneself so that, *heh heh heh*, one can be that egg. Thus, "Last one in's a good egg!" could be a good example of perverse incentive design. Or it might just be deceptive incentive design: it strongly seems to want to do something, and that very seeming is what makes it do something else. But then, at the other extreme, imagine a day of broad consensus that being a rotten egg is as bad as it gets. On such a day, a single yell of "Last one in's a rotten egg!" and in we all splash, not so much as stopping to take off our socks and shoes. So that's good, transparent incentive design in a sense, although the results are again quite homogenous across the whole band of us. More about the socks and shoes in a moment. What we see in both examples is the power of naming, or more specifically the power of labelling within a hierarchy, to steer action and shape subjectivity. As the poet Timothy Thornton writes:

> eggs haribo
> eggs boxset
> eggs poirot
> eggs amagansett
>
> eggs powerful
> eggs underfunded
> eggs sporcle
> eggs countermanded (Facebook post, 15 April 2020)

It's this power of naming that probably tempts poets into cultivating wriggly, creaturely poems that seem to maybe articulate forms of social organisation different to those the poets have experienced and, in some sense, different to those they can imagine. What if instead of (say) laws or economies or bureaucracies, we had sonnets or stretchers? Because between these idealised extremes of infinite appetite and infinite aversion, there stretches a vast possibility space of diverse leaderboards (and leaderlessboards) where diverse armoured and storied embryos vie to define us, shape us, and steer us. "Third one in's an eggs toxteth," etc. "Penultimate one in's an eggs liar's paradox," etc. I think these floating ascriptions have a quality that first two earlier examples don't have. These ones filter and sort. In a very basic model, they filter according to a pre-existing distribution of desire and aversion, merely revealed in our response to the yell. We discover in what proportions each of us wishes to be or to not be which egg. In a more nuanced model, albeit with a neoclassical energy, these ascriptions filter *first* on that basis, and *then* on the basis of revised desire and aversion reflecting the various skinny-dippers' updated theories about one another's mental states and intentions, and then again, and then again, and so on, probably accommodating "strategic" action, and probably converging on various Splash equilibria. I'm not sure, but I do think you could probably rig a Turing machine out of skinny-dippers moving to and fro hesitantly, craftily, hungrily at the edge of the limpid plunge-pool in strategic search of their preferred egg statuses, implying that with enough time and energy you could *run an entire universe filled with conscious life* by shouting, say, "4th one in is a rotten egg, 3rd one in is a good egg, 6.022×10^{23}th one in is an egg amagansett!" etc. to *just* the right gang, *just* the right that one summer that seemed to last forever. Eggs nihilo: something comes from nothing when it is egged on.

Maybe that's a bit of a stretch though.

Jaden: "I don't got the time to put you on the stretcher (*stretcher*) I am here and I'm still flexing (*flexing*)."

The diversification and spread of digital social architectures in the 2000s and 2010s has probably both enriched but also colonised the social imaginary of the governance of the commons—the recipes Marx scorned to write because, as he perpetually pointed out, he didn't yet know about microwave ovens or for example activated charcoal—or at least the more abstract, ethereal regions of that imaginary. In the simplest version, you just add "social" or "networked" or "crowd" to some older aspiration. Let's simply crowdseize the means of production, etc. The virtual valorisation machines that make up the internet are still very much capital, capital more human than ever in its capacity to absorb and co-ordinate human and more-than-human investments of affect and cognition, in its capacity to twist a buncha-jewels-inna-bucket like it's a kaleidoscope of crystalline personality godhead, its capacity to make Wogan economies of Wonga economies. The interest in virality and permutability of several of Jeff Hilson's *Latanoprost Variations* (Boiler House 2017) is inflected by the voice of specifically digital algorithmic curation and suggestion. So the recommendation

"You might like" becomes "You might liken" or "You might not liken," spreading across the page like the proliferation and crumbling of fungi and algae / cyanobacteria symbiotic composite organisms, like *likens.* "A False Botanic—Forensic Poem for February" is a witchy eco-poem, a little redolent of Caroline Bergvall's Dante variations, and an extended meditation on Google's "did you mean to search for." That said, I don't really think it *is Google's* "did you mean to search for": it is a broader exploration of the concept of being asked if you meant to want what you did not quite manage to want. I think part of what is exciting about these poems is that they often manage to feel like they're not about the internet at all.

> ... & on the twenty sixth day I was up with the lark to root out the scottish dock I didnt find it instead I found a red star thistle I rubbed myself with which withered me to a stalk & on the twenty seventh day ... ("A False Botanic—Forensic Poem for February")

I was searching for an egg and "I didnt find it." There isn't actually an egg in *Stretchers* poem number nineteen, "...smile your in candid trench," but there *is* an *eggs conspicuously missing*. The line in "...smile your in candid trench" is "the last one in is a thistle." One of the ways that *Stretchers* often feels sort of curiously generous and inclusive is that even when it leaves things out, it keeps them in. The "correct" versions of the idioms, proverbs, collocations, scraps of nursery rhyme etc. faintly accompany their morphed and mutated versions. These unspoken words can be sinister presences too. The egg is missing, and so is the shell: "I've some blonde / bombs" implies the word "bombshell" and puts into interplay the objectification of femme bodies with the objectification of the enemy, the target to be neutralised. And the poem begins "smile your in candid trench": it begins, in other words, not only with a warzone, but with a hidden "camera." The candid trench could well be the stretcher itself. And of course a *camera* and a *stanza* share the etymological metaphor of being a *room*, perhaps a room stretched to capacity.

This failure-to-appear also appears in later writing. The Incredible String Band are a British psychedelic folk band formed by Clive Palmer, Robin Williamson and Mike Heron in Edinburgh in 1966. In *Latanoprost Variations*, what is missing from the title of "The Incredible Canterbury Poem" is "String Band." It is obviously a poem about how music can, like a room, bring people together. Music brings people together, for example, in the sort of somatic or subter-songfulness of language and of all semantic interaction; in dancing; in a kind of affective commoning where we mosh and/or emosh together in tandem; in dismissive, gatekeeping interactions like "Oh, you say love your daughter? Name her first four albums"; and in Spotify's recommendations and the broader patterns of digital persuasion architecture and surveillance capitalism in which they participate. It is a poem, in other words, like a lot of Jeff Hilson's poems, about how societies (or assemblages or networks or bands of individuals or dividuals) are put together or how they might be put together. If we read it as a utopian poem, then the "incredible strings" become the amazing and currently slightly implausible linkages that bind together utopian society. String Theory helps these implied ligatures to feel vaguely angelic and ectoplasmic. But these incredible strings are *not there*, they are only implied, they do not make us a band, we did not form a band. "I didnt find it."

Instead, there is the word "Canterbury": maybe recalling the Knight, Franklin, Summoner, Pardoner, Manciple, Canon et al. of Chaucer's *Canterbury Tales*, while the invisibility of "String Band" also allows an implied "Shrinking Man" to scuttle in or "Hulk" to smash in, along with the superhero genre generally, and its often flamboyant celebration of well-divided labour: cf. e.g. the Eggs-Men, this one scrambles brainwaves, this one fries you, etc. The gesture toward an estranged or detourned or evolved or utopian together-yet-apartness is (I think) quite a broad gestural sweep. Think of buying a song as a 1 and not buying a song book as a 0. Given enough time and energy, and an immortal listener, I think you could *run an entire universe filled with conscious* life on a Spotify playlist equipped with just the right recommendations algorithm.

> if you liken the incredible string band try hatfield and the north you listened to aphex twins heres an album you might not liken you listened to supertramp and kate bush you might not liken this song you listened to swell maps this week liken to try the wilde flowers? ("The Incredible Canterbury Poem")

Egging your MP is like detonating a small material symbol of a bomb. It activates associations of assassination. But whether you're shouting "Fuck you, here, the egg" or "Seventh one in is an eggs candid" or "Third one in is an eggs floaters," or whether you are shouting, "The first tranche of divers are gold eggs, the second are silver eggs, and the third are bronze eggs," the cultural form of the hierarchy will never be a neutral frame, but always an active agent. In other words, I had to clarify earlier that in my made-up scenario "everybody wants to be a good egg." That's because if you just shouted, "Last one in's a good egg!" where norms of individualist striving prevail, the meaning of "last one" would overwhelm the meaning of "good egg," and everyone would assume *eggs good* were the new *eggs anathema*. Contrariwise, if you just shouted "Last one in's a rotten egg!" where norms of solidarity prevail, the meaning of "last one" would probably overwhelm the meaning of "rotten egg," with everyone assuming *eggs rotten* were the new eggs *non-contributory assistance*. And again, it's in the middle territory stretching between these two idealisations where the precise force of the hierarchy (or leaderboard, procession, parade, queue, *race*, or something else) is various and probably unpredictable. It is somewhere in that vast stretch where you get the weird forms of equity that are not just inert negations of hierarchy, which are not just "horizontal organization" that are really the same old vertical hierarchies lying on stretchers. Where the first shall be last and the last shall be first, and stuff like that.

The worst liars are often the best liars. There is an essay at the back of *Stretchers*, "Why I Wrote *Stretchers*," that talks about that title *Stretchers*. The preoccupation with virality and the fractal is here too. "Each stretcher tells a story and each story contains many other stories." Do they really tell stories? Or are some of them just complete nonsense? A stretcher is where you lie when you are hurt. It's that old paradox: how far can you trust a liar sharing their lying practice? Maybe what is less well acknowledged is how leaky and spready that Liar's Paradox is. *Everything* that is said about lying is a bit suspect, because whoever is saying it is thinking about lying. And is there a kind of listening, adjacent to misinterpretation, that can also generate lies? If so then everything that is said about lying is doubly suspect, because whoever is *listening* is thinking about lying. Stretching and lying strongly imply yoga. Also, utopia: the thing the genre (if that's what it is) has been stuck on since More's *Utopia* is the enclave form. Who's the last one in before the gate slams? Who is outside? The ones who walk away, the ones who were not born in time, the ones who would tear it to shreds, etc.? The sleeper woken, the time traveller? What makes any utopia better than a billionaire's gated climate fastness? Is utopia constitutively stretched, always managing to include more than it reasonably should? The title of *Stretchers* comes from Mark Twain's *The Adventures of Huckleberry Finn*:

> YOU don't know about me without you have read a book by the name of *The Adventures of Tom Sawyer*; but that ain't no matter. That book was made by Mr. Mark Twain, and he told the truth, mainly. There was things which he stretched, but mainly he told the truth. That is nothing. I never seen anybody but lied one time or another, without it was Aunt Polly, or the widow, or maybe Mary. Aunt Polly—Tom's Aunt Polly, she is—and Mary, and the Widow Douglas is all told about in that book, which is mostly a true book, with some stretchers, as I said before.

A bit of a stretch. Entertaining ideas just over the edge of feasibility. Allowing things to work that shouldn't or don't really. Epistemologically, there may be an "OK just this once" aspect to anything that is a bit of a stretch: let it slide, but don't update your deeper convictions on the basis of what just slid by. *Don't* learn from it. When you stretch a piece of fabric, sometimes you control its translucency. If there are words or imagery printed on it, they may mingle with the imagery of the world below. Stretching an image can also reveal an infrastructure of threads, a sort of secret lattice or honeycomb shape bound together with the shape of the ink.

There is an experiment you can do where you hold your fingers in front of your face, and then keeping your gaze fixed forward, gradually draw your fingers apart. Eventually you'll come to a point where your fingers are in the "shadows" and you're sure if you can see them or not. Or, you can see them, but what you can see isn't the sort of phenomenon that stereotypically characterises the constituents of vision. Or they are neither "in" or "out" of the enclave of your visual field. Bataille writes in *The Story of the Egg*, "She played gaily with words, speaking about breaking eggs, and then breaking eyes, and her arguments became more and more unreasonable." In Dublin in 2008, a woman named Ann Dooley was blinded in one eye by an egg thrown by eighteen-year-old David Morgan. Before I got glasses, in order to bring distant objects into focus, I used to curl up my forefinger and look through the pinprick "lens," or more often just manually distort my eyeballs with my fingers. It was fine, we've all been brainwashed by Big Optometry. And when an eyeball is stretched wrong, visual field degrades. There is an essay at the back of *Latanoprost Variations*, "On 'Latanoprost Variations.'" Latanoprost is topical eye drop used to treat open-angle glaucoma. Glaucoma is becoming besieged by "shadows." They bunch around the periphery of your visual field and march inward. Latanoprost relieves pressure. "Latanoprost" was printed on a pen found by the poet under a bed. Something astonishing I've noticed is that darkness is literally not black. When I shut my eyes in the sun, of course I see a sort of taupe orange. But even in the middle of the night, I don't think what fills my visual field can be described as blackness. It's a flock of colour or colour-like qualia, and there *is* black, I think, but there is also at least as much silver and grey.

But does "...smile your in candid trench" tell a story that contains many other stories? It might be a time travel story. I am writing in 2020. A day ago Matt Hancock tweeted: "Thanks to the nation's resolve, horseracing is back from Monday. Wonderful news for our wonderful sport." A bit of a stretch. There are also questions of elasticity: that is, whether these poems unpinned from the page would snap back into another shape. If something has been stretched, energy was involved in deformation, and that energy may be stored in a specific pattern suitable to a specific agency.

Sometimes stretching the truth can be boasting. Is poetry a kind of boasting? British people supposedly don't like boasting. Walt

Whitman contained multitudes: did ye aye? But which *people* really say: "We love boasting, come round to ours and boast?" The USA? Cape Verde, Egypt, Ghana, Mozambique, Iran? I kind of don't think any do. If *Stretchers* are boasts, they are *mostly* very gentle and self-effacing boasts. More like the kind of naturally occurring boast when someone is very tired or drunk or high or just forgetful and they keep repeating themselves, and the repetition is actually a kind of odd (almost extra-linguistic) cognitive sharing, a kind of telepathy, insofar as it gives you a special kind of peek deep into their skull, behind many of the usually intervening layers of potential guile. Or like a toddler who runs into a room and shouts something strange. Or like when someone keeps repeating themselves.

If it tells a story, it might be a time travel story, partly because I am writing about it after almost twenty years. Partly because it raises the possibility of disordered or reordered time with *hysteron proteron*, the rhetorical trope where the first shall be last and the last shall be first, as in "I put on my shoes and socks" or "I took off my socks and shoes." How can the time traveller who visited utopia in a temporally disordered fashion avoid accusations of boastfulness upon their return? And if everyone has to see for themselves, is the utopian economy largely based on tourism?

And/or "...smile your in candid trench" might be a kind of pubescent sexual boast. The poem is queer-gently gender-jiggling: "your it ling-boy who / fingered his walnut for sunny / delight." This is one of the stretchers that first appeared in a chapbook in the early Naughties, the era of teen sex comedy box office dominance: *There's Something About Mary* came out in 1998, and the second *Stretchers* chapbook itself fills the gap between *American Pie 2* (2001) and *American Wedding* (2003). The American Pie franchise (continuing in 2020 with *Girls Rules*) springs from a virginity-losing pact of the hetero penetrative phallocentric kind: it's a movie about "the last one in." They are also movies about reasonable expectations of privacy being constantly confounded, about bodies brought shamefully into the light in ways that are somehow worse than anything the inspected figure could have possibly predicted, and yet not so bad.

The poem may end with a kind of biiig gesture toward polysemy, really a bit of a breakdown of meaning through multiplication of meaning. It is a candle burning at both fuses. Vowel variants are letters or pairs of letters that can make the same sound, and we're told elsewhere that all misspellings are intentional, so there's a possibility here that every word is actually pronounced like a different word. Maybe "peel" is pronounced "pale," and so on:

> ... vowel
> & variants all frail peel them
> like each other with our pen-

tricks move along or you
will lose it with that zee ...

It's the kind of thing you can usually only do at the end of something. In the game of tag, when you're "it" you chase everybody. *They fle from me that sometyme did, they fle from me that sometyme will me seke.* When you are "it," everyone who is "them," who are they, he, she, etc., flee from you. Maybe you are the expletive subject, the "it" of "it's raining." If reality absolutely consistently fled shrieking from a vacuum, would it be indistinguishable from its flowing shrieking into that vacuum to fill it? Last one in is *named*, last one in is "it," last one in doesn't really exist. When a game of tag ends, and you were the last it, you feel weird about that.

"[S]o shoot me"—that's what you say when you've done something bad, but not as bad as your interlocutor is making out. And/or to downplay something really bad you've done. The play on a photo shoot is elaborated throughout the poem: on the one hand, violence as epistemologically generative, producing knowledge and/or things to be known, and on the other hand, observation and image-making as violent processes. The trench of "...smile your in candid trench," especially so close to "some blonde / bombs" and "every good girl deserve," could be read as public space transformed into a theatre of war by misogynist gaze, expectation, and imperative ("smile"). Later, "hop hop has lost his lean his / wife could eat no floaters" is a reference to an old rhyme about a gendered division of labour (and / or dietary requirements: "Jack Sprat could eat no fat / His wife could eat no lean, / But, together both, they licked the platter clean"), altered to remove his name as well as hers, and perhaps to include suggestions of "hopping to it," of the collapse of individualist "lean-in" feminism, and of an inability to flash the shit-eating grins, or to let daily microaggressions be water off a duck's back, left behind in the workplace ("splashing off / sallys night feathers"). "Sally" is one of those names that feels plucked from folklore. It suggests a little attack, of course: so "sallys" is again one of those femme military puns. But it's also again about mutualistic swarming behaviours—ways of being together—and about the division of roles within collectives: mixed-species flocks often divide into sallying species and gleaning species.

Rivers, roads, trenches, are said to *stretch*, which is strange because they don't. Could it be a kind of weird metonymy, insofar as what stretches is the person who goes from one end to the other? Stretches their legs, maybe, but stretches their self, definitely, the elastic distortion of the self at the origin to the self at the end. The poem's interest in things being out of order could be understood as a provocation about lived experience, about how the legitimacy of any voice of lived experience, whether it is the self speaking to the self or the self speaking to others, is stretched and transformed by temporal distances from the experiences of which it speaks. XYZ. The "zee" is, within British English, the less likely, the less canonical, the surprise ending.

One thing about "last one in is a" as a model of surveillance is that you're not confident that anybody *will* actually be watching who the last one in is. Everybody will be in mid-air with arms and legs windmilling. "[L]ast one in is a" has the aura of the last evaluation before the revaluation of values, or the apocalypse. Not the Final Judgment, more like the opposite: the judgment that is made when it is too late for it to trigger any process. The very last time somebody pays for something with money. A moment later, through the membrane, they receive their purchase as a gift. The need to "move along" or you will "lose it with that zee" raises the idea of staying put too long, and getting cross, giving up on that surprise ending.

Is there such a thing as the "baseline avant-garde"? That statistically inevitable presence in *whatever* you are doing or experiencing of traces of things that will by sheer chance be more widespread and/or significant in the future. Maybe poets cling to that sheer surface or hammer things into it. What if these poems, lurking in the heart of a Liar's Paradox, haven't been stretched at all? What if they've been *hammered dense*? Just like "your" could be the final state that "you're" approaches, after only half the hammer blows. The blurring of the possessive "your" with the contracted pronoun and copula "you're" suggests reification, becoming blurred with the things that you own, or alienation, being unable to be identical with the things that you are. The hammering-dense can be seen in the tendency for the end of one phrase to flow into the start of the next: "that time at that time," which untangles to "that time at" (a stroll down memory lane) and "at that time" (some historical context). Nostalgia has an affinity with fascism—golden ages, decline and degeneration, purifying fire—but when society grows more fascist than it was, there's got to be such a thing as antifa nostalgia too. Which is like saying they don't make they don't make nostalgia like they used to like they used to.

Is there such a thing as a "degenerative avant-garde," associated with the collapse of possibility and the closing down of potential? As political possibilities fall, as the eye, or whatever it is, stretches, as the "shadows" march in from the edges, different sets of objects begin to welter and flicker and give up secrets. I'm not necessarily saying this is happening now, any of it. And I'm not really talking about immiseration. I don't think I'm talking about disaster communism either, or building things back better for all. I'm talking about something probably a bit more trivial, about quite good things becoming estranged through their wrecks and ruins, and for a moment conveying visions of even better things. By seeing x decay into not-x, we might discover the why and zee. Of course, on one level, e.g. Johnson might make May "look good in comparison," May might make us "miss David Cameron," algorithmically governed fake news ecosystems might tempt us to "long" for earlier more analogue phases of media ideology, the next phase of deepfake stretchers might tempt us to "long" for the epistemological larks of 2020, etc. I don't think that's what I mean either. But perhaps that process is mixed in ambiguously with the other one, the one where objects crumpling and distorting reveal their never-before-seen facets. And maybe these two processes are not really distinguishable after all.

The series *BoJack Horseman* is built around the never directly acknowledged pun, "Why the long face?" BoJack Horseman, on the home stretch of *BoJack Horseman*, is contacted by an old acquaintance. "You're tall. I need you to reach something for me."

OK, now you're just reaching.

Adrian Clarke

2 Drifters for Jeff

poet *lèvres bleues*
a blank sheet
sorrowful space carved
up not jade
exactly vanishing due
east obscure on
foot materials attendant
cherchant la clé
in a hole
through the language
Hokusai oscillates wind-blown
prints traced in
permanent black on
damp rock a
lost horizon time
regardless the winter
landscape going nowhere
fleshed in its
crevice the throat
blocked change colours
an uncertain prospect

*

intense thermals map
syntactic vision not
retinal strapped in
for galactic drift
literally an abstract
cortex as balcony
the last word
redacted bolt hole
and cockpit signal
enduring passion for
scriptural landscapes breach
a firewall visitors
welcome between conflicting
demands descent from
dust in the
rear-view mirror sphere
contextualised regardless of
origin oceanic under
erasure a Titian-blue
memory's farewell embrace

Misreading Stretchers

> *... up and over kerbs.*
> *...*
> *... people round mob-like*
> *open into a column*

In the wind tunnel created by the erection of the Shard, on my way to a Crossing the Line reading in Leathermarket Street - in 2011 I think, long after completion of the series anyway - I made a connection between tower blocks and *Stretchers* that has helped to garble my readings of the texts ever since. The shape of the poems emphasized by Bob Cobbing's original Writers Forum publication of sets 1-12 and 13-33 on vertically folded A4 sheets, the Canary Wharf starting-point and Jeff's account in *Why I wrote stretchers*, the afterword to the Reality Street edition, of the encounter in the bar in Centre Point that determined the 33-line form were enough to set me on an observation platform where vertigo may account for a lot.

For the afterword stretchers are "...more prose pieces with a frayed right margin. They are tatters, ragged flags ... The first stretcher in volume 3 seems to have the front of a ship sailing out of it." I guess to glimpse a cruise liner or maritime high rise approaching Tilbury would be stretching things too far. Start again. ...

... With an overview. Topographic rather than conceptual; hallucinatory as much as topographic. A voyeuristic offshoot of the *dérive*, psychogeography thankfully not in the frame. Michel de Certeau (in *The Practice of Everyday Life*, (U of California P., 1984): "The perambulatory gesture plays with spatial organisations, however panoptic: it is not foreign to them (it does not eschew them), nor does it conform to them ... It insinuates into them its multifarious references and citations ... whatever may surprise, cross or seduce its route." Down below *it is not oxford street*.

Apparently, the French poet starts with God and ends with anything, the English vice versa, while Margate Sands is the place to connect nothing with nothing. The kinds of thing that get linked in a stretcher are mostly to be found along *clean london lines / out to Croydon-on-the-fringe*: the view extends to *windows all over wandsworth, sudbury hill, maida vale, huge essex, south london, london, london* ... specific to general. The metropolis's increasingly indistinguishable micro-identities survive in language, some of it " ... verbal detritus heard or seen on journeys through this city" that the poems incorporate.

But why do the poems so often *prefer to live in a tree a leafy house* ? Andrew Lawson *On Modern Pastoral* (in *fragmente* 3, Spring

1991): "In the twentieth century the country becomes indistinguishable from the town, both ruled by industrial processes and the rural idyll a dormitory for a managerial and executive elite." Evading "Cambridge pastorale" and its "phenomenological impasse," subversion here involves a steady attention to an unstable surface, agitated time-frames, skewed glimpses of folk song and pageant history, "taken from books ... another kind of reading which was partial, discontinuous and manic," plus on-line sources from the start. ...

Jeff's initial notoriety was as the author of a thesis on Zukofsky he abandoned after 10 years. Quoting the fourth stretcher, Andrew Duncan (in *A Poetry Boom 1990-2010*, Shearsman, 2015) doesn't find it "easy to recognise Zukofsky," though " ... there is no recognisable speaking figure. No attempt at creating a sociological narrative full of ethical interactions." So if Ron Silliman is right that for Zukofsky poetry "is not deferred to any hierarchic abstraction such as character, plot or action," there may be room for a trade-off here.

In contrast to High Modernism, Projective Verse and the School of Cambridge, if Zukofsky approaches Major Themes he does so increasingly rarely and obliquely. By *80 Flowers* David Levi Strauss (in *Code of Signals*, North Atlantic Books, 1983) finds words "unbridled, flex, shift from noun to verb to adjective to sounder, break to form other words, recombine, all still held in the suspension of *words together*." No surprise that L=A=N=G=U=A=G=E approved. - *Stretchers* is a long way from most of the output of that group, though not Charles Bernstein's to the extent that, as Andrew Duncan notes, "it is very cheerful and makes everyone very relaxed." (And despite Andrew having seen a photo, of a T-shirt with the slogan Hilson School of Poetry, Jeff is no André Breton.) Trying to pin down "the avant-garde thing," Andrew offers " ... if we say that the expectation is to be critical, to be didactic about how the power order is failing, and to disrupt patterns, that is a start. Hilson's work does not fulfil these expectations ... ." Certainly *Stretchers* is not didactic, while its overviews stop some way below high seriousness; disruptive shakings-up can be tricky for the classifier. From *Stretcher 44*:

(special guest monarchs
& wars of the nineteenth
century & wars of the
twentieth century may
well begin with wars of
the twentieth century
(result (the wars of the
finches the wars of the
finches yachts & piler n
has tried to quit even
this small advance (em

dash dash cram it all in
to made four errors four
hundred errors of the
wars of the rosses and
monarchs and the like
they serve as a.) cause
b.) result of wars of the
rosses (never end a line
with a dollar sign bracket
parenthesis bracket periods
complete sentences ...

Michel Serres' smartphone-savvy *Petite Poucette* (Editions Le Pommier, 2012) "chattering in the hubbub of her chattering contemporaries," has all the facts at the tips of her thumbs. "The voice of the past is no longer required—unless someone, original and rare, invents."

Back to the afterword: " ... specialised languages are more often than not allied to specialised practices which solidify into accepted practices, practices which obscure possible alternatives as well as obscuring actual histories and deliberately sabotaging alternatives. These 'official' languages need to be broken into by poets and deliberately misused as much as possible."

Which suggests *Stretchers* challenges the regulative practices to which this piece has been struggling to conform.

Ken Edwards

Mostly a true book, with some stretchers

The Reality Street Book of Sonnets (2008), edited by Jeff Hilson, has been one of my press Reality Street's biggest hits. To date it's sold more than 1,000 copies—big numbers for a small press.

It had its origin as far back as July 2003, when I read from my newly completed poem sequence *eight + six*—as the title suggests, using the sonnet form, but in non-standard ways—at the Poetry Café in London. At that time, the post-avant poets were allowed to assemble in the narrow basement reading space. I was reading with Rob Holloway. After the reading, I had a conversation with Jeff in the course of which he suggested there was an anthology to be made of contemporary poets' innovative spins on the sonnet form. I found it hard to believe, but he convinced me, and boy was he right—the main problem, once Reality Street had commissioned it, was keeping the book within bounds, there was so much material.

It was a long time taking form—Jeff fed me contributions at regular intervals. He thought it ought to cover contemporary "sonnets" in English from Britain, the USA, Canada, Australia and New Zealand at the very least. There were and are several contemporary sonnet anthologies, but pretty conservative on the whole, none that have taken the radical approach we did. In fact, "The Radical Sonnet" was an early working title, though never a serious contender. Jeff, together with Tim Atkins, came up with "I LOVE YOU and the sonnet is not dead" (a quote from Ted Berrigan's *The Sonnets*)—which I vetoed as a title. Finally, Jeff and I were having yet another discussion about what on earth a Reality Street book of sonnets could be called, and I can't remember which of us said "Why not just 'The Reality Street Book of Sonnets'?" That was it.

While all this was happening, I also invited Jeff to submit a manuscript of his own for Reality Street to publish. I'd heard him reading from a new set, "Stretchers," but I can't remember where that was. Not a sonnet sequence, this, but one of 33-line poems, a form invented by Jeff because 33 was his age when he composed it. Huckleberry Finn is made by Mark Twain to describe *Tom Sawyer* as "mostly a true book, with some stretchers." Just as much fun as the sequence itself is Jeff's afterword "Why I wrote stretchers." The cover incorporates his graphics. So that came out in 2006, but meanwhile work on *The Reality Street Book of Sonnets* continued.

Jeff kept feeding me more and more contributions, and when the number of contributors exceeded 80 I panicked and told him to stop. He wrote an excellent and very useful introduction, and, as he had done for *Stretchers,* also designed the front cover. I did the layout and typesetting, which was challenging at times. Together, we sorted out any copyright problems: there were a few high-profile names among the contributors and at least one publisher insisted on payment, though other copyright holders waived this when they learned what a small operation the press was, and that this book had no funding to back it up, just the advance subscriptions from the Reality Street Supporter Scheme.

Sixty-five people subscribed to the book—about twenty fewer than the number of contributors, but enough to pay for the basic print-on-demand setup. Even with print-on-demand, a book of over 350 pages is a big deal without subsidy or working capital (paying 83 worldwide contributors in free copies alone was a big outlay in this context). But we both believed in it. And eventually sales picked up, and the book made back its costs over the years—it's still selling steadily today.

After publication, Jeff recorded a contribution about the anthology for BBC Radio 3's *The Verb* with Ian McMillan—a loyal supporter of Reality Street from the early days, as it happens—which was broadcast in May 2008. In September Ron Silliman posted a review to die for on his blog (then read by thousands), comparing Jeff to the great anthologists such as Donald Allen and Jerome Rothenberg, which naturally Jeff was ecstatic about. On 25 October it received an "official" launch at the Small Publishers Book Fair at the Conway Hall, London, with no fewer than 19 of the contributors reading!

July 2020

Scott Thurston

A Stretcher Birder for JH

...the disaster is necessary
can't work without him he
announces himself: why
am i not a hilson?
dragging his sleeves in the river
puts his hook in joy
drops all his spit there on
handy little biscuits the devil
page 1 is unseen
a new Harley in slim forms
happy you year
everyone's poems have jeff in,
even mine
i am not a jeff, i am a hilson
how we missed ye, dropping
the Ikea orrery on yr ft
the shiny round alternatives u need
the ground is sedating
you *are* the special, i mean that's not what
happens in hilson, trace, this staggering,
this standing out
he said I need longer words
i fucking love you Jeff i write like this
don't go there for lines or limbs
fun is not the only fun
ling-boy who tickled his peanut
your dancing skin
their word is not a crystal or
kinder guard
a bird with no name
for parade in being a poet shame
why this is all a write error
we call him the third jeff

Bird bird

Jeff Hilson

A PEEPSIAN MALADY

or

nothing is so lonely in the countryside as the shining stars

I wasnt always a door I am full of holes a country door unbendy against the swollen tone poem in the 1970s men in the fen peer at french moths le papillon de nuit upstairs & downstairs with my lily white hands in the 1970s men in the fen appear as french moths sucking their plums in a leisurely exchange I wasnt always amour I am mull of kin tired in the 1970s men in the fen are la phalène I wasnt always a door I am mull of kin tired & so full of holes against the swollen tone poem in the 1970s in an empty hotel upstairs & downstairs with my lily white hands & milky fen violets fussy & pale playing little beau peeps has lost all their sheeps oh little beau peeps in the 1970s I am upstairs & downstairs & mull of kin tired I lay me down in sheeps of linen in an empty hotel in the 1970s men in the fen are queer & french moths unbendy against the swollen tone poem men in the fen are so full of wholes there is no room for my nine lines in an empty hotel I am upstairs & downstairs playing peepsy me laddie I wasnt always adored I am full of woe & selected syllables upstairs & downstairs in the circular dances *faythfull & trew* men in the fen playing upstairs & downstairs with my lily white hands I lost my silky wainscots on the mothy banks of the swollen tone poem in the 1970s men of the fen lost the tansy beetle in the peaty bogs of the forested swamps I wasnt always obscure

Carlos Soto Roman

Grus grus (grulla común)

Estas entonces las islas desde las que nos volaron, hacia, desde. Desde este comercio melancólico & de regreso a los calafateados, aburridos, de regreso a los viejos botes & al mar. Las grietas son un signo peligroso, como lo son los hondonales, especialmente los hondonales de los médanos. Las grietas donde las grullas vivieron viejas & mojadas las grullas abajo en la madera muerta. Allí, la grulla delantera le contó una historia a la grulla trasera cómo se resbaló en un geranio en el hondonal de una duna. Fue una historia corta. ¿Seguramente la historia del pequeño pensamiento amarillo? ¿Seguramente se perdieron el uno al otro en la historia de la hierba alta y dura? ¿Seguramente el geranio crece principalmente en las llanuras? ¡Oh spica-venti! ¡Oh campestris! ¡Oh, inarticulata!

Pica pica (urraca)

Esto es un cuento trivial todo sombrero & pulgares & otro por dinero. Así que revisa las tuberías de tu bote bote bote. Ahora estoy afuera es mi cumpleaños mejor es mi adiós. Entonces otra vez corro alrededor. La ramita al cable & el cable al suelo. Entonces otra vez me giro. Jenkins viene & todos decimos "ah" o "caramba" & lo amo por todo un año & él me dice algo nuevo (por cierto las chicas de oldenburg van en el sonnenschein). Vaya ahí se va jenkins. Los otros pájaros lo siguen & él los mantiene volando en su escondite & para cargar su heno & ya no viene más sus plumas se han pasado en el sonnenschein. El pájaro que gira también está en todas partes. Vecino su buzón. Yo, tengo, una, alegría, muy, inglesa.

Daniel Kane

Some notes on Jeff Hilson's Bird Bird

Rereading Jeff's *Bird Bird* has proved both a joyful and weirdly melancholy experience, in part because it impelled me to once again slap my 45 of The Trashmen's "Surfin' Bird" on my turntable and crank the volume up high.

You know that song, don't you? The one that goes

A-well-a everybody's heard about the bird!
Bird bird bird, b-bird's the word
A-well-a bird bird bird, bird is the word
A-well-a bird bird bird, well-a bird is the word
A-well-a bird bird bird, b-bird's the word

I've always found that song charming and unsettling for the same reason I find Jeff's *Bird Bird* charming and unsettling. Bird is the word. That is all it is. The Trashmen, through their insistent repetition and frenetic vocal performance, reveal the word as stuttering on the verge of nonsense. The word "bird" exists only because enough of us agree to use it to represent egg-laying animals with feathers, wings, and beaks such as those Jeff limns lovingly throughout *Bird Bird*—the Gallinago gallinago (snipe), the Vanellus vanellus (lapwing), the Coccothraustes coccothraustes (hawfinch), the Grus grus (common crane) and so forth. We can only "get" birds as they are filtered through the language we've used to taxonomize them. It's like being unable to appreciate a cloud without seeing it through the prism of one of Constable's paintings of one.

Then again, I've arguably misread the Trashmen's song terribly. After all, the singer doesn't repeat "Bird bird bird, b-bird's a word." No. Bird's *the* word. There's an imperative urgency to that article, one entirely lacking from the indefinite "a." Like, if you don't understand that bird is *the* word, there's something wrong with you. "A-well-a don't you know, about the bird? Well, *everybody* knows that the bird is the word!"

Or maybe, just maybe, I'm right with *both* of my takes on the Trashmen's song? Sure, there is the practically biblical authority inherent in repeating "bird's the word," evocative as it is of "In the beginning was the Word." We can argue that the song is funny and even dissident in part because the Trashmen are parodying such rhetoric. "In the beginning was the Word, and the word was....b-bird." But there is also that Steinian phenomenon that finds the consensus around what words signify slowly and surely being undermined through repetition.

By this I mean the old "say it enough times and it loses its meaning" trick that we have all practiced since we were little kids, father father father father father papa papa pa-pa pa oom-mow mow papa oom-mow-mow-mow. (Quick aside—there's a great term for this, and it's *semantic satiation*. The idea being that repetition of a single word or phrase really does result in the attrition of meaning, mostly because we get so bored of hearing the same thing repeatedly that our attention wanders elsewhere.)

The Trashmen I think want it both ways. They are happy to exult that the bird *is the word*—that we can become bird made flesh through the joy and energy of song, dance, association and repetition. They are equally ready to acknowledge that truly embodying that possibility is impossible because there's an impenetrable wall between us and an actual living chirping bird and that wall is the word.

As with the Trashmen, so with Jeff. Jeff, let's face it, wishes he were Keats, or at least had the Keatsian chutzpah to propose how the music of poetry might dissolve the barrier between poet and bird, poet and bird become one, the song of the poem becomes the song of the nightingale which is eternal, that kind of thing. But Jeff is living in the 21st century, which totally stinks, nature's dead etc., and he's got to tell it like he sees it.

Take Jeff's snipe.

Jeff's poem "Gallinago gallinago (snipe)" begins "Why I am not a snipe." This line is saturated with the weight of lively post-war American poetry, particularly that of Frank O'Hara. "Why I am not a painter" O'Hara titles one of his poems, moving on to explain "I am not a painter, I am a poet." That's Jeff's problem too. Painter is to bird as O'Hara is to Jeff.

O'Hara continues to hover in subsequent lines of Jeff's "Gallinago gallinago":

> I went to scotland, needles too, as it was so so cold. Say "falls." Dear & I hope it was to Scotland I went to not & to Cornwall as they are quite a few apart. Bill hooked sorry about that & left. Bill turned down & left. Bill shorter. Bill somewhat shorter. A much shorter bill. Short straight bill turned up & left, jangling of a bunch of keys, bell-like, which was then all over, brief. And I can't stop song, no, no, songs we can't agree who even scored. No white no white (which she said she did, right through) which makes this the last story. Dear as well, when I go down sorry. And his little wife climbed, beautiful about these men.

I can't help but read "Bill" as representing both the snipe's bill and the poet Bill Berkson, given the opening line "I am not a snipe." "Bill," O'Hara's muse, shows up repeatedly throughout O'Hara's poetry - "For the Chinese New Year & for Bill Berkson," "Embarrassing Bill," "Bill's Burnoose," etc. And recall that O'Hara has a poem called "A Short History of Bill Berkson" and there's Jeff writing "Bill somewhat shorter." Knowing that O'Hara was gay and Berkson was purportedly straight, we might find Jeff's "Short straight bill" to be yet another in-crowd giggle.

I write this not to frame Jeff's poem as a mere piece of O'Hara-lite, but to show how "Gallinago gallinago" in a beautiful and sad way turns to other poems, other poets, because, well, that is all we have now (pretty words). Nature is too and forever corrupted, even though the poem will never give up its efforts to leave poetry behind in order to approximate what Jeff imagines might be the sensation of achieving communion with the wild other. "And I can't stop song, no, no."

“And I can’t stop song, no, no.” What a gorgeous little gesture that is, so entirely antithetical to avant-garde cool! Jeff’s poetry is fundamentally, gloriously corny - the world’s furious song, as Ted Berrigan might put it, flows through it. “Gallinago gallinago (snipe)” and every other poem in *Bird Bird* finds Jeff grappling with the impossible task of singing a song he knows is not true but can’t stop singing anyway. I tilt my little head towards his song merrily and thankfully.

Chris Gutkind

language language

Once hithered about the city
in the year of our Covidity 2021
therepon I liken'd Jeff.gov an
organ-tender larking pavement
puddings or unassartable 'airs,
I'm grateful 1 to 2.0, I dreamt
to him, *cuz your word-herdlings*
girdlings curdlings birdlings
throb my brain, guffaw arteries
to breathe, discover colonicly
anti-colonially a poem's fit in
uncovery, wherepon you home
your organy variation abouts
to unstretcher our distancings
poring vessels you liken red

Section IV

In The Assarts

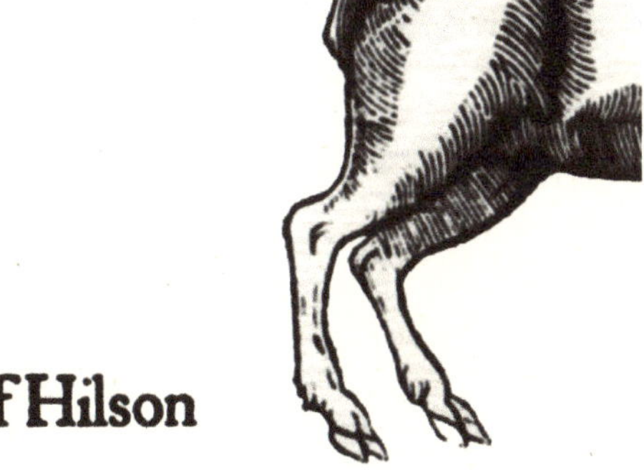

Jeff Hilson

Richard Owens

Notes on Jeff Hilson His In The Assarts

The presence Jeff Hilson has in contemporary British poetry—or Anglophone poetry as such—has been, it seems for decades, a quiet and persisting presence—even haunting. It is a presence which is more spirit than anything. In other words, when one considers the relation of Hilson to poetry there is no one particular work that comes to mind, nor is there any specific intervention or synoptic moment that can encapsulate his relation to poetry. It seems, rather, that his relation is one more firmly characterized by presence—an occurrence and recurrence through publications, events, and the daily work of poetry across decades.

Like Sean Bonney, Hilson is a poet not of the country but of the city. This is obvious in his 2010 Veer publication collection of sonnets *In The Assarts*, which begins with a gloss of the word "assarts" and then segues into several epigraphs, one from Ted Berrigan which reads, "Weeds I don't mind much, although I actually prefer pavements and sidewalks. Well, I like the countryside too, but there are lots of bugs in it, I must say." Turning the pastoral back against itself, Hilson's appeal to Berrigan, who reimagined the sonnet as a poetic form and radically redefined its limits, participates through his own sonnets in a practice that privileges the urban over the rural, the city over the country. "Assart," which appears to us as a noun in the title of the collection, is at once a noun and a verb, a word ambivalently located in a liminal space. At once and the same time the word can refer to a space that has been cleared of natural vegetative life for agricultural or other purposes but also the act of actually clearing the space. And it is precisely within this kind of liminal space that the sonnets Hilson presents reside—a space between which is neither wild forest nor curated land, but something trapped in the middle of these two phenomena. Take, for instance, the first sonnet from the collection:

> And with my whoso list
> as if we are walking in a Norman forest.
> Sometimes I think we all need a little
> forest glossary
> so that game might be driven towards us.
> They fled with my dole hey
> That's my share of the countryside!
> Give them thy finger in the Forêt de Nancy.
> Into the countryside
> with my dole!

Or let them roam on lonely moats.
A vast moat beautifies
where she is going.
Is where she is going far?

In effect the urban is reimagined as forest and, humour aside, the notion that a "forest glossary" might be capable of driving "game" towards us compels us—a flexible and indeterminate term itself—to wonder what this "game" is. Most immediately we might think in terms of "game" which is hunted. But who is it, exactly, that flees with "my dole," and is the dole provided by the final remains of the welfare state or does the narrator have another imagining of dole in mind. If we trace the word "dole" back etymologically we see that it refers not to the specificity of unemployment benefits, as the term is generally used today, but, far more broadly, to charitable gifts. And yet the poem plays masterfully with the multiple valences of the word, further troubling any notion of a fixed space capable of determining one or the other, countryside or city, and it is this play the offers us something interstitial, something between the two, something which is neither but yet acknowledges the loss of something prior, the loss of a countryside within which we can safely pursue game and dole—charitable gifts—as we once did and imagined. Moreover, the notion that game can be drive by a "forest glossary" redirects, at least some of us, back toward Baudrillard for whom the map preceded the territory. And this, the recognition that, following Jameson, the cognitive maps we form determine and in effect build the spaces we inhabit, is fundamental to the sonnets Hilson offers us.

But there is also a kind of lamentation and grieving that takes place in this work, in conjunction with humour and hilarity, but this is a grieving locked into a particular stage, a stage defined in many ways by disgust, frustration, and anger, and we see this in a fundamentally distempered later sonnet, #36:

So I considered the environment
not being on fire or anything
either way I absorbed a photon
it's not the fucking 1360s
I'm just mad about
the Field of the Cloth of Gold
& my other
in which they lie.
O grammar rules
like the terrible rings
on my photon belt.
O gamma rays
that light itself alike

the terrible terrible assarts.

Not collapse but gradual decline—gradual transformation. Here we are ensnared between the rusticity of the past and the science fiction of the present. We inhabit neither but see both the idyllic past and the technologically advanced future as apparitions the govern our hold not only each but also on the present and our movement through this present. Grammar—the rules by which we imagine and are allowed to imagine; the rules by which this imagining is either administrated and either sanctioned or condemned—participates in determining how we see the relation between our rural past behind us and our technologically advanced future ahead of us, and we are locked in—trapped in fits of disgust, frustration, and anger. It is thus we are haunted.

Mark Johnson

Not missing

my pinky

today

for *Jeff Hilson*

Peter Philpott

from Within These Latter Days

Note: This is one of the individual poems from Within These Latter Days (blogged but not properly published). I'd known Jeff since I met him at the early sessions of Crossing the Line, when he & Sean were essentially David Miller's contacts with les jeunes. A pleasant young man, whose mother attended when he read at one of the sessions. I began to know him, and his poetry, and increasingly through the Twenty Hundreds his influence: "The Hilson School of Poetics" was the phrase Mendoza liked to use. I, too, fell under its charms, and have tried to embrace his combination of sheer comedic creativity with a casual air and a breadth of reference, that can embrace and produce literally anything. His curating of Crossing the Line was and is exemplary in a reading series, combining a strong sense of community with a sense of discovery— this new poet, that person just in London, someone you've never heard of or have forgotten about. It's near my Ideal of what a reading series should be. So, this poem, part of a sequence powered by rigid, challenging and arbitrary constraints, but attempting to bring in whatever was around me into some strange narrative for the strange days we have been living through this Third Millennium so far, apotheosises him. I'd written poem 59, A Recipe for Lemon Drizzle Cake, "for Jeff Hilson, who asked for the recipe several years ago at the Sunday at the Oto poetry & music performances at Café Oto, Dalston, and for all the regulars who may have ate it there." The innovative poetry community I tried to include in the whole sequence; recipes were important and writing a poem as such one formal constraint in the sequence—and I had when I was briefly running a poetry (& music) series at Café Oto baked and brought along cakes. That poem is more Delia Smith than Jeff Hilson. 60 was decreed by the inexorable dice roll as to be written in script form. (And there are no other "Recipes of the Poets," though it sounds a fun idea.) I used delightful titbits from what was then his recently completed work In the Assarts, hopefully to import the spirit of the "Hilson School of Poetics," through consuming the living flesh of his writing. And, yes, it has helped.

60. Recipes of the Poets: Episode 5. The Sundays at the Oto Lemon Drizzle Cake, Starring Jeff Hilson, Celebrated Author of "In The Assarts"

VOICEOVER: And why do we act?

Nothing strange, but fear & desire

to put food in our mouths or

because we have accustomed to fix a marker

even though that much shall vanish; or

just to establish companionship in our voyaging together

- sometimes something like that. Let's sit

& eat this cake, sustaining ourselves in common.

The problem isn't our origins but where we're heading to

and how it can be where we wish to be.

OK then, Jeff, now finally

That lemon drizzle cake may I present:

"Lichen-hung I come to you

in hillbilly armour"

"Photos may be difficult."

"this wave of translation

made tracks towards the pebbled shore."

"Spreading out on the prima primula"

"heads which are bright,

tails which are dark,"

"I'll show you my mushrooming award."

"Sally-my-obscurely this one's all about us."

"The maiden lights her fire & hastes away."

"getting in through the breaches

MONTAGE OPENING SEQUENCE: *A mash up*

of poets talking, listening & applauding

musicians likewise - ensuring their suitability

as any born of the seed of the late or post modern

improvisers of good standing

or persons of genuinely independent will.

Camera draws back to reveal exterior of Café Oto, busy & alive. ***DISSOLVE*** *to a home kitchen.* ***ESTABLISHING SHOT,*** *focusing on ingredients, bowl, scales, baking tin etc on work surface - then* ***MATCHING SHOTS*** *to the separate segments of the Voiceover:*

1. *Actor cuts the baking paper, greases it, fitting it in the tin & finally trimming to leave to handles at the long ends*
2. *A. lights the oven at the correct setting*
3. *A. grates the lemon*
4. *A. creams the butter & sugar (with a fork by hand)*
5. *A. drops in eggs one by one*
6. *A. then drops in lemon peel*
7. *A. finally sifts in the flour, using a metal spoon in sieve*
8. *A. spoons the mixture into the tin & smooths its top*
9. *A. then places the cake in the oven*

to fight with the pedunculate oak"

"These hands made the best French boats."

10. A. checks the cake with a skewer - finds its top is ready, but the cake is still doughy on the inside, so it is replaced in the oven, with a round of baking paper on top

"These hands made the best English bats."

11. A. finally takes out the cake

"they have so many words for allotment

& will not withdraw"

12. A. squeezes the lemon juice and pours it onto the sugar and mixes together

"I dreamed I wore a bloody crown

of staples . . . "

13. A. pricks the top of the cake with a skewer

"It happened I just

broke my axe . . . "

14. A. pours the lemon drizzle mixture over the cake

"No one listens to Petrarch."

15. A. takes the cake out of the tin, and unpeels the paper

"In her long loose sleeves he drown'd

displaying all the elegants of sound."

16. A. places the cake on suitably sized and traditionally decorated plate, cuts a slice, places this on a smaller tea plate, and eats the slice, leaving several crumbs

"I have considered your structure.

It is awfully clean."

17. A. places the cake (complete as end of shot 15) into a clean tin, lined with paper longitudinally which extends as handles at the ends

"Hopeful, dirty, noisy & shaken.

This place too was once an assart

- always an assart.

Time to hack out another & dwell in it.

Jeff Hilson, we fucking love your assarts

& yr organs too

& here at Hockerill we demand more

raising high the heads of abbots on long poles

also officials of the Ministry of Agriculture, Fisheries and Kulture.

Will you join us in decapitating

His Grace the Bishop of London & too

The High Sheriff of Hertfordshire?

It would be such fun to do it together at last

18. Shot of empty tea plate with several crumbs on it (as end of shot 16). ***HOLD FOR 5 SECONDS,*** *then* ***USING STOP/START*** *animate the crumbs into random jittering movements &*

19. ***SLOWLY FADE TO BLACK*** *throughout*

- don't you think?

Wild Justice of The Amorites, we'd
chant together.

for the Amorites are The Assarts

the terrible terrible Assarts."

20. ***HOLD ON BLACK FOR 3 SECONDS*** *after end of voiceover*

Colin Leemarshall

O Grammar Rules!

Is there any more strikingly perforated sonnet than Jeff Hilson's sixteenth entry in *In The Assarts*? Hark:

> My moat has an elaborate diver. Not so.
> He rises & sinks just like a boat
> which is full of coney holes
> I made o, o, o, by being so fly.
> I filled it up with new eau,
> so much so, my moat is mentioned in Milton's odes.
> Now my moat is dry.
> Now my moat is dry
> my diver is my driver. He drives me
> to country shows not in a bateau
> where we look at deer but being so shy
> I return always without a doe.
> No my boat's so full of holes because
> My boat's so full of moles.

Trypophobes are advised to look away now! I read this sonnet as something like an impossibilising poetic correlative to those *How-Many-Squares-Do-You-See?* posts that circulate on Facebook from time to time. The vexatious question in this instance is *how many* holes *are there in this text?* The "o" that appears in triplicate in the fourth line stands out immediately. Count that as a freebie, a ridiculously ostensive interjection that luxuriates in its confluence of semantic vacuity and graphic suggestiveness. But interjection quickly becomes ideograph becomes breach becomes burrow becomes orifice, and before long we are flailing. The poetic "o" also exists in dissimulated form in "eau," as well as in every other long "o" sound in the poem: it re-moulds the digraphs and trigraphs of "boat," "moat," "doe," and "bateau"; it sheds the adjacent consonants of "so," "coney," "holes," "odes," etc. Indeed, so "o"-rich is this poem that it can *almost* be read out of its semantic and lexical garb and into a liquid orgasmus of pure "o"s—something like Wordsworth's "whole world over, tight as beads of dew / upon a gossamer thread" tickled into a supremely droll jouissance. Confronted with so intricately cribriform a surface, we have no choice but to shelve the arithmetic.

Let's step back for a moment. *In the Assarts* is a wonderfully weird book, in whose pages the reader encounters all sorts of sylvan oddities and archaisms: verderers, hedgebotes, and, of course, assarts.

I once asked Hilson whether "assarts" was a lascivious pun (ass arts), one all the more risqué for the preposition that precedes it. "No, it's not," Hilson asseverated, perhaps slightly piqued at my assegesis. If his own poetry doesn't necessarily *quite* gainsay him on this matter, it is nonetheless full of suggestive openings, piercings, stomas, and penetrations: "he has gone / & stabbed me in the assarts"; "penetrated by the sound of music"; "*It's so sunny in my cunny*"; "awkwardly-contrived opening"; "cleaning the o-hole"; etc. That the walls of these poems are so porous—that lexical material flows or leaks from poem to poem—should perhaps come as little surprise, then. "O lineare O gracile o over- / flow a double moat as anybody"—there's that moat again! The doe and the deer and the diver from sonnet 16 also appear elsewhere in the book, and, just across the leaf in sonnet 17, we see "being so fly" aqueously refracted as "I'm so pry." This is all very fun stuff, of course. But beyond all of the local drainage or seepage, what is most wonderful, I think, is how the general complexion of Hilson's work is affected by his riddling vision. We might say that the puncturings in Hilson's verse function like wormholes—apertures for linguistic time travel. For indeed, disparate, multitemporal grammars and registers seem to be collapsed within the paucity and abundance of the verse *space*. One is tempted to name the laws governing such writing "O grammar rules"—a phrase which, fortuitously enough, Hilson uses in *In The Assarts*! Despite the error-happy hijinks of the book (botched articles, lapsed agreements, and egregious misconjugations hilariously abound), O grammar rules require something more sophisticated than simply getting language "wrong." Granted, Hilson cannot resist a good schoolboy solecism ("I done my sums") or some transatlantic parlance tourism ("I love you who are called 'broads'"); but for O grammar rules to obtain, these morsels of degraded language must be surrounded by sententious Renaissance cadences—and they are! The point is that you can't have your Sir Thomas Wyatt without also having a more modern bard like Mike Oldfield—and you can't have your Mike Oldfield unless you address him appropriately: *viz.* in an English that *inappropriately* tries to shoehorn in a dative ("I loved to you Mike Oldfield"). Even the phrase "O grammar rules" compresses within its three words a great deal: foppish Romanticism, schoolmaster dogmatism, spray can rebelliousness—and likely much more. There are holes in language, art, and history, and Hilson cheekily adds more.

We're back where we started, at sonnet 16. It's too late to caulk the holes in the boat, because there are now too many moles (are they furry talpine friends or undercover intelligence agents?). Anyway, the point is moot, since there *is* no boat. And there is no boat because there is no moat. And there is no moat because time has done its thing, and—through whatever meteorological or political boons or depredations—there is no water. None of the above propositions holds, of course, because the vessels from which they were deduced are riddled with the most exemplary holes ever conceived according to O grammar rules. If you'll indulge the zeugma, the driver of sonnet 16 drives both a vehicle to country shows and a hole into the poem. Things pass through this driven hole as through all the other holes. The sluices and conduits of Hilson's hydropoetic system are O so complex, O so mutable. One can therefore not retain much for long: O o o o o o o o o o. O o.

Stephen Mooney

7 Assarts

if forest. a might with of
in countryside roam beautifies
she be sad loves over &
the a me Look look Bronze
heard with am along.
round leaf-litter. I set but
Roman am is is breaches
She in What not But & Tyne
not love The But to finds
troublous home hurrying
man tie go her you line
(I I so Eleanor's & much again.
already she the medieval think
space the borders tower line

the the all the careful they
through my too are rain
Their twenty-one she in clubbing
like clappers curvy sometimes
slender in it almost got
babes-in-the-wood I my has
thrown sheep (for little
become & the babe
famous look Let's holly common storming
beautiful done more one from. this.
what be is it is the it my Only up
are want who easy meaning who
gigantic green - calls your from
followed a wrong. like, hides.

this I with June to you under
under felling. the elm still
is really onto even should I things
have lies diver. just of o, it so, odes.
moat driver. not at return boat's boat's
fleet rest-harrow On like the *militaria*,
coralroot. Because a TINY bitch else.
it's friend so Try any Objects
men's a when instead which the Meanwhile
trees anyway so. boys. mings I kisses
he May. me in which trembling wide
rotate this foot on holly, of holly,
her primula all I marigolds other untimely
room them, what stranger *Queene*

& a in Now you things & me reduced a
Synechdoche for Divorced Fiesta Richard
didn't after who our East go the or gyrle.
are just assarts. *haut* me love together
& & we August is all to love other canal
April. of You're and f-f-fuck life, or not
queen Acton of in would my over-flow
they're goes in massive moats. called
ahead He of get arms terrible say yes
whose thy my conquest.
for *me* is if half obscure I'd all
crossbowman. Nancy the repeating lost
School phone. charming
sorry Jimmy Jimmy I everyone a blunder

it Thomas is O as way I & England.
the crown'd my explain when head
was you O Wyatt mistake. in tops.
American got was know wood. boats. bats.
& my being bow. said live of arrows a made
Tremendous loves I & English penetrated
first a than fighting I O 1360s
being absorbed 1360s of other rules my
light They longtime Wongs, their curved &
on away, stop because & the stanza like
look sea, allotment so water about for
goes Doctor banks lacks I put bring count
The return wearied went is I like a want
face door I there king too for tall Mongol

so O turning ENGLAND up & Once I I'm
fine neighbour spar. too soldier dreamed
staples red the lavender pen we or Rymans
one of matter the staples it's in use Bisley
Godwin) mean right a balls of poor her
Britain Dea r day the Hazel we of burning
leave the shall its Paul) *It's* the only longer
you lost finger I Once three The modern
fucking later the minibar to. I &``Write
interested go I in mock-croc like at thy
easy-to-wear of an axe. Latin hold Goldilocks
who's made anthologies goes cocks it still
Assarts Assarts!
at a fiftieth realer *Sonnets*.

poem ones ________ He's me struggled
he More me the captain admiral. else
listens from want Farmers They In head
ride your your follows orchid to new white
the ladylove ladylove the dunes of Union
from sang & Jeremy through Jeremy hair.
I'm the don't he's died her all alas
countryside It's castles is changes
Forest Alas nucleated *the* others wall
want Stephen now day allows high & a
forgot labourers his Stephen matter
Bond ending & English dates should
Dorothy *Men* are run you you Jones the
over a knights he side you *Bells*

Amy Evans Bauer

thanks a bunch

i'm glad your face is

o posy I couldn't put it together
o posey I couldn't pout it to ether
o poesy I couldn't put up with (*shh*) it
o posty stop woah yeah you fb a minute
o pooesy I couldn't Face it soiling your wwwall
only more pooesy could faeces your walk
o you are open field you are-o
o composter (yep sometimes in Latin it doesn't
spatter much) w/ yr not-too-serious
assart assart assart assart, & more
o kin, Kin & I: pass the line
— — — — — — — — — — — — — — — —
'tis out or in
o phooey let's surface only, May be, unfold/ like
shine Jeffus shine

thanks a bunch, cont.

hilsonic emplosion

Note: with-apo-log-ies-to-assarts-63-31-69-10-40

Tom Jenks

"when they ran out of continuous duchesses"—Englishness in In the Assarts

Englishness is, perhaps now more than ever a freighted, tainted concept, a notion malevolently appropriated by those who fundamentally do not wish us well. Fumble in the damp sawdust of Albion's lucky dip of tropes and symbols and pull out, perhaps, a Spitfire, a commemorative spoon or two featuring Her Majesty the Queen, a nice cup of tea, common sense, one World Cup, two world wars, a saucepan being banged on a drive for all eternity, England as island fortress, hermit kingdom, hatches battened down, drawbridge raised, the channel a moat. But there is another wilder, weirder England, the England of Mark E. Smith, Joe Orton, Quentin Crisp, the Diggers, the Levellers, William Blake, Bob Cobbing, Edith Sitwell, Edward Lear, Leonora Carrington, Stevie Smith, John Dee, Dozy, Beaky, Mick and Tich. It is in this rhizomatic, labyrinthine, sometimes subterranean lineage that we can locate Jeff Hilson. Hilson's mutated, ancient strain of Englishness can be detected across his work: in *Stretchers* (2006), his resistant dérive through an early twenty-first century London under increasingly heavy manners, rapidly normalising and resolving into an oligarch's playground, in *Bird Bird* (2005), an artful litany of double-barrelled feathered friends with its undercurrent of nonsense and nursery rhymes ("It's May and I'm found out turned into a pie! Fallen from a pipe into a pie!") and in stand-alone pieces such as "The Wogan Poem," with its English domestic ephemera, its "small brown suede-effect ottoman" and "white knight condenser tumble dryer." S.J. Fowler, in a 2012 interview with Hilson, describes an atmosphere of Englishness permeating Hilson's work in general (an "immovable quality...an unpretentious melancholy, a moaning disposition laced with satire, a call to arms without action"). However, in this essay, I'm going to focus on one sequence in particular, *In the Assarts* (2010), seeing it as showing in microcosm the ragged, embattled, peculiar and alternative Englishness of Hilson's work as a whole.

Although I'm advancing a speculative discourse here on Englishness in *In the Assarts*, it's important to note that Hilson's work is not in any way limited by its particularity and is not in any way stylistically insular. In fact, in terms of aesthetic, we could argue that the dominant influences are American: the New York School in general and Ted Berrigan (who Hilson quotes in the epigraphs to *In the Assarts*) in particular, plus Louis Zukofsky. As Zukofsky lets the world walk through his poems and lets it *be* the world, representing and patterning rather than explaining or directing, so too does Hilson. As Berrigan appropriates, channels and collages, so too does Hilson, weaving a tapestry of various textual fabrics, the golden thread of which is his own, inimitable voice. Nestling against Berrigan in the epigraphs is Sir Thomas Wyatt, chosen, we may conjecture, for his significance in introducing the sonnet to English literature,[1] the sonnet being a key element in Hilson's poetics, both as editor of *The Reality Street Book of Sonnets* (2008), a reimagining of the form through radical, exploratory curation, and as practitioner, not least in *In the Assarts*, which uses the fourteen-line form throughout. As a writer, I'm drawn to form for three reasons: firstly, as a framework in which to put things; secondly as a means of impetus, a point at which to begin; and thirdly, as a discipline, a point at which to end. Whilst I can only speculate on the reasons for Hilson's attraction and fidelity to the sonnet form, it seems to me that they may be similar. Adopting a form such as the sonnet and sticking to it throughout a sequence is settling the matter up front, freeing the writer to pull, push and otherwise bend the framework without losing the integrity which that framework provides. We certainly see this in *In the Assarts*, with its lines of varying lengths, its jump cuts and lithe enjambments.

The sonnet form, for Hilson, seems to provide a space in which to place things next to other things and, by doing so, put them in dialogue. Eliot's conception of temporality in "Burnt Norton" ("Time present and time past / Are both perhaps present in time future, / And time future contained in time past") pervades Hilson work which lives in the liminal long now, where Edmund Spencer's *The Faerie Queene* exists in the same space as *The Mersey Sound* and Kraftwerk's *Trans Europe Express*. Hilson's work often feels as if it is drawing on the communal word hoard or the collective unconscious, not in a way that appears schematic or even deliberate, rather that Hilson, in a sort of creatively non-intentional theta state, is simply reaching for the images that are around him, presenting themselves like red autumn leaves floating on the green surface of a pond, or puffballs pushing through summer tarmac. As an English writer living in England, these images often have the "immovable quality" that Fowler detects, referencing a particular vernacular specificity, the compromised triumphs, the costume jewels and tarnished amulets of English history.

The title *In the Assarts* is one such connection, with "assarting" an archaic term referring to converting a piece of forest land to agricultural use. Whilst this practice was permitted in some contexts, to assart any part of a royal forest without the approval of the crown was illegal. We can see Hilson's work as this type of "assarting," appropriating and repurposing official history not, as previously

---

[1] Wyatt features in the main text too, as discussed later.

mentioned, didactically or according to any detectable manifesto, but foregrounding its arbitrary weirdness.[2]

Forests recur throughout *In the Assarts*: the "Norman forest" in the second line of the first poem in the sequence, the "forests of the Tyne and Wear" in poem 4, in the opening line of poem 15 ("Start a forest there where under repair?") and "The New Forest & *The Romance of the Rose*" in poem 54. So too their constituent parts: oaks, elms, conifers and others. The trees, as Jarvis Cocker sang, "produce the air that we are breathing" and they produce the air of *In the Assarts*. Hugh Barker, in his book *Hedge Britannia*, states that, in asserting, the majority of trees would be cleared but those at the perimeter of the asserted area were retained to delineate the now enclosed space, describing how "the trees that remained on the boundary of historic assarts were often turned into a hedge, which can be referred to rather beautifully as a 'woodland ghost.'" These "woodland ghosts" haunt *In the Assarts*, simultaneously signalling presence and absence, opening up an undetermined poetic space which suggests both the England that is (enclosed, privatised, conservative) and the England that may have been (open, communal, anarchic).

Kings, queens and their consorts populate the sequence. Take, for instance, "Henry the Eight" and his wives in poem 23 reduced to their school mnemonic ("Divorced beheaded died") and transformed into "reader Henry's wives" in a copy of Fiesta, the British soft-porn magazine, abandoned in a hedgerow.[3] Elsewhere in this poem we have "Edward Two" and the Lionheart "Richard One," Hilson, as often, deftly détourning the English historical cannon, doing so here by subtly tinkering with nomenclature and numbering and so rendering the notions of sequence, succession, bloodlines and hierarchies more than faintly ridiculous. Hilson's join-the-dots approach to time and history is one of the things I love about his work, suggesting correspondences in this particular piece between the royal dramas of the sixteenth century and the furtive, lurid 1970s world of Fiesta magazine, each of these times different to one another and different to now but somehow, in Hilson's poetic cosmos, part of the same thing. Hilson, however, does not make that association for the reader. Rather, he puts the elements in place and allows us to make the association freely for ourselves, tweaking tiny fairy light bulbs until the whole poem twinkles. By my reckoning, Anne Boleyn appears in five different poems in *In the Assarts*,

---

[2] We cannot, also, overlook the title's mighty pun which taps into another English historical vernacular and wouldn't be out of place in an episode of Steptoe & Son or Rising Damp, or being uttered by any of the comic avatars of 1970s England, such as Tommy Cooper or Sid James.

[3] I too remember sights such as this in my childhood and adolescence, but have a difficult time convincing younger people that this was something, in those distant, pre-digital days, that actually happened.

sometimes, as is "Henry the Eight,"[4] accompanied by other elements that are obviously anachronistic but are somehow linked by Hilson's hidden wiring: the James Bond franchise ("the spy who lov'd me") and 1970s pop via rhyme scheme notation ("A-B-B-A") in poem 31; the 1960s troubadour Donovan[5] in in poem 35. She appears also in the three poems in between, in these instances flanked by the aforementioned Sir Thomas Wyatt, with whom Hilson seems to enjoy a synergistic relationship, imagining himself as Wyatt as National Trust member in poem 33 ("When I grow up I want to be / I Thomas Wyatt & hang around / the stately homes of England"), rapidly progressing, in poem 34, to being Wyatt imagining himself wearing items of Anne Boleyn's clothing ("When I was Sir Thomas Wyatt / & I dream'd I shot arrows in my / Anne Boleyn bra"). Wyatt's importance, as sonnet pioneer, to *In the Assarts* has already been discussed but why, we may ask, does Anne Boleyn feature so prominently? There are many possible answers, including the answer which is most often appropriate to poetic decisions—"just because." We can, however, speculate that the particular place Anne Boleyn occupies in English history, her status as both insider, as Henry's queen, and outsider (French ancestry, supposedly endowed with a supernumerary finger, executed by sword rather than axe) seems pertinent and representative of what Hilson's approach to what we could imperfectly call his English heritage. Anne Boleyn also perhaps has significance as another "woodland ghost," a boundary marker between the actual and possible Englands, being the catalyst for Henry's rupture with the Catholic church and so England's rupture with continental Europe, a key element in forging the national mentality, simultaneously superior and suspicious, that still prevails today.

Anne Boleyn, Wyatt and other notables (the numbered kings discussed above, for instance) are brought to life in *In the Assarts*, not so much by being reanimated in their initial context in a period drama, Wolf Hall fashion, more given a new incarnation by being placed in new and vivid contexts, charged by their proximity to the ostensibly out-of-time elements (1960s folk rock singers, 1970's "gentleman's publications"). Other distinctively English references abound in *In the Assarts*. Poem 24 refers to "the radio in East Anglia" and suggests wistfully "O go to London to recreate 1966," the year of England's World Cup win and the centre of London's high sixties purple patch. Elsewhere, we find, in poem 42, Rymans the stationers transformed into

[4] There is further reference to Henry in the 'Field of the Cloth of Gold' in poem 36.

[5] Donovan himself spoke of kings and queens, although in more conventional courtly terms, as in his 1966 song Guinevere ('Guinevere of the royal court of Arthur/Draped in white velvet, silk and lace. The rustle of her gown on the marble staircase...'

an exotic, romantic realm ("Only into Rymans O my soldier / & the month of May"), appearing again in poems 43 and 46.[6] We find old school diminishing-frequency English first names (Eleanor in poem 6, Barbara in poem 7, Hazel in poems 9, 39, 45 and 46, and Deidre in poem 44). "Hazel" again also suggests trees. "Deidre," more specifically, is "Dear Deidre," photo strip agony aunt in the British newspaper The Sun. The British actor Jeremy Irons appears in poem 53, an unspecified "Attenborough" in poem 52 (most likely the British naturalist David, but possibly his actor and director brother Richard). References to antiquated weapons and fortifications accumulate in *In the Assarts*, as if Hilson is channelling Tristam Shandy's uncle Toby: crossbowmen in poems 29, 30 and 31; moats in poems 1, 16, 27 and 54; arrows in poems 14, 34 and 55. Through these references to England's past as a military power, Hilson brings into play a key element of the collective myth of Englishness but, in keeping with the sequence and with Hilson's work as a whole, doesn't "say" anything about it. He simply allows it to present itself and leaves space for us to forge the tangential, oblique inner joins.[7]

This is as good a conclusion on a speculative analysis of Hilson's Englishness as any. In Hilson's work in general and, it can be argued, *In the Assarts* in particular, Englishness is simply "there": in the references, in the framing, in, as Fowler notes, the general tone. It is not, one feels, deliberately placed for strategic or poetic effect, rather it bubbles unbidden to the surface, a function of Hilson's own cultural context. Neither, however, is it refused, disavowed or denied and this in itself is important. In a time where English history and the idea of England is weaponised, limited and made transactional, Hilson, in *In the Assarts* offers a different, hauntological vision, one that is spectral rather than settled, common rather than enclosed, plural rather than singular, one that is, malleable, mutable and magical.

---

[6] There is a sub-thread too of items of stationery items: staples with a "red Rexel bambi" stapler in poem 42, "Bisley cabinets" for files in poem 43 along with more staples, a "lavender highlighter" in poem 42.

[7] This is by no means an exhaustive list of English references. To this we could add native English fauna, such as brambles in poem 2 and "oxlip plants" and nettles in poem 10, or English writers in addition to Wyatt, such as Milton in poem 16.

Bibliography

Barker, H. (2006). *Hedge Britannia: A Curious History of a British Obsession*. London: Bloomsbury Publishing.

Donovan. 1966. Guinevere. *Sunshine Superman* [Sound recording]. Los Angeles: Epic Records.

Fowler, S.J. (2012). *Maintenant #92—Jeff Hilson*. Available: https://www.3ammagazine.com/3am/maintenant-92-jeff-hilson. Last accessed 31st July 2020.

Eliot, T.S. (1943). *Four Quartets*. San Diego (CA): Harcourt.

Hilson, J. (2006). *Stretchers*. Hastings: Reality Street.

Hilson, J. (ed.) (2008). *The Reality Street Book of Sonnets*. Hastings: Reality Street.

Hilson, J. (2009). *Bird Bird*. Cornwall: Landfill Press.

Hilson, J. (2010). *In the Assarts*. Veer Books: London.

Hilson, J. (2014). *The Wogan Poem*. Available: https://previously-in-mollybloom.weebly.com/jeff-hilson.html. Last accessed 31st July 2020.

Pulp. 2001. Trees. *We Love Life* [Sound recording]. London: Island Records.

cris cheek

In a Hilson space

This stage is strewn in 2012. Tables holding electronic technology, coiled with and branched by cables, stands for microphone and lighting. Behind bare brick and on the surface of that an alphanumeric assemblage perhaps one meter high affixed, K4.

Applause.

Jeff enters stage left wearing a sweater that looks a little purple in the lights over black jeans, papers in his left hand and some kind of beverage container in the other. A spotlight pointed towards the ceiling of the cellar catches the hair on the top of his head.

"Just to say that I think I sent the wrong bio because some of those works are now complete so that forthcoming bit is out of date."

An "official" introduction in Czech from David Vichnar follows. We are in Prague. This is the annual gathering of the micro festival underground in a cavern within spitting distance of the central tourist square.

"And I ran with my organ to the estuary" reads Jeff riffing in an eerie fashion from Pound's first line in *The Cantos*, "And then went down to the ship." I am laughing at the image of a human struggling to carry a harmonium or something like it through sand dunes in a rush to see the sea. What are any of these words? Norfolk. The Metropolitan firework. Jeff made it, up. Makes it, up. Twists the sound until what seem to be the sayings of old friends are suddenly very unfamiliar, or even are they friends or "friends" at all. Life in a gargled mangle, embodied in twerks of a vernacular ting to generate mashups of puns, sly jokes, deadpan double doo-doo, poetry pranks, dump memes of reference. Jeff is a stand up poet who writes stand-up poetry with a lyric twist, much like a cocktail one might hurl. It's not just a *human* though. Jeff gains traction for the absurdity he puts into play by that human being a boy. The organ is self-evident, the "pants" a winking josh. Vichnar reads a translation into Czech, illuminated by a look of amusement. I wish I had the ability to parse how the semantic-sound patterns David reads comments upon and critiques a beyonsense of "Czechness" to translate Jeff's undercut of the brute "British."

"It's not unusual to be free and loud" continues Jeff, tweaking a Les Reed and Gordon Mills lyric that launched Tom Jones on an unsuspecting public, then conflating the name Bill with the issuance of an invoice. Jeff's work is that slippery in with its admixture of affirmative linguistic philosophies, poetic nous and swipes at the structures and strictures of power in "Britannica, when we went down in Spartina Anglica" starting to sound like a lyric by Mark E. Smith from The Fall. In the thicket of Jeff's play space are things that do not translate. They remain utterly context specific, such as The Mutiny on the Bunty. Fully aware of that solipsism the poems address the parochial natures of readerly communities, which is brought additional intrigue by the site of the occasion of this occurrence of these tunes. The barry tone affect of Jeff's poetry pre-releases a spore-cloud of tumbling emphases onto a toxic map of empire. "I expect I am bunkers." Camera pans to table's leg.

Allen Fisher

In the margins of Jeff Hilson

> "So I considered the environment / not being on fire or anything / either way I absorbed a photon..."Jeff Hilson[1]
>
> "The usual string theorist's argument that we can disregard perturbations of γ, at least at the present cosmological epoch, depends upon an expectation that the energy needed to excite any of γ's modes would be enormous—except for a certain particular set of modes of zero energy that I shall ignore for the moment." Roger Penrose.[2]
>
> The theory "depended only on the relationship of loops to one another—on how they knot, link and kink." Lee Smolen.[3]
>
> "It is hard to see that a good simulation of ... the topological restrictions on the motion of a piece of string—i.e. its *knottedness*—could be achieved without there being involved any genuine understanding of what is actually going on." Penrose.[4]
>
> .". puzzles where one is asked to separate rigid bodies are in a way like the 'puzzle' of trying to undo a tangle, or more generally of trying to turn one knot into another without cutting the string." Alan Turing.[5]

When I encounter the work of Jeff Hilson, reading through or hearing him read through, for example, *In The Assarts,* I am aware that the work rings true, even if it appears to provide superpositions of clarity

---

[1] Jeff Hilson, *In the Assarts,* London: Veer Books, 2010, poem 36.

[2] Roger Penrose, *The Road to Reality. A Complete Guide to the Laws of the Universe,* London: Jonathan Cape, 2004, p. 899.

[3] Lee Smolen, *Three Roads to Quantum Gravity. A New Understanding of Space, Time and the Universe,* London: Phoenix, 2001, p. 129.

[4] Roger Penrose, , *Shadows of the Mind. A Search for the Missing Science of Consciousness,* Oxford &c.: Oxford University Press, corrected 1995, p. 60.

[5] Alan Turing, "Solvable and Unsolvable Problems", in Jack Copeland (ed.), *The Essential Turing. Seminal Writings in Computing, Logic, Philosophy, Artificial Intelligence, and Artificial Life* plus *The Secrets of Enigma*, Oxford: Oxford University Press, 2004, p. 585.

and obscurity or at least alternatives from being clear and being unclear in the same comprehension, I am still confident that it is not lying to me. Now that sounds extreme, but it is important for me because it means that I can rely on it, even if it does not always tell the truth, "Stretchers also as a pack of lies."[6] Its criteria for deciding to shift from the truth has a truth value, has, as Michel Foucault introduced to me, parrhēsia.[7] That is Jeff Hilson's work demonstrates a care and knowledge of the self and has the art and exercise of substantial poetic practice in relationship to the reader, that is it has the capacity for truth-telling and has the obligation to speak the truth on the part of the reader. This could sound inflated, but the work demonstrates that this is the position it has. This is achieved in a combination of ways which I can only touch base on. In summary, firstly, this is a matter of consciousness and its reciprocation in aesthetic performance; secondly it is the necessary and difficult regard to arrive at truth in situations with a strong reliance on ideals and ideal forms, a strong reliance on what we want the situation to be or presume what it must be or are even misled into thinking are the case. If poetry is to have substance, any weight for me, it rests here. This is not a pre-Socratic matter of being true to yourself, but a matter of recognising that the self is constructed and continues to be in a flux of construction. The worry readers have with critique of coherence and logic begins here.

Let's start by removing the logic box. The quantum origin of our comprehensions is largely chemical and govern our neurotransmitter substances that transfer signals from neuron cluster to cluster across synaptic clefts. This raises the importance of quantum effects in synaptic action, effects sited, by John C. Eccles, in the presynaptic vesicular grid—a paracrystalline hexagonal lattice in the brain's pyramidal cell—that anyway we could have guessed, even if we reject the conventionalist notion of "signals." For example, light-sensitive cells in the retina, directly elaborated by the brain, can respond to a small number of photons—sensitive even to a *single* photon, in appropriate circumstances—and to speculate that there might be neurons in the brain that are also essential quantum detection devices. Many scientists, Roger Penrose included, like many poets, want coherence. In quantum terms that refers to circumstances when large numbers of particles can collectively cooperate in a single quantum state which remains essentially unentangled with its environment. (Penrose thinks "coherence"

---

[6] Jeff Hilson, *stretchers*, Hastings: Realty Street, 2006, p .75.

[7] Michel Foucault, *The Government of Self and Others: Lectures at the College de France 1982–83*, edited by Fr.d.ric Gros, translated by Graham Burchell (Basingstoke: Palgrave Macmillan, 2010) and Foucault, *The Courage of Truth: The Government of Self and Others II, Lectures at the College de France 1983–1984*, edited by Gros, translated by Burchell (Basingstoke: Palgrave Macmillan, 2011.

refers, generally, to the fact that oscillations at different places beat time with one another. Here, with *quantum* coherence, he is concerned with the oscillatory nature of the wavefunctions, and the coherence refers to the fact that we are dealing with a single quantum state.[8]) The characteristic ingredient of such phenomena is the presence of an *energy gap* that has to be breached by the environment if it is to disturb this quantum state. He also notes the unlikelihood that quantum coherence effects have any relevance to a "hot" object like a human brain. Much of this correlates to the conventionalist notion that messages move from one neuron to another and chooses to not remember that messages presuppose coherence.

Jeff Hilson's work does not lose its place and demonstrates that coherence is not part of the poetic parcel. As a significant aesthetic practice his work provides a pattern of connectedness that can only complete in the reader and furthermore, that it has the potential to be new with the same reader and each reader on every occasion that they encounter the work. There is no need for metaphors of "signals" or "messages" across "synapses." How is this achieved? There are many answers none of which are correct because none of the answers can be complete.

My first foray was prompted by Jeff Hilson when he enquired about John Conway's problem where two knots can't cancel each other out. The world is four-dimensional if we include time as a dimension, so it is not awkward to ask if there is a corresponding theory of knots in 4D space. This isn't just a matter of taking all the knots we have in 3D space and plunking them down in 4D space: with four dimensions to move around in, any knotted loop can be unraveled if strands are moved over each other in the fourth dimension. To make a knotted object in four-dimensional space, you need a two-dimensional sphere, not a one-dimensional loop. Just as three dimensions provide enough room to build knotted loops but not enough room for them to unravel, four dimensions provide such an environment for knotted spheres, which mathematicians first constructed in the 1920s. Some mathematicians find it hard to visualise a knotted sphere in 4D space, but it helps to first think about an ordinary sphere in 3D space. If you slice through it, you'll see an unknotted loop. But when you slice through a knotted sphere in 4D space, you might see a knotted loop instead (or possibly an unknotted loop or a link of several loops, depending on where you slice). Any knot you can make by slicing a knotted sphere is said to be "slice," an object without object-hood. Some knots are not slice — for instance, the three-crossing knot known as the trefoil. But there's a wrinkle that lends richness and peculiarity to the four-dimensional poetry: in 4D topology, there are two different versions of what it

---

[8] Penrose, 1995, ibid. p. 351.

means to be slice. Then mathematicians discovered that 4D space doesn't just contain the smooth spheres they intuitively visualise — *they also contain crumpled spheres* that could never be ironed smooth. The question of which knots are slice depends on whether you choose to include these crumpled spheres. The Conway knot problem was solved this year (2020) by Lisa Piccirillo in Boston who showed that the Conway knot was not slice.

Penrose discussed knots in 2004. He noted that "the loop-variable picture of quantum gravity leads us into that field of mathematics which is concerned with the topology of knots and kinks."[9] The ingredients for the poetics was untangling bits of string. Penrose had to decide "whether or not a closed "loop of string" is actually *knotted* (where "knotted" means that it is impossible, by smooth motions within ordinary Euclidean 3-space, to deform the loop into an ordinary circle, where it not permitted to pass stretches of the loop through each other)." This leads him into asking "for criteria that decide whether or not two or more distinct loops can be completely separated from one another—so they are *unlinked*."[10]

The geómetrical ideas that are needed in order to understand a piece of string—i.e. its "knottedness"—may not too difficult to decide. Penrose used simple manipulations with his hands, and applying his common-sense understanding, comprehended "whether or not a closed but tangled loop of string is knotted or unknotted."[11] "Now knots are very familiar to anyone who has ever tied shoelaces or ropes or worn a tie, and the notion that there exists a substantial body of mathematical theory devoted to knots might seem rather incongruous."[12]

In "The Incredible Canterbury Poem" at the beginning of *Latanoprost Variations*, Jeff Hilson writes, "people who listen to marvin gaye are also listening to/ perry como since you listened to marvin gaye you might/ liken this new release by bing crosby ..."[13] and then line 5, "if you liken marvin gaye we recommend dean martin you listened to the talking heads ..."[14] and line 36, "you listened to marvin gaye heres an album you might/ not liken since you listened to the feelies ..."[15] and line 58, "you listened to marvin gaye heres an/ album you might not liken ..."[16] then line 66, "if you liken marvin gaye

---

[9] Penrose, 2004, ibid., p. 943.

[10] Penrose, 2004, ibid. p.899.

[11] Roger Penrose, 1995 , ibid., p. 60.

[12] Jim Baggott, *Quantum Space. Loop Quantum Gravity and the Search for the Structure of Space, Time, and the Universe*, Oxford &c.: Oxford University Press, 2018, p. 164.

[13] Jeff Hilson, *Latanoprost Variations*, Norwich: Boiler House Press, 2017, p. 3.

[14] Hilson, 2017, op. cit. p. 3.

[15] Hilson, 2017, op. cit. p. 4.

[16] Hilson, 2017, op. cit. p. 5.

try gavin bryers ..." and line 91, "you listened to marvin gaye this week liken to try again/ perry como?"[17]

You can pick up *In The Assarts* before you have any notion of medieval or Elizabethan lyrics. You can read play with the text and then the sonnet form locks in. The poems use sonnet structures to dismantle the structure. They unknot and knot again. It sent me back to Alastair Fowler's *Silent Poetry. Essays in numerological analysis,*[18] with various authors' works on Chaucer's *Book of the Duchess,* on *Sir Gawain,* on *The Fairie Queene,* and *Amoretti,* and particularly I guess Christopher Butler's "Numerological thought" and as a consequence, Butler's work on number symbolism and Greek and Renaissance thought and what he goes onto in "Aesthetic Assumptions" and "the Aesthetic of Proportion."[19] In 1967 an anonymous author notes, "The connection between mathematics and poetry may not be obvious to our modern world, in which many people would probably regard them as extreme representatives of each of Lord Snow's two cultures. The romantic idea of the poet as a prophet rather than a conscious, rational and deliberate craftsman is still with us. We are not easily fooled when eminent mathematicians declare that higher mathematics is an art rather than a science, and that what they pursue is beauty rather than truth. The day is past when philosophical theories could be presented in verse form, and we do not, as Milton and Dryden did, use "numbers" as a synonym of "verses."

"But though we must reject the idea that in some 'deep' sense mathematics 'is' poetry and the other way round, perhaps we can establish another kind of connexion between the two. Mathematics is often said to be the language of science. Some would even maintain that only those branches of inquiry are worthy of being called scientific whose fundamental concepts are capable of being handled mathematically. As *science* and *scientific* are positively loaded words in our society, mathematical methods spread everywhere—not only in astronomy, physics and chemistry, but also in biology, psychology and sociology, not to speak of philosophy, essential parts of which are nowadays indistinguishable from mathematics. We should therefore not be surprised to find mathematics being used to describe and analyse

[17] Hilson, 2017, op. cit. p.6.

[18] Alastair Fowler, *Silent Poetry. Essays in numerological analysis,* London: Routledge & Kegan Paul, 1970.

[19] Christopher Butler, *Number symbolism,* London: Routledge & Kegan Paul, 1970.

poetry."[20] In 1988 Alain Badiou noted, "The Greeks did not invent the poem. Rather, they *interrupted* the poem with the matheme."[21]

"Each stretcher is nominally a 33-line unit. The decision to use a 33-line form was ultimately banal, based on my age at the time of writing the first set of them, although one night I was sitting in the bar underneath Centre Point just off Tottenham Court Road when a French woman there asked me my age. When I told her, she told me to watch out because Jesus had died at 33. The 33-line form was thus also talismatic, though not all the poems are 33 lines long because sometimes I miscounted."[22]

---

[20] "Numbers and Verses", *The Times Literary Supplement*, February 9, 1967, p. 106.

[21] Alain Badiou, *Being and Event*, translated by Oliver Feltham, London and New York: Coninuum, 2005, p. 126.

[22] Hilson, *stretchers*, 2006, pp. 70-71.

L A T A N O P R O S T V A R I A T I O N S

JEFF HILSON

BOILER HOUSE PRESS

Robert Kiely

A Note on "The Incredible Canterbury Poem"

> *[...] what the algorithms capture and emphasize can be different from what users value. Think of all the actions that aren't captured or that aren't monetized. What's key is to think through that gap and to enlarge it. [...] How do your actions not only affect the kinds of recommendations you get but affect each other? If you consider the ways in which we're massively correlated to other people (if you like X, then you like Y, based on the actions of people who are deemed to be like you) that also means that what you like and how you act can affect the scripts and possibilities that somebody else receives.*

Poetry is probably best defined as that textual substance which shuttles between the impossible dipoles of what we call first and second nature. "The Incredible Canterbury Poem," the first poem in *Latanoprost Variations* (2017), lists a number of bands and musical artists, linking them with interpellations of a listener, or perhaps a user, saying that "if you liken" a certain artist "we recommend" this other, with a few variations. It is a transcription of the kind of textual cues generated by any number of online digital recommendation systems. The only weird aspect of it is the word "liken." The slide from *like* to *liken* seems to enact a kind of cod-middle-Englishness by way of the title's indirect reference to *The Canterbury Tales*, Chaucerian English creeping into the language and subjecting the recommendations to homeopathic defamiliarization. In the *OED*, the etymology of *liken* asks us to "Compare [...] Middle Low German līkenen to resemble, to compare, to make equal." The emphasis is on likening as a homogenising force which makes equal as it compares. Perhaps the title of this poem also recalls the Canterbury music scene, a label which homogenizes and draws together a disparate group as if it was a genre, whose members themselves have no idea why they are grouped together. Labels, genres, borders. Recommendation systems rely on the idea that like begets like, the law of *homophily*, which has been aetiologised by Wendy Hui Kyong Chun. Homophily has been taken for a law of human behaviour by network designers and programmers. Hilson's poem is partly a dramatic re-enactment of the slow ossification of novelty to habit, and from there further on to something like a law of nature, even if of second or third or n^{th} nature. When media are no longer new, they have become habitual, almost automated, and thereby unconscious. Homophily has moved from observed fact in a constructed environment to application and prescription, from happenstance to a spuriously constructed human nature, from second nature to first nature. People are not defined in any meaningful sense by the enormous quantitative accumulation of their data, nor are they delimited by their aesthetic choices or judgements. This is negative anthropology. To say that people are not defined by their online data feels like an insane claim in the context of a successful redirection of collective struggles into something like a culture war, where battle lines are drawn by likes. Homophilic groups reinforce each other's belief, false or not. They produce ever more sameness in clumps, reinforcing their respective bubbles. These bubbles are also the scourge of benevolent liberals, who shrink in horror as centralized authority structures lose control of the crumbling middle ground, and while they bemoan this they turn in compensation to covert and overt authoritarianism to reconstitute that middle ground. If online life and networks are premised on, extrapolated from, and modelled on physical life, they also completely determine that physical life. Homophilic systems determine who gets access to good rates for health care, to credit or mortgages, who gets released on bail. It is not just a matter of taste, or what you like, but who you're like. Who you're like and who your likes are like is all about class, race, gender, and other determinants. Homophily claims to be nothing but an index of leanings, of mere choice or innocent preference. It thereby indirectly naturalizes racism and obscures that which has conditioned these choices or preferences, namely institutional and economic factors. It is for this reason that "The Incredible Canterbury Poem" leads Hilson inexorably to a poem about borders and migrant deaths, "A Final Poem with Full Stops." It is August 2020, Sky News livestreams desperate migrants in a sinking boat crossing the English Channel, and people are acting as if *algorithms* have autonomously decided that kids in poorer postcodes would have done worse than those in richer ones. Hilson knows, and has highlighted for me, how these are consequences of the same malevolent force.

[Written early July to mid-August 2020.]

An email

Reading *Latanoprost Variations* (2017) was a real pleasure. It is impossible to read it without hearing Jeff's distinctive voice and tone, which is not really the case for *In the Assarts* (2010) (or maybe I haven't seen him read that enough) or *stretchers* (2006). I especially enjoyed "The Incredible DIY poem" erasure and "Latanoprost Variations (abandoned)," which both feel madder and more freewheeling than the utterly weird poems preceding them. Enjoy is a difficult word with any poem, and definitely w/ these ones. What I mean is that I also find the whole book incredibly difficult. It is the sort of difficulty which is close to Beckett's *Watt* (1953) in spirit, though probably that's because I know Beckett better than Stein, who serves as one epigraph, and so just see it everywhere. *Watt* is one of my favourite Beckett texts. But texts like the Wogan poem and the rest seem like a *Watt* without <u>any</u> let up. If *Watt* is a weird building I wander around, these are tiny panic-inducing gaps between floorboards where I fear I'll fall forever, and so while I am staggered by their seductive rhythm I also have to dip in and push back out as I go, in case I end up thinking in its tone and rhythm, which strikes me as infectious. Halfway through a poem in this book, I feel like I might panic and believe the poem will go on forever, that this rhythm won't stop. It's quite a weird experience, one I haven't come across in poetry ever before. But maybe that's just all the coffee I've had.

[This is revised slightly. It was originally sent to Jeff Hilson on 6th May 2019.]

Frances Presley

Brexitland

for Jeff Hilson

the Wash is red hot red lines against the sea
shingles red pock marks red pox
chickens pecking each other red in a coop

especially noticeable in Lincolnshire no con hire
the fens are dry and red can't breathe in Boston for the fire
out Holland out
Holland

we were four in Rusk (ington) other babies were fed rusks
beck rushes over our boots

Leaf below Rusk is (S) leaf (ord) river Slea
deep asleep far below the bridge
she was talking talking about the stopped lorry
a small body bleeding in her arms

Even when Even is (Kest) even what is odd?

kest Celtic ced wood ceded
even Norse stefna meeting place

Kesteven is progressive *keep it independent*

(our bumper sticker)

kest is for keeps I am cast in

cast adrift by kest

even rusk leaf

in co she

Bodleian, Oxford
Dec 19

[Stephen Walter's map, Brexitland, hand painted with watercolours, takes the 2016 EU referendum and shows "Leave" areas in red and "Remain" areas in blue under water:
altered place names reveal new words for Brexit.]

Virna Teixeira

Poema Optotípico Incluindo Art Garfunkel

para testar se meus olhos estavam funcionando um dia eu tentei olhar para art garfunkel eu queria ver a luz inclinada em volta dele o cantor & às vezes ator art garfunkel que não é um letrista & realmente apenas uma excêntrica anomalia ali sobre o coreto americano na clara luz do dia eu tentei olhar direito para ele como se ele fosse uma bebida láctea ou apenas uma superfície plana brilhante mas enquanto meus olhos moviam-se o perfil elipsoide de art garfunkel moveu-se & eu não pude vê-lo em lugar nenhum rolando meus olhos de um lado para o outro eu comecei a perceber que o cantor adulto contemporâneo art garfunkel era uma verdadeira anomalia & por causa da sua cabeça eu não podia olhar para ele de forma alguma ou no grau de aperto do seus braços mal definidos ou na sua pequena região central & mais cedo ou mais tarde todo mundo percebeu que art garfunkel somente tinha valores aproximados no espectro observado & mesmo na luz invisível poderia apenas sempre ser parcialmente imaginado cantando os olhos brilhantes eu queria apenas olhar para art garfunkel eu não queria tocar ou ouvir Art Garfunkel antes de vê-lo — Nigel Farndale, *The Daily Telegraph* Por que eu não poderia ser um ourives? — Art Garfunkel, *Still Water 32* mesmo fotografar sua cabeça de estrela distante cabelo modelado se eu pudesse eu certamente teria sido destruído por binóculos olhando na direção de garfunkel & então na direção de seu pequeno quente companheiro simon sobre o coreto americano certamente teria sido como olhar um milhão de velas padrão ou ter um corpo estranho no meu olho ou uma emergência real como a instabilidade do comprimento do jeans de art garfunkel não é fácil conceituar mas se a é igual a r mais g onde g é o maior número de sucessos & r é o comprimento crítico somente quando reformulamos a como g a massa do jeans é igual a r não é fácil conceituar não é fácil ouvir art garfunkel cantar eu apenas tenho olhos para você eu apenas tenho pelos flamingos quando ele não sabe se está nublado ou claro ele nem mesmo sabe ou numa avenida lotada novamente eu penso que ele deve estar colapsando no seu frio companheiro simon que não tem energia eu não sei porque em condições ideais de visão ele quer tentar fazê-lo aparecer tão distante talvez seja por causa da ponte na sua cabeça de cabelo problemático talvez seja porque na sua juventude simon & garfunkel realmente eram traças notórias por comer vestir & voar em direção à luz mas eu não acredito que garfunkel é a maior traça no mundo eu não acredito que seu pequeno denso companheiro voe apenas entre junho & julho olá escuridão olá se você diz mais & mais art garfunkel torna-se uma variável luminosa eu não o descreveria exatamente como o sol eu o descreveria como uma lua eu estava apenas tentando olhar para ele para testar meus olhos para ver a luz curva em volta dele pensando que talvez ele vai direcionar seus jatos na minha direção agora ele é o objeto mais escuro em 33 no universo o que é afinal um coreto americano quais são as condições ideais de visão em qualquer dia claro eu definitivamente não deveria tentar olhar para art garfunkel através do telescópio gigante de Magalhães não quero que os fios próximos do seu cabelo de sálvia ou salsa sejam a última coisa que vejo, afinal, sou especial e difuso também com minha educação em estado sólido e coração de ouro quando eu estava uma vez num coreto inglês com meu olho desamparado eu não conseguia descobrir a diferença entre garfunkel e simon um minuto um deles bamboleava no outro o outro estava embaçado e apenas um padrão arejado a milhares de quilômetros de casa apenas nos meus sonhos art garfunkel é um novo planeta brilhante exigindo que eu dê uma espiada rotineiramente olhando para ele por uma espiada nos meus sonhos me ajudam a entender a atração de suas pernas empoeiradas como elas são extensas & irregulares & mesmo embora haja às vezes milhares de platôs em sua cabeça de cabelos redistribuídos todo mundo chorou quando no seu solo difícil usando rima como tycho brahe art garfunkel disse é fácil todos nos precisamos de um pouco de espaço & tempo para nos separarmos, mas secretamente eu sei que todo mundo chorava porque ele não tem nenhum ombro ao contrário do seu rigoroso companheiro simon que está sempre bem mesmo em um barco a remos que viaja para & de todos os shows na vizinhança art garfunkel não tem ombros para deitar sua cabeça sua cabeça imaginei inclinar meus ombros em art garfunkel verdadeiro ou falso sequestro & comecei a chorar também olhando no espelho para minha própria cabeça de cabelos brilhantes e óbvios & o volume de feedback positivo descontrolado ao redor dela reorganizando meus olhos para sobreviver ao volume de 34 sendo um poeta de poetas sozinho num reencontro de simon e garfunkel & se afastando de toda uma revolução de música americana porque simon e garfunkel são uma dupla de folk rock duo & eu sou um poeta de poetas como edmund spenser subindo & descendo nos olhos de keats de volta ao vigésimo primeiro século tudo o que posso pensar é a distância entre os pupilos de art garfunkel que não querem olhar para nenhum dos meus poemas ou para a luz entre eles não art garfunkel não eu não poderia ser um ourives ou em cujo tempo eu sou um idiota & suas mãos estão tremendo simplesmente para me repetir suas mãos crescentes estão tremendo mas os olhos são meus em cada um destes poemas um após o outro eu vejo que suas mãos reluzentes estão tremendo obrigado art garfunkel obrigado afinal os olhos estão bem

Matt Martin

"trying to cross the border. & drowned.": Appropriation and Representation in Jeff Hilson's "A Final Poem with Full Stops"

When Jeff Hilson's "A Final Poem with Full Stops" appeared in issue 5 of the online journal *Datableed* (September 2016), it immediately stood out for its political urgency. Hilson's work often conveys political subtexts, but this piece is explicitly, even primarily, activist in nature. "A Final Poem..." later reappeared as the concluding part of the titular prose-poem sequence from Hilson's collection *Latanoprost Variations* (2017); it also featured in *Wretched Strangers* (2018), an anthology of poetry by UK-based writers born overseas.[1] Three pages long in book form, the text lists causes of death (and some associated data) for refugees who perished seeking safety in EU countries.[2] The ending may give a flavour of the poem:

> died of thirst. died of bullet wounds. died of anxiety psychosis. & drowned. drowned in the seine fleeing from police. drowned in the rhine. drowned in the river thames. found dead. roma. found dead in the snow. found dead after sixteen days at sea. ignored by NATO. no name. SOS ignored by NATO. no name. suicide. found dead. ignored by NATO. & died. SOS. died or killed. killed. drowned. killed. (Hilson, *Latanoprost Variations*, 37.)

This essay explores how information about actual refugee deaths underlies the poem and discusses the challenges of appropriating such data into poetry. As Hilson's conclusive "killed" suggests, these fatalities are deliberate, resulting sometimes from individuals' malice, but also

---

[1] Citations here are from Hilson, *Latanoprost Variations*, 35–37, but the anthology text (Hilson, "A Final Poem with Full Stops," *Wretched* Strangers, 125–27) will also serve, as will the online manifestation (Hilson, "A Final Poem with Full Stops," *Datableed* 5, at https://www.datableedzine.com/jeff-hilson). For footage of Hilson performing the poem, see SJ Fowler, "Jeff Hilson—Prose Poem Poetics," https://www.youtube.com/watch?v=mmZcumawCFU.

[2] Legally speaking, a refugee is someone who has been formally granted the right to asylum within a country's borders, whereas an asylum-seeker is attempting to attain this status but has yet to succeed. However, it seems evident that many asylum-seekers have a right to refugee status but are prevented from lodging claims, while others have their applications wrongfully turned down. This essay thereby follows Amnesty International's practice of extending the term "refugees" to people legally classed as asylum-seekers (Amnesty International, *The Human Cost of Fortress Europe*, 5).

from national and supranational policies. The mechanisms of this structural violence can be clarified by exploring the poem's documentary sources. The tragic narratives thus uncovered, though, contrast Hilson's collage of fragmented, minimalist sentences. How do such techniques enable him to represent realities of refugee struggle in ways that more detailed, nominally "truer" documentation cannot? Building upon discussion of the text's distinguishing features by Robert Hampson, the essay proposes that Hilson's extreme condensation of narrative, reducing each life to the moment of death, allows a non-literal but emotionally resonant story to accumulate. The poem, using the same devices that enable hilarity in much of Hilson's other work, movingly represents the scale of the ongoing disaster while remaining faithful to the truths of individual refugee lives.

The poem's epigraph, "These deaths are not inevitable," is from the Amnesty International report *The Human Cost of Fortress Europe* (2014). "Fortress Europe," a World War Two term originally denoting areas of the continent under Nazi occupation, here names the sum total of policies adopted by the EU and its member states (which in 2014 included the UK) that aim at discouraging migration, and that exacerbate refugee deaths:

> With safer routes into the EU being closed off by fences, increased surveillance and the deployment of more and more security forces, people are being forced to take ever more dangerous routes, sometimes with tragic consequences. Women, men and children are drowning at sea or suffocating in trucks. They face violence at EU's borders and are denied their right to seek asylum. Those seeking to enter the EU end up trapped in countries such as Libya, Morocco, Ukraine and Turkey, where their rights are at risk. (Amnesty International, *The Human Cost of Fortress Europe*, 6.)

The fortress exists not only at borders, but in destination countries' administrative systems, causing deaths by withholding proper health care, refusing protection from racist violence, driving refugees to suicide with bureaucratic obstacles, or repatriating people into danger. In 2016, when the poem first appeared, Europe was experiencing what the media habitually labelled a "migrant crisis," and a widespread panic stemmed from perceptions that unmanageable numbers of refugees were fleeing into Europe to escape crises such as the Syrian Civil War (in some quarters, these perceptions doubtless endure). 2016 also saw the 23 June "Brexit" referendum where the UK voted to leave the EU. Far from expressing horror at excesses of EU border control, this decision was in part motivated by desire to withdraw from EU freedom of movement, thereby (it was hoped) making it even harder for refugees to enter the country; advertising by the far-right campaign group Leave.EU included a much-criticised poster that implied a legion of brown-skinned refugees was marching across Europe towards Britain (Stewart & Mason, "Nigel Farage's anti-migrant poster reported to police"). The goal was not to dismantle Fortress Europe, but to build a yet more impregnable Fortress UK.

A likely source of information for Hilson's catalogue of mortality is UNITED for Intercultural Action, an Amsterdam-based charity that, since 1993, has maintained and updated a list of "documented deaths of refugees and migrants due to Fortress Europe." Collating media reports from throughout the EU, UNITED has made this information easily accessible online.[3] At the time of writing this essay, the most recent incarnation of the list (up to 11 June 2020) enumerates 40,555 deaths. The document includes the date and number of fatalities for each incident; victims' names, ages, and regions of origin (where available); and how each death occurred. Hilson's poem's lexicon almost completely overlaps with the list, and numerous incidents in his text (precisely enough described for coincidences to be unlikely) are found in UNITED's document. It remains conceivable that Hilson researched the same sources rather than accessing UNITED's work, but given the variety of media and languages involved, this would have been a colossal task. The thoroughness of the charity's list certainly makes it invaluable for understanding the realities informing Hilson's poem.

Some causes of death account for huge numbers of refugees. UNITED's current list includes 1,836 drownings (many killing several people); accordingly, Hilson uses the words "drowned" and "drowning" 30 times, as well as incidents like "fell into the sea" where drowning seems probable. Likewise, UNITED records 408 incidents of "suicide." Hilson uses this word six times, in addition to deaths where suicide either seems likely or, by cross-referencing with UNITED's list, can be demonstrated. For example, Hilson's "jumped from a church tower" invokes an unnamed, 13-year-old Bosnian boy who died on 19 September 2000, listed by UNITED as "suicide, jumped from church tower in Villach [Austria] out of fear of deportation." (Hilson, *Latanoprost Variations*, 36; UNITED, "List...," 57.)

Other deaths mentioned by Hilson lead to stories that are no less heart-breaking. A victim "run over by a car reaching the italian beach" was a mere baby from Kurdistan, killed on 1 January 1994

---

[3] UNITED for Intercultural Action, "List of 40,555 documented deaths of refugees and migrants due to the restrictive policies of "Fortress Europe"," http://unitedagainstrefugeedeaths.eu/wp-content/uploads/2014/06/ListofDeathsActual.pdf. More information on the list is at UNITED for Intercultural Action, "About the "List of Deaths"," http://unitedagainstrefugeedeaths.eu/about-the-campaign/about-the-united-list-of-deaths/.

(Hilson, *Latanoprost Variations*, 35; UNITED, "List...," 68). The person who "suffocated eating money to avoid being robbed" is Olivier, who in 2003 tried to avoid robbery at a military checkpoint in Agadez (Niger) by swallowing cash he had saved to pay people-smugglers; he died before even leaving his homeland (Hilson, *Latanoprost Variations*, 36; UNITED, "List...," 51). Solyman Raschid, a 28-year-old Iraqi who perished in Kirkuk on 6 September 2007 after his asylum claim was rejected and he was deported from the UK, is Hilson's "killed by a roadside bomb" (UNITED, "List...," 39; Hilson, *Latanoprost Variations*, 36).[4] An unnamed Kurd was "frozen to death and mutilated by wolves in the forest near Nimfopetra [Greece]" on 29 December 2008, leading to the poem's "eaten in the forest by wolves" (UNITED, "List...," 62; Hilson, *Latanoprost Variations*, 37).

UNITED's list lets some deaths be researched more thoroughly through reference to other sources. Hilson's refugee "touching an electric cable" is Selliah Jeyakularajah, a 25-year-old dying in Görisried, Germany (Hilson, *Latanoprost Variations*, 36; "List...," 66). He committed suicide on 16 August 1995 by climbing a utility pole, deliberately grasping the cable. Jeyakularajah was from the Tamil minority in Sri Lanka, where civil war then raged. He feared persecution by the Sri Lankan army if he returned. Contributing factors to his death include his illness with paranoid psychosis, and the refusal of his asylum claim (a decision his lawyer was contesting).[5] Each individualisable death in Hilson's poem, if investigated fully, might yield background just as full of tragic detail.

The UNITED list is emotionally moving (traumatising, even) despite its list format, for it individualises lives and deaths that might otherwise be obscured by an ocean of statistics; it thus acknowledges the specificity of human lives. The list's political impact derives from this power as literature, and it has indeed been used in artistic contexts. Turkish artist Banu Cennetoğlu (who works closely with UNITED) has frequently displayed and distributed the list, for example in her 2018 exhibition at London's Chisenhale Gallery, and in the 2018 Liverpool Biennial (where it was plastered along a 280-metre-long hoarding on Liverpool's George Street).[6] The hoarding was repeatedly vandalised,

---

[4] There is uncertainty about Raschid's story, since a separate entry on the list describes him as "killed by a car bomb in Kirkuk" a year later, on 6 September 2008, "2 weeks after voluntary repatriation"—perhaps a case of conflicting sources (UNITED, "List...," 36).

[5] Jeyakularajah's story is explored in depth in Herzog and Wälde, *Sie suchten das Leben*, 87–93, and summarised at Anti Rassistische Initiative, "Bundesdeutsche Flüchtlingspolitik und ihre tödlichen Folgen," http://www.ari-berlin.org/doku/text_95.htm.

[6] Cennetoğlu's Chisenhale Gallery exhibition ran 29 June—26 August 2018; see Chisenhale Gallery, *Banu Cennetoğlu at Chisenhale*, PDF,

including the application of racist graffiti—proving Cennetoğlu's point that racism against refugees is endemic across Europe, experienced "while individuals are in Europe and are in detention centres, hospitals and refugee accommodation, or ... facing hate crimes." (Chris Sharratt, "Liverpool Biennial"; Grieg, "Interview with Banu Cennetoğlu," in Chisenhale Gallery, *Banu Cennetoğlu at Chisenhale*, n.p.)

Cennetoğlu is painstakingly ethical about sharing UNITED's documentation; she is adamant that "The List should not be represented or aestheticized in an attempt to make it an artwork," and is keen to avoid "'appropriating' The List." (Grieg, in Chisenhale Gallery, *Banu Cennetoğlu at Chisenhale*, n.p.) Aestheticization and appropriation, however, are intrinsic to Hilson's collaging of refugee narratives into a poem. His good faith seems evident from his contribution of the text to *Wretched Strangers*, an anthology dedicated to "celebrating the contribution of migrant writers to British poetry culture." (Welsch, "The Stranger's Case," *Wretched Strangers*, 8.) Nevertheless, for the poem to successfully memorialise the deaths it catalogues, and to further the struggle against injustice, it must articulate something that UNITED's documentation does not. Since the list so forcefully registers the horrifying scale of the disaster, while still maintaining a sense of individual tragedy, an obvious angle on the topic might be to transfer this fullness of detail into poetry. This could involve further research into particular deaths (as demonstrated above in the case of Selliah Jeyakularajah), and the working of these narratives into verse, perhaps akin to how Charles Reznikoff created a poetry of extreme trauma from legal transcripts in *Testimony* (1934–78) and *Holocaust* (1975).

In fact, Hilson deliberately avoids many factors that make UNITED's document such a powerful condemnation of Fortress Europe. Narrative details are shed, often leaving the most basic information about cause of death, so that only the rarer causes let an individual be identified from the poem. This brevity results in a staccato succession of short sentences, interspersed by full stops that (outside of the epigraph) are the poem's only punctuation. Nobody is named, despite a large minority of the dead being readily identifiable; "no name," abbreviated to "N.N." in UNITED's list when a deceased person cannot be identified, is one of the poem's several refrains. Hilson omits all information about genders, ages and dates, as well as most data about locations, ethnicity and nationality ("roma" is one recurrent exception).[7]

---

https://chisenhale.org.uk/wp-content/uploads/BC_Exhibition_Handout_FINAL-1.pdf. Information on Cennetoğlu's Liverpool installation is at https://www.biennial.com/2018/exhibition/artists/banu-cennetoglu.

[7] Other than in abbreviations or its epigraph, this poem uses only lower-case letters. Lack of capitalisation for "roma" therefore connotes no disrespect.

During an essay that touches briefly on Hilson's poem, Robert Hampson describes the affects achieved:

> The "full stops" are not just the method of punctuation; they are also these premature deaths: the suicides, the accidents (because of the dangers of the journeys undertaken), the murders. The recurrence of the term "Roma" recalls the documentation of reasons for arrest in the third Reich. Another recurrent item, "no name," emphasizes the de-humanization these migrants have undergone. (Hampson, *Border-crossing*, 124.)

The point about "no name" seems indisputable; the migrants' dehumanisation consists not only in the difficulty of identifying bodies, but in how Fortress Europe frames them as unworthy of compassion, and in how they are regarded by racist inhabitants of destination countries (such as the vandals targeting Cennetoğlu's Liverpool installation). Even among Europeans who imagine themselves as anti-racist, the individual identities of refugees tend not to register (this may be compounded by how such migrants are represented in the media). On UNITED's list, this reader recognised the name of Aylan Kurdi, a 3-year-old Syrian boy who drowned after the boat he was on capsized near Bodrum (Turkey) on 2 September 2015; images of his corpse were widely published in international media (UNITED, "List...," 24). Also recognised was Joy Gardner, a 40-year-old Jamaican woman who "died of brain damage after struggle with immigration officers on deportation in her flat in London" on 1 August 1993 (UNITED, "List...," 68). She is probably the figure in Hilson's poem who "died of brain damage" (Hilson, *Latanoprost Variations*, 37). In total, then, two recognised names out of 40,555 dead. The absence of names in the poem does not perpetuate such erasure but depicts and implicitly condemns it.

Hilson's repetition of "roma" is undoubtedly influenced by historic and ongoing persecution of Roma, including genocide of Romani people under the Third Reich, as Hampson claims. Fortress Europe partakes of this legacy, as an administrative system designed to cause deaths among already marginalised peoples. However, the number of Roma deaths recorded by UNITED is surprisingly low—13 in total. Of course, this figure should not distract from the severity of anti-Roma bigotry throughout Europe, nor the horror of Roma deaths that did occur (one suicide by self-immolation, eight murders, three drownings, and one baby who died of a heart attack during a police raid). Furthermore, many Roma may be among the unidentifiable dead, or their ethnicity may not have been noted in UNITED's sources. Nevertheless, there is a startling discrepancy between the recorded data and the frequency of "roma" in the poem (at 12 occurrences, nearly as great as in the complete list).

Perhaps the Roma are repeatedly invoked by Hilson due to their intrinsically diasporic culture. Discussing roadside campsites and "stopping places" frequented by Roma in the UK, Romani writer Damien Le Bas notes:

> Such places symbolise the misunderstood truth of many Traveller lives, which is that they are neither permanently nomadic, nor ever truly static. Howbeit these yards provide a base, the highway is right beside them, ready for the times when family ties, work, a wedding, a funeral, the fair season, beckon. ... Every family is haunted by stories of relatives, too often toddlers, who have been knocked down and killed by their literal closeness to roads. (Le Bas, *The Stopping Places*, 28.)

There are major differences between this life and becoming a refugee; for many travelling Roma there is a conscious choice to follow this path, plus a sense of communal belonging, and participation in a continuing tradition. There remain parallels, however: interspersion of staticity with travel, physical danger (especially for children), awareness that one's rights of habitation are always at the mercy of local authorities, and discrimination from an area's long-term residents. To become a refugee, Hilson intimates, is to share the peripheral, precarious role into which Roma are often swept by the mainstream of European society.

This mobility is contrasted by the poem's full stops. As Hampson proposes, these marks certainly convey "premature deaths," each tiny black circle suggesting ripples where a refugee vanishes below the page surface. However, the punctuation also operates on a deeper level of allegory. The text relates strikingly to points about the more general experience of migrants, articulated by Ágnes Lehóczky in endnotes to *Wretched Strangers*:

> The notion of homecoming inhabits the security that lies both in the struggle of naming and silence, Heidegger writes: and so as soon as one gives thought to this "homelessness, it is a misery no longer." If we, only temporarily, find solace in this premise, then it is true that what binds these works together is the attempt to fill in such elliptical constructions—silences, erasures, or more precisely the space or *lack* between appearances and disappearances—of "arbitrary" reveries, peripatetic meanderings, off-track mobilities, from the experience of being lost in this motioning, dissipated in disappearing surfaces of structure, or in the "reading" of the *note*book, one's "notes on oneself." (Lehóczky, "Endnotes," *Wretched Strangers*, 313; Lehóczky's italics.)

For Heidegger, this "homelessness" is a universal experience where one "still does not even think of the *real* plight of dwelling as *the* plight"—and the plight is that mortals "*must ever learn to dwell*." (Heidegger, *Poetry, Language, Thought*, 161; italics in the translation.) In moving between cultures, the migrant (Lehóczky argues) lives a reified version of this ongoing quest to fully inhabit one's own being. If this is the case, then refugees undergo a yet more concrete manifestation of the process, since their "peripatetic meanderings" and "off-track mobilities" are frequently literal; "silences, erasures, or ... *lack* between appearances and disappearances" are constant threats. These dangers may come in the form of dehumanisation (erasing the refugee's subjectivity), but can also represent physical death, particularly by drowning (literally becoming "dissipated in disappearing surfaces of structure"). Hilson's full stops thus depict textually the "silences, erasure, or ... *lack*" that his subjects' "meanderings" and "mobilities" strive to fill, each new sentence suggesting repeated movement towards safety and belonging. However, the very structures of both the poem and Fortress Europe mean every effort will be met with another full stop, another point of erasure. Arrival and even receiving asylum in the destination country still do not free one from alienation, discrimination or outright violence. The quandary for refugees, *contra* Heidegger, is that they assuredly do think about the "plight of dwelling," but that "learning to dwell" cannot be pursued at leisure while their existence remains under threat of metaphorical and literal annihilation.

The full stops here must also be compared to their absence from the rest of the sequence "Latanoprost Variations." "The Wogan Poem" features a few question marks, but all the other poems consist of massive, unpunctuated paragraphs implying non-stop continuity of thought. In "A Final Poem...," the interruptions are stark by contrast. They underscore another difference from the rest of the sequence, and from Hilson's work as a whole. His sense of humour has long distinguished his opus, as illustrated by another "Latanoprost" poem, "Optotypical Poem Including Art Garfunkel":

> to test if my eyes were working I tried one day to look at art garfunkel I wanted to see the light bend round him the singer & sometimes actor art garfunkel who is not a songwriter & really only an eccentric anomaly standing up there on american bandstand in the clear light of day I tried to look right at him as if he was a milky drink or just a bright plain surface but as my eyes moved ellipsoid profile art garfunkel moved & I couldn't see him anywhere (Hilson, *Latanoprost Variations*, 31.)

This poem makes serious points about living with eye problems like early onset glaucoma, for which Latanoprost is a medication (Hilson,

Latanoprost Variations, 60). The text is also insightful regarding the polymorphous identity of Art Garfunkel and, by extension, human beings in general. However, such messages are conveyed through laughter provoked by the incongruous collision of ophthalmic illness and celebrity homage. Conversely, "A Final Poem..." is completely unfunny—as is appropriate, given its topic. It is as though all the full stops—those deaths, silences and erasures—have migrated from the rest of the sequence into the concluding section, bringing along their melancholy and leaving uninterrupted, comedic improvisations behind. The difference becomes stark in performance. Hilson usually reads his poems in a deadpan voice that accentuates comedic elements, with confusion and vulnerability sometimes cutting through in response to surreal aspects of the text. When he reads "A Final Poem..." in the same register, his delivery suddenly comes across as completely earnest (Fowler, "Jeff Hilson").

Being unfunny, though, is not the same thing as lacking humour. The humour in this poem consists in the piling-up of incongruous, surprising details that do not create laughter, but add to the text's embittered urgency. Bathetic, deflationary details, of the sort received as jokes in Hilson's other poetry, here impart a feeling of authenticity even before one verifies that they are genuine; the person "found on a cucumber lorry," for example, was an unnamed Iraqi who suffocated in the vehicle and was "found on ferry in Venice ... coming from Greece" on 27 June 2008 (UNITED, "List...," 37).

An especially powerful, unfunny but humorous affect emerges through collaging together these fragments of lives and deaths. When reading the sentences in a continuous paragraph, one instinctively construes every event as befalling a lone protagonist in rapid succession. Hilson's elision of names, ages and nationalities serves this purpose, and the impact is heightened in performance, where a single voice unifies the experiences. There is disjunction, though, between this continuity and the variety of deaths, some of which are contradictory in nature: "blown up in a minefield trying to cross the border. & drowned." (Hilson, *Latanoprost Variations*, 35.) An individual protagonist is constructed but dies repeatedly and ceaselessly. Ampersands and other connectives intensify this impression by combining multiple, irreconcilable deaths within a single sentence: "killed in a factory fire & killed on a freight train & killed in the middle of the road" (Hilson, *Latanoprost Variations*, 36). In a more fictive scenario—a cartoon, computer game, or Hollywood action movie—for one character to suffer so many traumas, each fatal in itself, might seem like slapstick comedy (or at least *grand guignol*) due to sheer excess of brutality.

A comparison may elucidate matters and is intended not to make light of refugee deaths, but to demonstrate how context affects reception of imagery. At the end of the thriller *Con Air* (1997), an archvillain (played by John Malkovich) dies by hurtling through a glass bridge, falling onto live electric cables, then being crushed by a piledriver (West, *Con Air*). The audience is expected to cheer this demise or laugh at the ridiculous accumulation of violence. The scenario's obvious artifice, and the way the character has been dehumanised through portrayal as irredeemably evil, short-circuit the sympathy one might instinctively feel for a human being subjected to such agonies.

Hilson's poem likewise presents a sequence of lethal disasters befalling one notional character, but paradoxically humanises the protagonist in doing so. Individual fates might sometimes feel abstract against the sheer scale of Fortress Europe's death toll; in letting readers access the accumulated tragedy as though it were a single person's experience, Hilson expedites empathy and thereby counteracts the racist dehumanisation of refugees. A technique that causes laughter in action movie depictions of violence, or indeed in Hilson's other poetry, here underscores the seriousness of the situation. It does this by implying something fundamental about living (and dying) as a refugee. Whereas the UNITED list confronts each person with only one hazard (that person's cause of death), the reality of refugee journeys is that dangers, many potentially fatal, follow one after the other. It is therefore perfectly plausible that an individual could encounter a long sequence of risks, rather as the poem depicts. This also recalls the allegorical significances described by Lehóczky. Each death or full stop is a metaphor for dehumanising erasure of subjectivity, an occurrence that might well coincide with physical danger, such as when bureaucratic systems deny access to healthcare, when asylum-seekers face racist attacks, or when a rightful claim to refugee status is disbelieved and the claimant is repatriated into danger. All of the poem's resources—its stripping away of narrative particulars, its parallels between refugee and Roma experience, its barrage of violent imagery, its assembly of staccato sentences into fluid prose—are marshalled towards articulating this experience of constant threat. From this perspective, Hilson's procession of fatal hazards may feel like hyperbole, but given the perils and anxieties that accompany the seeking of asylum, it is utterly true—and in light of continuities in European and British policy, the poem's call for empathy sadly remains as urgent today as in 2016.

Bibliography

Amnesty International. *The Human Cost of Fortress Europe: Human Rights Violations against Migrants and Refugees at Europe's Borders*. London: Amnesty International, 2014. PDF. Accessed 31 July 2020. https://www.amnesty.org/download/Documents/8000/eur050012014en.pdf.

Anti Rassistische Initiative. "Bundesdeutsche Flüchtlingspolitik und ihre tödlichen Folgen." Accessed 30 July 2020. http://www.ari-berlin.org/doku/text_95.htm.

Chisenhale Gallery. *Banu Cennetoğlu at Chisenhale*. Exhibition handout and PDF. London: Chisenhale Gallery, 2018. Accessed 30 July 2020. https://chisenhale.org.uk/wp-content/uploads/BC_Exhibition_Handout_FINAL-1.pdf.

Fowler, SJ. "Jeff Hilson—Prose Poem Poetics." Filmed 25 November 2018 at Torriano Meeting House, Kentish Town, London. Video. https://www.youtube.com/watch?v=mmZcumawC.FU.

Hampson, Robert. "Border-crossing—These deaths are not inevitable," *Crossings: Journal of Migration and Culture* 10, no. 1 (April 2019): 119-128.

Heidegger, Martin. *Poetry, Language, Thought*, trans. Albert Hofstadter. New York: Harper Colophon Books, 1971.

Herzog, Heike, and Eva Wälde. *Sie suchten das Leben: Suizide als Folge deutscher Abschiebepolitik*. Hamburg and Münster: Unrast Verlag, 2004.

Hilson, Jeff. "A Final Poem with Full Stops." *Datableed* 5. Published September 2016. Accessed 30 July 2020. https://www.datableedzine.com/jeff-hilson.

Hilson, Jeff. *Latanoprost Variations*. Norwich: Boiler House Press, 2017.

Le Bas, Damien. *The Stopping Places: A Journey through Gypsy Britain*. London: Chatto & Windus, 2018.

Lehóczky, Ágnes, and JT Welsch, eds. *Wretched Strangers: Borders Movement Homes*. Norwich: Boiler House Press, 2018.

Liverpool Biennial. "Banu Cennetoğlu." Published 2018. Accessed 30 July 2020. https://www.biennial.com/2018/exhibition/artists/banu-cennetoglu

Sharratt, Chris. "Liverpool Biennial: artist Banu Cennetoğlu's memorial to dead refugees daubed with graffiti in third instance of vandalism." *A-N*. Published 10 September 2018. Accessed 30 July 2020. https://www.a-n.co.uk/news/liverpool-biennial-artist-banu-cennetoglus-memorial-dead-refugees-daubed-graffiti-third-instance-vandalism/.

Stewart, Heather, and Rowena Mason. "Nigel Farage's anti-migrant poster reported to police." *The Guardian* website. Published 16 June 2016. Accessed 30 July 2020.

https://www.theguardian.com/politics/2016/jun/16/nigel-farage-defends-ukip-breaking-point-poster-queue-of-migrants.
UNITED for Intercultural Action. "List of 40,555 documented deaths of refugees and migrants due to the restrictive policies of "Fortress Europe."" PDF. Published 20 June 2020. Accessed 30 July 2020. http://unitedagainstrefugeedeaths.eu/wpcontent/uploads/2014/06/ListofDeathsActual.pdf.
UNITED for Intercultural Action. "About the 'List of Deaths'." Accessed 30 July 2020. http://unitedagainstrefugeedeaths.eu/about-the-campaign/about-the-united-list-of-deaths/.
West, Simon, dir. *Con Air*. Los Angeles: Touchstone Pictures, 1997.

Colin Herd

Another Poem About Jeff Hilson

once I rode a poem by Jeff Hilson it was any poem from *LATANOPROST VARIATIONS* & I rode it carelessly in a library and a bookshop without the proper controls & it kept stopping at the Local Interest section and the Non Fiction section and the Travel section and the poem was trying to sniff out a Poetry section (which it seemed to think resembled its own butt or that was a joke it was playing for its own pleasure) & I rode it wilfully by roundabout sentences and other units of meaning to lead to pleasure to lead to the pleasure of the text & there I suffered those who were anti-pleasure and pro-suffering but the poem it was any poem by Jeff Hilson was so thick and panting at this point it was any poem from the *LATANOPROST VARIATIONS* and I entered the play area of its language which emerged fully formed like a building by Arakawa and Madeline Gins and the poem rode me into itself or I rode into the language of the poem carried by itself & said "why do people have to die" & Jeff Hilson's poem was a better place where maybe they didn't or didn't for the same injustices & inequalities as they do in other places & the mirage of a poetry section was there it was a poetry section so big it couldn't exist & it became this vast gorgeous edifice but also just a prose poem any prose poem or any other poem by Jeff Hilson whose presence was in the poem and whose poetry which here was synonymous with pleasure so that we realised bookshops needed a pleasure section were sorely lacking a pleasure section so the first activities of my newly funded Centre for Decentred Pleasure where the reading lists were heavy on Jeff Hilson poems were to campaign for better Pleasure Sections in bookshops & these activities involved mint green book jackets and pamphlet production and hosting recitals in mint green buildings and painting shops mint green we chose mint green because of its capacity to both wake people up and help their digestion both desirable for the pleasure of poetry as enacted in the reading of a poem by Jeff Hilson from *LATANOPROST VARIATIONS*

Jessica Pujol Duran

Un Poema Ritual Contra el Mar

El problema és que m'assetgen els galions naturalment ningú dóna la benvinguda als galions que s'interposen en la vida normal el submarí d'atac també és difícil d'ignorar sovint faig mans i mànigues per evitar-lo el vaixell hospital al qual retorno invariablement com al gundalow que està endreçat "a la perfecció" a diferència del trimarà que és forassenyat i irracional comprovo repetidament el petrolier d'hidrogen el problema és que m'assetja quan el toco com el transbordador encara que el transbordador i el galió no tenen res a veure netejo el transbordador una vegada i una altra el canoner és difícil d'ignorar inevitablement retorno al restaurant flotant a rellegir el menú ningú li dóna la benvinguda al restaurant flotant rellegeixo el menú fins que queda net com l'horrorós vaixell de vapor de rodes bàsicament el transatlàntic no està bé i m'assetja en tocar les baranes de les seves escales invariablement retorno a les baranes i als mànecs de les portes els homes de guerra també són difícils d'ignorar encaixar-los les mans no significa que no siguin homes de guerra a diferència del trencaglaç que és "perfecte" a diferència del patruller que és "perfecte" no com el vaixell de càrrega a granel que és "perfecte" ningú dóna la benvinguda als homes de guerra que no són intrínsecament agradables el problema és que m'assetgen en comptar-los i cridar els seus noms com general beauchamp duff o clive el conquistador d'índia i encaixem les mans el problema és que faig tard a la feina al clíper que també està contaminat a netejar el transbordador una vegada i una altra invariablement hi retorno encenc i apago els llums del vaixell de càrrega fluvial invariablement retorno al creuer de batalla que és difícil d'ignorar pensa en els creuers de batalla en què t'has escurat la gola en l'HSM invencible escurant-te la gola en l'HSM indomable escurant-te la gola en l'HSM inflexible el problema és que m'assetgen naturalment ningú dóna la benvinguda als indiaman que són més fàcils d'abordar que els crommesteven invariablement sóc descurós en el vaixell de vapor com en el vaixell de durham intento no pensar en ells ni en els bergantins hermafrodites homes i dones deixo les finestres obertes equitativament i faig mans i mànigues per evitar els telèfons que s'interposen en la vida normal em dutxo repetidament en abordar la barca longa pujo i baixo de la passarel·la del gran vaixell de càrrega una vegada i una altra i deixo les portes obertes això és difícil d'ignorar com el dragamines naturalment ningú dóna la benvinguda al dragamines que no es pot aturar el toco a la feina o a la universitat el problema és que m'assetja invariablement retorno a l'hotel flotant invariablement sempre que sigui possible retorno a l'hotel flotant per a una recuperació completa a l'hotel flotant que és difícil d'ignorar a diferència del showboat que és absolutament segur tot i que en el fons vull l'hotel flotant per avançar ràpidament el comprovo repetidament comprovo el petrolier d'hidrogen que es va deteriorant progressivament naturalment ni vull ni dono la benvinguda a la nau nodrissa ni al clíper també està contaminat i m'assetja sovint faig mans i mànigues per bloquejar-lo com a l'astronau que és forassenyada i irracional com caminar pel tauló del vaixell pirata una vegada i una altra la qual cosa sempre s'interposa en la vida normal el problema és que el vaixell pirata està brut i els pirates s'han d'esquivar o posar-los en ordre fins que quedin "perfectes" cridar els seus noms ben alt com calico jack o redlegs greaves o netejar el vaixell pirata una vegada i una altra fins que quedi net com l'increïble hulk sovint durant hores o dies aquesta és la millor manera bàsicament el vaixell pirata no està bé com dinar a la cafeteria d'un creuer de 1a classe intentant no pensar en el quetx o el knarr intentant no pensar en el koff o en el kotx especialment el kotx donant voltes pels vàters del vaixell hidrogràfic fent mans i mànigues per evitar el vaixell d'aprovisionament logístic tot i que el vaixell d'aprovisionament logístic i el vaixell hidrogràfic no tenen res a veure m'assetgen sempre que faig quelcom pecaminós sempre enverinen el menjar a la nau de transport de tropes que és difícil d'ignorar tot i que ningú dóna la benvinguda a la nau de transport de tropes em dutxo amb els soldats i els abraço o em planto davant de les tropes amb l'objectiu de fer-los mal temo que dec estar predestinat no serveix de res demanar ajuda al vaixell frigorífic ni al junc que s'interposa en la vida normal ni tan sols puc desfer-me de la meva barqueta de rems inevitablement hi retorno vaig d'un cantó a l'altre per alta mar on s'esgota l'espai amb el portaavions de camí intentant no pensar en ell ni en el cuirassat que s'apropa enviant missatges de text al capità perquè apagui el gas perquè jo sóc el capità de la barqueta i no em dirigeixo a terra ferma tot i que el petrolier d'hidrogen m'hagi travessat naturalment he fet una parada d'emergència per raspallar-me les dents seguint un moviment d'escombrat circular primer les dents superiors després les inferiors parant especial atenció a la línia d'aigua i també raspallant-me la llengua per refrescar l'alè realment tinc traça és difícil arribar a les dents de darrere i són fàcils d'ignorar a diferència del destructor naturalment ningú li dóna la benvinguda ni al vaixell fantasma que emet llum fantasmal a la deriva cap a l'horitzó veritable el problema és que m'assetja com els bots salvavides absents jo invariablement hi retorno i m'hi agafo ben fort amb totes les mans rentant-me-les una vegada i una altra

Andrew Spragg

Some Notes on "Latanoprost Variations (Abandoned)" (Abandoned)

The poem from which Jeff Hilson's *Latanoprost Variations* (Boiler House Press, 2017) takes its title—"Latanoprost Variations (Abandoned)"—is a prose piece. Such intricate turns of the heel are true to the gambol of Hilson's particular vernacular, one refined and revisited throughout his "late" work. The diary that is "thin & muscular." The explanatory post-script unread or unnecessary. The indeterminate is the thing. The title ("Latanoprost") suggests a sic neologism—what rare or sick mind would contemplate *In Search of Lost Time* retrofitted and "writ in latin in the latin language"?

"Latanoprost Variations (Abandoned)" is jammed with these compounded misrecognitions—

"you wont know this without you have seen a tv/ no I am lying again I mean a fridge"

"yesterday sheila I mistook modern history for marsden hartley"

The examples accumulate, the prose becomes a place of unlocated locatedness

"lanes like workhouse lane which is in many towns in england sheila"

"no kettering is not a country sheila it is in the country on its own"

This oscillation is instrumental to Hilson's best work, his finest gambols, and we experience the pleasure of being simultaneously sincere and silly. There is a great yearning in "Latanoprost Variations (abandoned)," not quite tangible enough to be biographic, and traced in lines like:

"in wildwood flower it doesnt make sense to say *a pale and a leader* but all the singers are dead 320 years after thomas campion and thats that"

"this left me in ruins"

"lanes like the lanes you walk you walk down in your dreams with high banks of sedge and wild parsley and where you then fall into a reverie in your dream"

This motif of the past has a melancholy current and is idealised by its undetermined distance. The reader exists 345 years and 320 years after Thomas Campion simultaneously, is led into an obscure debate on the origins of the song "Wildwood Flower," before a desultory "thats that." Likewise, the reverie of the dream, so close to the poem's coda, is edged by a doctor doctor joke. This perpetual snapping shut of the line could be read as Hilson's refusal to give over to poetic impulse, a natural lyric sensibility, or it could be ascribed to a firm commitment to give us both worlds as once. Latanoprost is, in fact, a drugs company. The unfixed possibilities wrench back and forth between the sublime and the banal.

The cumulative effect of "Latanoprost Variations (Abandoned)" is the weariness of the returning world, the returning world experiencing its own weariness:

"in my house you must smoke outside and the wind takes the smoke to heaven otherwise it goes onto the curtains"

"he goes look at this they will soon knock it and she goes how the world for me is like this"

Hilson's associative refielding of the prosaic recalls his much-loved Robert Wyatt. Like Wyatt, his routes into (roots in) surrealism are too sophisticated to be wholly British in origin, but too embedded in the quirks of the English language to be benign pastiches of the European school.

It is tempting to do a retrofit of our own—not least when thumbing through the book to this opening line of another poem: "to test if my eyes were working I tried one day to look at art garfunkel" ("Optotypical Poem Including Art Garfunkel"). Opportunists might describe Hilson as a Cassandra figure, a state of the nation poet, even overextending themselves into a convenient (and wholly false) dialectical reversal: first as farce, then as tragedy. However, his is the same simple impulse that drives the work of collagist Cold War Steve, another artist for whom the world of day-time celebrities seems to burst forth with chimerical grotesqueness. By chance or design, Hilson's receptors have picked up a quirk of the English sickness, one that throws itself at our petty obsessions, our mistaking of daytime hegemony for consensus, our vaulting hubris in the face of inoperable under-achievement. It is no more a sign of the times than a recognition of these times *having always been here*. A buffoonery acquiring terminal velocity. A course of lemons, or a treatment such as "The Latanoprost Variations (abandoned)," may not offer a cure but it serves the senses with sharpened attunement.

Ágnes Lehóczky

Theorising The Final Poem

But look, Jeff, surviving what exactly; there is a passage somewhere in Hannah Arendt's *The Life of the Mind,* a book designed in three parts out of which the third book's first page was left in the author's typewriter in the eve of Arendt's death on the 4th of December 1975, a composition still incomplete (even though who is to say what completion is) or more precisely a piece of writing still in the making, a manuscript suspended abruptly, arrested in time, in other words, a piece of auto-writing still patiently waiting to be written up *by* the typewriter, in other words, by itself, specifically in the chapter entitled "Mental Activities in the World of Appearances" in book 1, in which Arendt, while still typing, by which I mean, while still alive, deconstructing "metaphors," suggests that *metaphor* when (being) constructed has the capacity architecturally, a process the modernist poet Ágnes Nemes Nagy, again, after Goethe refers to as "architectonic," to *metapherein,* that is, to build a bridge between disparate entities, i.e. to connect two or more incongruent, i.e. unrelated, estranged words estranged even by themselves which, Arendt, in her chapter, adds, standing by and in themselves are purely frozen concepts, paralytic things between which the distance or correlation, or intricate network, i.e. contours of a sort of mental arc we must be able to draw – as if with an invisible pencil – in order to conjure any preambulary meaning, as if by way of telepathy, into the empty space which stands between them, and here by "them," i.e. by "words," I also mean a collective "we" or "us," animate and inanimate, real and spectral, visible and invisible beings, who, without such a space or bond or connection, and by connection I and by "I" I also mean "you" might mean "familiar," a type of lexical or semantic or just simply linguistic familiarity or intimacy I imagine to be more impersonal than personal, or a type Susan Howe in the book called *The Midnight,* a collection of poem-documentaries, describes as more "factual" than "private," will remain purely words as volatile as paralytic "stones." "To be," in the essay *Building, Dwelling, Thinking,* Heidegger suggests, "is to take place." A kind of being, it occurs to me, which, ideally, must or should take place in a paradoxical home, or controversial house, or on the fence or border between two such paradoxons, say, in an invisible room or unapparent residence or a place of such subtle lodging which motions between *not yet belonging to* and a *place already possessed,* simultaneously always already domiciled and addressless, a house kind of lived in, kind of left behind, still semi-secret and already also civic property, half *still* habitat or habitation and half *ready* to be bulldozed, re-named, re-functioned, a sort of small museum or library or lyceum, or perhaps something we may call *agora*, a place of a quasi-nostalgic/spectral gathering which unexpectedly turns up from the past, where the disclosed is undisclosed and the undisclosed is disclosed, where say, things exist as living anamnesis, by which I am thinking here of a storage place with memories accumulated, the type of memories, which, like fugitives, or like secrets, do not belong, or some sort of a spatio-temporal memorial – or quasi-vacant tomb – where there is plenty of forensic evidence – as if an indication as to how productive or counterproductive one has been while being there – i.e. seemingly random and insignificant clutter collected through the many years by someone who is by now absent having left the house half vacant, half obstructed by some sort of still living, but already posthumous, unmovable and removable data which proves that this someone *actually* and factually, but also secretly or intimately, *was* dwelling in here / there but also a room or store which already performs as an archive or some other sort of liminal place storing, preserving and eventually displaying pseudo museal objects, where these objects left behind appear already as qua objects, i.e. as "dead metaphors," holding meaning only to and in themselves, i.e. emptied of their former idiosyncratic meaning, by which I also mean an idiosyncratic functionality, which used to belong to them and their holder only, yet a room of by now some communality, too, one which, Denise describes in *Time Lived*, as a space of "a loss held in common among people," in other words, what I might name for now, a room of lived-in, filled in, or inhabited lack, i.e. a room of my own, by which I mean a room of, or a space for some collective co-writing, collaborative not-writing or what Boyer in *The Undying* reconfigures in the image of a universal weeping wall designed mainly for women or, a room of, what Denise also tentatively contemplates in *Time Lived* [on p67 and on p74], a literature of consolation. But what makes this unfamiliar familiar bond, this correlation, this factual privacy, this *Room, Raum, Rum*, which Heidegger in the same essay describes as a place cleared or freed for settlement and lodging, a [new or alternative] space as something that has been made space for, after, I should add, melancholically, the former owner is gone with all its random archival clutter (e. g. worn garments left on the chair, or random collections of endless series of facsimile swimming pools – as a result of a lifetime long compulsive gathering, storing, amassing, an obsession deriving, what Derrida claims in *Archive Fever*, from some death or anti-death, i.e. tomb or anti-tomb drive, all mimicking the real pool, the macro pool, the qua swimming pool) taken to the local dump – a process or time you may call post demolition, post clearance, a space that offers freedom, not a bondage, an area or premise cleared and free, a space of sort of margin or circumference, perimeter in other words, from Greek *peras*, a would-be boundary "which is not that at which something stops but, as the Greeks recognised, is an un-prohibitive room, Raum, Rum, where something begins its presencing," which you may call bond between words, or the border, the edges of objects, their outer – rough – edges, I mean, or even our own boundaries, of our own bodies, present and absent, active – i.e. in motion – or paralysed, doing or being, or *between* these bodies we own, i.e. one's own vista, diverse and abundant, *horismos*, which motions towards these rough edges of the outside, protected from the inside, a horizon simultaneously shared and approached from different angles by the "neighbour," "the near-dweller." The eleatic stranger I find, *nunc pro tunc*, one early summer morning in and around the limits of my own poem.

Robert Hampson

"It's behind you": A Barry Bendy Poem and Cambridge in the 1970s

In *A Barry Bendy Poem* (2015), Jeff Hilson offers an extended prose poem that accumulates a succession of paratactic statements beginning with the assertion "like rolf harris in the 1970s I didn't go to Cambridge."[1] This sentence which is repeated through the poem (with some variations) as one of its structural components opens onto the darker side of the history of the 1970s. In the summer of 2014, Harris had been convicted of 12 indecent assaults on underage girls between 1968 and 1986, and so the poem had an immediate topical significance, as Harris became yet another figure from 1970s popular culture arrested for historical sexual offences as a result of Operation Yewtree.[2] To give a sense of Harris's prominence in the popular culture of the 1970s, the *Rolf Harris Show*, for example, was broadcast on the BBC from 1967-74, and he was the BBC commentator for the 1967 Eurovision Song Contest, the year Sandie Shaw's "Puppet on a String" was the winner. He was twice the subject of *This Is Your Life*, the first time in 1971; the second time in 1995, when Michael Aspel had taken over from Eamonn Andrews.

However, as that repeated sentence suggests, the work initially presents itself as a poem about Cambridge. From one perspective, *A Barry Bendy Poem* is a site-specific poem. The second sentence begins "if in the 1970s I had gone to cambridge," and the third sentence picks up this conditional mood to observe: "I would have asked but where are jesus green & the university arms hotel." Subsequent sentences trace various possible routes through central Cambridge, walking "from the railway station to tennis court road" or from the station to the Institute for Manufacturing, or else citing particular locations such as "christ's pieces & the lammas land" or the University's Botanic Gardens. It is perhaps significant that Jesus Green, Christ's Pieces, the Lammas Land and the Botanic Gardens are parks or recreational areas—public spaces rather than the undergraduate world of the university.

---

[1] Jeff Hilson, *A Barry Bendy Poem* (Hunstanton: Oystercatcher Press, 2015)—no pagination.

[2] The Harris case was not actually part of Operation Yewtree, but the complaints against Harris were prompted by publicity relating to Operation Yewtree. Harris was found guilty of molesting four girls, ranging in age from 7 to 19, and of a catalogue of abuse against another victim whom he had groomed from the age of 13. See the *Guardian* (1 May 2015).

There are other motifs that Hilson works with throughout the sequence. For example, he repeats the phrases "jumping up and down" and "on all fours" in various contexts. In both cases, when Hilson reads the poem, the undignified actions gain a resonant inappropriateness from his deadpan delivery and resolute immobility as a reader.[3] There are also the names of various women that occur in the course of the poem: "walking with grace from the railway station," walking "with ruth down tenison road," walking with "nancy down amherst road," culminating in the speaker's imagining not so much being with Rosa, but rather "breaking everything with her in a second rate taverna"—although it is not quite clear whether this means breaking off the relationship, breaking plates in a Greek taverna or smashing the place up (as the University Arms Hotel was "trashed" in the opening section). In the first two instances of walking, there is a different kind of ambiguity, both in performance and on the page (given the use of lower case throughout), since "with grace" and "with ruth" might have an adverbial function to describe the manner of his walking rather than naming his companion. In effect, there is a diminution of ambiguity as we progress through "grace" and "ruth" to "nancy," since it is quite possible to imagine walking "with grace" as an alternative mode of mobility to "jumping up and down" or going "on all fours."

The topographic aspect of the poem also includes repeated references to Cambridge hotels: the University Arms Hotel, the Varsity Hotel and Spa (with its roof terrace), and the Garden House Hotel. In fact, these early references to hotels build up, in the context of 1970s Cambridge, to that mention of the Garden House Hotel. On 13 February 1970, as the climax to a "Greek Week" in Cambridge organised by the Greek Tourist Board, there was a formal dinner for 120 guests at the Garden House Hotel. Several hundred protesters against the Greek military junta besieged the hotel, which was invaded and damaged. Fifteen students were arrested, eight of whom were convicted and given harsh sentences by Justice Melford Stevenson. In the poem this is alluded to in the sentence "surely I would have stayed at the garden house hotel burning it down," where "stayed" probably does not mean booking a room, but rather remaining to take part in the demonstration outside.

This chimes with another set of associations brought into the poem by the epigraph from Anna Mendelssohn's *Implacable Art*. In this

---

[3] Hilson's deliberately low-key performance of his work should be compared with the foregrounding of performance by cris cheek and Caroline Bergvall, the dynamic reading style of Ulli Freer or the dramatic rhythmic performances of the late Sean Bonney. For this aspect of poetry (and, in particular, the place of performance in the work of Allen Ginsberg, Denise Riley, Eric Mottram and Allen Fisher), see Juha Virtanen, *Poetry and Performance during the British Poetry Revival 1960-1980* (Palgrave Macmillan, 2017).

context "walking with grace" inevitably suggests Grace Lake, the name under which Anna Mendelssohn published much of her poetry. However, Mendelssohn did not move to Cambridge and become "Grace Lake" until the middle of the 1980s. (She changed her name to Grace Lake by deed-poll in 1983 and became an undergraduate at Cambridge in the same year.[4]) The reference to walking down "amherst road with nancy" is similarly slippery—particularly in performance. In fact, there is no Amherst Road in Cambridge, but Amhurst Road, Stoke Newington, was where Anna Mendelssohn lived with Hilary Creek and John Barker in 1971.[5] At this time, she was using the name "Nancy Pye." The three (along with her boyfriend, Jim Greenfield) were arrested there in the summer of 1971 and, eventually, charged (along with four others) for carrying out bomb attacks on government buildings, embassies, corporations and the homes of Government Ministers. (The trial of the "Stoke Newington 8" ran from May 30 to December 6, 1972 and ended with heavy sentences for all four for the lesser, more general charge of "conspiracy to cause explosions."[6])

The first reference to "amherst road" in the poem reads: "walking with her down amherst road I should have asked but where are your grundig tape recorder and bicycle bomb." This is followed by the rejection of this imagining (or, perhaps, a revisioning as the use of "should" to express the conditional is retrospectively turned into the use of "should" to express obligation, which is then subjected to self-censorship): "& not doing so because I am only comic lead joining instead the spangly brigade." At first glance, the "grundig tape recorder" sounds like an innocent period detail.[7] Grundig was founded in Germany in 1945 as an electronics company producing radios and televisions. In the 1950s, the company developed a portable tape

---

[4] Information from the Anna Mendelssohn Archive, University of Sussex. She reverted to the name Anne Mendelson in 1997, but her collection *Implacable Art* (Cambridge: Salt / Equipage, 2000) was published under the name Anna Mendelssohn. Her last publication *Py*, was published by Oystercatcher in 2009. See the essay by Sean Bonney, "'Minds do exist to agitate and provoke / this is the reason I do not conform'—Anna Mendelssohn," *Poetry Project Newsletter* #226 (February / March 2011), 17-19.

[5] In the *Latanoprost Variations* (Boilerhouse Press, 2017), where "A Barry Bendy Poem" is reprinted, Hilson uses the spelling "Amhurst". Perhaps there was interference from the ghosts of Cambridge and Amherst, Massachusetts. Tom Raworth also lived in Amhurst Road—as did Sean Bonney and Francis Kruk in the 2000s.Tom Raworth's correspondence with Anna Mendelssohn is in the Anna Mendelssohn Archive.

[6] See Gordon Carr, *The Angry Brigade: A History of Britain's First Urban Guerrilla Group* (1975; Oakland, CA: PM Press, 2010) and Stuart Christie, *Grannie Made Me An Anarchist: General Franco, the Angry Brigade and Me* (Scribner, 2004).

[7] It is also another citation from *Implacable Art*.

recorder, and in 1960 opened a factory in Belfast to produce tape-recorders. However, in December 1973, the manager of the Belfast plant, Thomas Niedermayer, was kidnapped and killed by the Provisional IRA. The "bicycle bomb" confirms this context. Bicycle bombs were first used by the IRA in August 1939; in August 1976, Robert Borucki, a member of the Parachute Regiment, was killed in Crossmaglen by a bomb placed in the basket of a bicycle. In addition, the "spangly brigade" suggests, through assonance, "the Angry Brigade" (the anarchist group to which it was alleged Mendelssohn belonged), but this affiliation is rejected by the speaker for something more appropriate to a "comic lead": perhaps the glitter and sequins of Marc Bolan and glam rock that kicked off in 1971—or, for reasons I will mention later, possibly the similarly flamboyant New Romantics of the 1980s.

There is a submerged link to another sentence which further confirms this line of reading: "I should have turned off miss world as I turned off victoria avenue." The speaker might have "turned off" Victoria Avenue to cross Jesus Green, but the sentence pivots on that wordplay on "turning off" which, with an effect akin to zeugma, turns from switching off a television to changing direction while walking through Cambridge. Again, the reference to "miss world" is not quite as innocent as it first appears. During the November 1970 Miss World contest, the BBC hired a bodyguard to protect Michael Aspel because of fears that he would be abducted by feminist protesters. The feminist protest, with its flour bombs and leafletting, is now well known.[8] Less well known, however, is that security at the Albert Hall, the venue for the event, was increased after a bomb (a small amount of TNT wrapped in a copy of *The Times*) was detonated by the Angry Brigade underneath a BBC Outside Broadcasting lorry parked there to record the Miss World contest.

As this account should by now have suggested, the text is constructed from a number of repeated sentences, phrases and motifs which appear, with variations, in various combinations. These repeated elements also include references to "the motto," "the cambridge men," "all my life," and the colourful language of heraldry. References to "the motto" draw in the Latin phrase "*volans propriis*" (flying by our own wings), which is (perhaps coincidentally) the University of Buckingham's motto. This motto is also a link to the heraldic language in the poem, since "volant" is used in heraldry to describe a bird, emblazoned as a charge, supporter or crest, depicted in flight. Thus, a mention of the Cambridgeshire police is followed by the words "a bend wavy" and then (after an invocation of "the men of understanding") the words "flory counter flory gules." The first term ("bend wavy") refers to a

---

[8] It is the subject of the 2020 film *Misbehaviour*.

band running from the upper right corner to the lower left corner of a shield with wavy rather than straight edges. The term "flory counter-flory" refers to a series of fleur-de-lys alternating between the left- and right-hand side of a line. ("Gules" means simply red.) A later passage refers to "the men of girton rampant and regardant," where the heraldic term "rampant" (rearing up) refers to animals depicted standing on one hind leg with forelegs outstretched as if attacking, and "regardant" describes an animal with its head turned backwards as if looking over its shoulder. The former is very appropriate to the Garden House Hotel riot; the latter fits with the poem's own stance and its repetition of the pantomime warning "it's behind you." At the same time, "rampant" also has its colloquial sense of something intemperate and uncontrolled—in this context, suggesting both riot and male sexual desire—while "regardant" is not without a hint of self-regard. The sexual connotation links with a later reference to "a salient rolf harris erect in the knowledge," where "salient," in heraldry, describes an animal leaping with both hindlegs on the ground and both forelegs in the air and "erect" is used instead of "upright." More obscure is the statement "after all I am not engrailed," where "engrailed" is the heraldic term to describe a line made up of a series of arcs, curving in the same direction, meeting at angles, forming points outward. Perhaps this describes the poem's own form, those points created by a series of connecting arcs.

Heraldry also takes us back to the title of the poem. What is "A Barry Bendy Poem"? It sounds like a trademark ("a Walt Disney Production"). It also sounds as if it might be foregrounding a persona. Is "Barry Bendy," Hilson's version of Allen Fisher's "Pam Burnel" or Robert Sheppard's "Wayne Pratt"?[9] Neither of these is the case. In heraldry, "barry" signifies a field marked with a series of horizontal (fesswise) stripes. When the field is marked with a series of diagonal stripes (bendlets) from top left to bottom right, the field is described as "bendy." That is, "bendy" refers to a variation of the field consisting (usually) of an even number of parts created by these stripes. Merriam-Webster defines "barry bendy" as a field "divided with bars and bends with tinctures alternate." When the field of the shield is divided by both barwise and bendwise sinister lines, by horizontal and vertical lines, a field of lozenges with alternating colours like a skewed chessboard is produced. In the language of heraldry, "barry-bendy

---

[9] "Pam Burnel" published a sequence of fifteen poems, "Political Speeches for Jean Jacques" in *Rawz 2½* (1979); Wayne Pratt flourished in the period 1983-89. He was the author of a number of pamphlets. His work is most readily found in Robert Sheppard, *Complete Twentieth Century Blues* (Cambridge: Salt Publishing, 2008), 322-27, or in his *History or Sleep: Selected Poems* (Shearsman, 2015), which includes "Three poems by Wayne Pratt from *The Penguin Book of British Parrots*," 46-48.

lozengy" involves dividing the field barwise, each piece being subdivided bendwise also, with the tinctures counter-changed. The titular invocation of "barry bendy" should prepare us for the formal complexity of Hilson's text.

if I had gone to cambridge in the 1970s

The first speculative response to the thought "if I had gone to Cambridge in the 1970s" introduces the curves of the Cam, Jesus Green and the University Arms Hotel—the "university arms" perhaps being the prompt for the later turn to heraldry. The second speculative response produces a more detailed engagement with the topography of Cambridge through imagined walks with Grace and Ruth. It introduces mottos, Cambridge men and the (non-Cambridge) Michael Aspel. It concludes with an extended topographical riff on the surrounding area which takes off from the repeated second (answering) refrain ("but I didn't go to cambridge in the 1970s like rolf harris") with a series of unlikely assertions: "nobody even heard of cambridge then forgetting east anglia completely not remembering bury st edmunds overlooking warboys & failing to notice saffron walden." East Anglia, Suffolk, Huntingdon, and Essex, linked by these near- synonymous present participles, provide a framing for the Cambridge setting. This leads in turn, via a reference to Pink Floyd's 1973 album, *The Dark Side of the Moon*, and an apparent memory of "falling into the cam," to "plans for the reform of the constabulary of cambridgeshire & the isle of ely." In 1965, all five forces that covered the Cambridgeshire area (including the Cambridgeshire Constabulary and the Isle of Ely Constabulary) were amalgamated to form the new Mid-Anglia Constabulary. The Local Government Act (1972) created the new non-metropolitan county of Cambridgeshire with the same boundaries as the Mid-Anglia Constabulary area. Like the reference to Pink Floyd, this fixes a time in the mid-1970s. A figure in the poem's carpet here is, perhaps, Syd Barrett, who left Pink Floyd in 1968, played a few gigs in Cambridge in 1972 and moved back there permanently in 1978. His withdrawal from public life provides a subject-rhyme for Anna Mendelssohn's (dis)similar retreat to Cambridge.

The third speculative section is introduced by a muted version of the refrain ("not knowing in the 1970s because I didn't go there") and then picks up a reference to "outfitters of uniforms & sportswear" at the end of the previous section to refer more specifically (and problematically) to "the school girls of the hills road," referencing Hills Road Sixth Form College, a co-educational college set up in 1974 on the site of the former Cambridgeshire High School for Boys. This is juxtaposed to Michael Aspel and the Miss World contest. The fourth section intercuts walking "with Nancy down amherst road" (and the associated Angry Brigade and IRA material) with references to "the cod war." This looks like a typo for "the cold war," but the Cod Wars were a series of conflicts between the UK and Iceland over fishing rights in the North Atlantic. The First Cod War was from November 1958 to March 1961; the Second Cod War ran from September 1972 to November 1973.The second war began with the Icelandic Coast Guard using net-cutters against the trawling lines of non-Icelandic vessels ("cutting all my nets"). The Third Cod War ran from November 1975 to June 1976. In each of these wars, Iceland achieved all its aims, because of its strategic importance to NATO. The UK lost all three wars, which is perhaps why they are largely forgotten by the British. Nevertheless, they had a significant impact on the UK economy. As a result of these wars ("small wars are the best wars she said"), British fisheries were excluded from the Icelandic fishing grounds, and this furthered the decline of northern fishing ports like Grimsby and Hull.

There are other references in this section which serve as period markers. "Climax trucks," for example, probably refers to the 1960s Dinky toys, but it could mean the original products of the Coventry engineering company which was merged with the Leyland Motor Corporation in 1968 and nationalised as British Leyland in 1975. Kid Jensen takes us back to 1970s rock. Jensen joined Radio Luxemburg as a teenager in 1968; in the 1970s he presented a popular progressive rock programme at midnight on Luxemburg; in the 1980s he was presenting an indie-rock programme on BBC Radio 1. The fifth section begins with similarly topical markers - the decimalisation of the coinage in 1971; the introduction of buses with front doors and paying on entry—before arriving at the Garden House Hotel and "the girl from argos." Again, Hilson has an acute sense of the period: Argos shops were founded in July 1973 as a rebranding of the Green Shield stamps catalogue shops.

This same section introduces "whippet coaches," not a piece of surreal imagining, but a local, Cambridgeshire bus company which provided summer services to the coast—Great Yarmouth, Lowestoft, Clacton-on-Sea. Indeed, the epigraph from Anna Mendelssohn begins "go Whippet / coach, driven by male." The fleet of Whippet coaches merges with Cod-War fishing fleets in the speaker's voiced desire "to see her whole fleet sailing upriver" like some latter-day armada before suffering a diminuendo to the unheroic world of the "day return & weakly explorer" of Stagecoach. In the same way, the myth of the original *Argos* (and the quest for the Golden Fleece) is replaced by the diminished world of a catalogue retailer.

The sixth section introduces Baroness Butler Sloss, who has no obvious connection with 1970s Cambridge. Her presence in the poem is indebted to events nearer the time when the poem was written. She chaired the 1987 Cleveland Child Abuse inquiry, but her official title at that time was Lord Justice Butler Sloss: she did not become Baroness Butler Sloss until June 2006. More relevantly, for the poem, in July 2014, she was named by Theresa May as the chair of the forthcoming Independent Inquiry into Child Sexual Abuse, to investigate accusations of sexual abuse within government and other institutions. Six days later she resigned.[10] Since she was the sister of Sir Michael Havers, who was the Conservative Attorney General at the time of some of the alleged abuses, questions were raised about her independence, since she might have to adjudicate on his failure to prosecute child abuse cases. Her nephew, Nigel Havers, tweeted in her support. This earns him his place in this section: "not even nigel havers would read my poem from end to end." This penultimate section clearly brings to the surface the theme of child abuse, cover-ups and official inquiries which has been implicit since the first mention of Rolf Harris.

its behind you

The poem's seventh section begins by significantly changing the refrain (and the time frame): "if I had gone to Cambridge in the long 1970s." The speaker now asks "where are your class of 1970" (much as Villon asked where were the snows of yesteryear). In a similar mood, after a negative review of the Rock View Hotel, the speaker observes that "sometimes the stars don't come out in cambridge england and don't even shine"—apparently a rewrite of Chris Stapleton's 2015 song "When the stars come out," which evokes "one of those LA nights" when "the stars come out and shine." However, the Rock View Hotel is another nod to Syd Barrett, who lived a few streets away from the hotel until his death in 2006. There is an ironic link between the hotel's name and Barrett's reclusiveness. In this context, "the stars don't come out" refers to Barrett's withdrawal from public view, while "and don't even shine" can be seen to play on the words of the Pink Floyd song, "Shine On You Crazy Diamond," which was written about Barrett's mental collapse.[11] The speaker also rephrases a sentence from the previous section ("I would never read my poems aloud in cambridge not in the 1970s"): this now becomes "I would never read my poems aloud in cambridge not in

---

[10] She was replaced by Dame Fiona Woolf, who was appointed on 5 September 2014 and stepped down on 31 October, because she was a neighbour of Lord Brittain, who, as Home Secretary had been in receipt of a dossier of alleged high-profile paedophiles. She was replaced on 4 February 2015 by Dame Lowell Goddard, who resigned on 4 August 2016. On 11 August Professor Alexis Jay became the fourth chair of the Inquiry.
[11] "Shine On You Crazy Diamond" appeared on their 1975 *Wish You Were Here* album.

the obscure 1970s to the serious men of the twentieth century." As in the previous section, the time has shifted from the 1970s to the contemporary moment, to a time from which not just "the long 1970s" but also "the twentieth century" can be viewed as distant.

That reference to "the serious men of the twentieth century" gestures towards early-twentieth-century modernists and the more recent "class of 1970" who were present at the Garden House Hotel against whom the speaker has presented himself as a "comic lead," a member of "the spangly brigade." Wyndham Lewis famously called the group of writers that included himself, Ezra Pound, T.S. Eliot and James Joyce "The Men of 1914," and there is a whiff of that phrase around here.[12] These "serious men" (of whichever generation) are then described as "floating on the pound," which again might suggest a play on the name Ezra Pound, but is primarily a reference to economic policies in the early 1970s. From 1946 until the start of the 1970s, the post-war Bretton Woods Agreement had made fixed currencies the norm. During 1971 the US Government under Richard Nixon decided to discontinue maintaining the dollar exchange pegged to the gold standard. In June 1972, the Conservative Chancellor, Anthony Barber, after deterioration in the balance of trade, floated the pound rather than remain within a broad band linked to other currencies. The floating pound was allowed to fluctuate in relation to foreign exchange market events. This was criticised by Labour MPs as the first step towards devaluation, and, indeed, a quick devaluation of the pound followed. This floating of the pound also brought to an end the sterling area, which had fixed the exchange rate of member countries against the pound. (In January 1973, Britain joined the European Economic Community.)

At this point in the poem, there also seems to be a shift in the intellectual climate: the "obscure 1970s" is replaced by "the new era of light," but it is not at all clear when that "new era of light" was or what it involved. And the transition to "like rolf harris in the light of the bishop's hostel" is far from re-assuring (unless the "light" is the exposure of historical abuses). The reference to the Bishop's Hostel initiates a final flurry of references to Cambridge topography and perambulation: "passing through hobsons passage on the way to the buttery or passing through the buttery on the way to the maids causeway." Of the Cambridge colleges, only Clare, Fitzwilliam, St John's, Newnham, Pembroke, and Trinity have butteries. This is a much more arcane and intimate knowledge of Cambridge than was on display in the earlier sections with their new arrival's anxious enquiries: "where are jesus

---

[12] See, for example, Erik Svarny, *"The Men of 1914": T.S. Eliot and Early Modernism* (New York: Open University Press, 1988) or, more recently, Colleen R. Lamos, "The Men of 1914" in Vincent Sherry (ed), *The Cambridge History of Modernism* (Cambridge University Press, 2017),478-92.

green & the university arms hotel" or "where are christ's pieces & the lammas land." At the start, the speaker told us that, in the 1970s, he "would also have asked where are the curves of the river cam," but now he affirms "the knowledge of the 1980s & the curves of the river cam."

That reference to "the knowledge of the 1980s" tips the wink to Hilson's private joke that has run through the poem: it is true, as he has repeatedly stated in the poem, that he did not go to Cambridge in the 1970s, but he was at Cambridge. He went to Girton in 1985. This has an immediate impact on the reading of one small detail in the poem. As he would know, Girton became co-educational in 1976—so "the men of girton" could not have been at the Garden House Hotel in 1971. The phrase "with the men of girton" has to be disconnected from the Garden House Hotel context and read as initiating a new unit of sense. There is also a more significant re-adjustment: Hilson's time at Girton coincided with the period when Grace Lake had returned to Cambridge and had started writing poetry. His evocation of Cambridge in the 1970s (and particularly the poem's topographical dimension) presumably draws on his own experiences (and knowledge) of Cambridge a decade later. Perhaps this is also where the New Romantics might come in.

Meanwhile, both Cambridge of the 1970s and Cambridge of the 1980s are written from the perspective of 2015. This gives the poem its double sense of belatedness: the "knowledge of the 1980s" laid over remembered or researched details from "the obscure 1970s." The former knowledge seems perambulatory, the product of spatial practices and personal relations; the latter knowledge depicts a time of political and financial change and uncertainties—and an older generation's committed and embattled engagement in contemporary politics. Perhaps this is how Cambridge undergraduates in the 1980s looked back at their predecessors in the early 1970s. Either way, whether it is the political engagements of the 1970s or the personal relations of the 1980s, as the poem repeatedly reminds us, "its behind you."

on all fours

There is, however, a further dimension to the poem, which has become less apparent as time has passed. That early reference to Jesus Green is another non-innocent detail. In fact, it has a direct connection with Rolf Harris, with his trial at Southwark Crown Court, and with the poem's repeated refrain. During the trial it was claimed that, among other things, Harris had indecently assaulted a teenage waitress during a 1978 episode of the ITV programme "Star Games."[13] He had been "on all fours barking at a dog" outside the marquee where she was working, and, when she had gone outside to see what was happening, the assault had occurred.[14] The game-show episode had taken place on Jesus Green, but, in his defence, Harris denied that he had ever been to Cambridge in the 1970s. This defence becomes the poem's refrain "I didn't go to cambridge." During the trial, however, a video emerged of the "Star Games" episode, which showed Harris as captain of one of the teams. It also showed him "jumping up & down" like a kangaroo. Michael Aspel was the co-host of the show, as he had been of Miss World, contributing to the concatenation of hidden connections on which the poem is constructed.

The refrain "I didn't go to cambridge," which was a playful misdirection in the mouth of Hilson as the implied speaker, now carries a very different weight as a lie, spoken in a court of law, intended to discredit the victim of an indecent assault. It also gives a different turn to other parts of the poem. The riff that begins with the statement "nobody even heard of Cambridge then" (which follows the words "like rolf harris") now becomes a send-up, a *reductio ad absurdum*, of Harris's defence. At the same time, the assertion "but I didn't go to Cambridge in the 1970s like rolf harris" now reveals a second meaning: not that neither Harris nor the speaker were in Cambridge in the 1970s, but rather that the speaker wasn't there then—though Harris was. The repeated statement "I would be jumping up & down too" now clearly refers to the visual evidence that demonstrated Harris's lie and, as a result, loses some of its lightness. Harris's subsequent claim that he didn't know the show was in Cambridge, because "the stars" were often bussed into a town and then bussed out again without necessarily knowing where they had been, provides a context for those early anxious questions ("where are jesus green & the university arms hotel") but also for the common-sense riposte: "I would have asked where are I going." Harris's statement also provides another set of resonances for the assertion "sometimes the stars don't come out in cambridge."

A Barry Bendy Poem, then, initially presents itself as a humorous poem about an imagined Cambridge of the 1970s. Through what seem to be topical details designed to produce a "reality effect," Hilson implicates us in a history of protests, bombings, harsh legal penalties, economic uncertainty and forgotten wars. At the same time, in part through its repeated refrains, the poem also registers the revelations of historic child abuse at the time of its composition. It becomes a poem about concealment and forgetting. Three time periods

---

[13] "Star Games" ran from 12 September 1978 to 26 December 1980. It was ITV's short-lived response to the long-running BBC family programme, "It's A Knockout" (1966-1982).

[14] *The Guardian*, 2 June 2014.

are brought into play: the 1970s, the 1980s and the contemporary moment of the Harris trial. This contemporary frame is always present, but also steadily comes into view as the poem nears its close. The field of the poem is divided by the stripes of those resonant refrains, and each of the resulting sections might be described as one in a series of narrative arcs, meeting at angles, and pointing outwards. Finally, the poem shows how flippancy—the apparent lightness of a self-described "comic lead," a member of the "spangly brigade"—can successfully engage a range of serious topics.[15]

---

[15] For more on the political uses of flippancy in poetry, see Prudence Bussey Chamberlain, *Queer Troublemakers: The Poetics of Flippancy* (London: Bloomsbury, 2019).

JEFF HILSON
organ music

Zoë Skoulding

Celeste Stop

> And is the church organ itself not a hauntological instrument, simultaneously both backward and forward looking? Old-fashioned in its outmoded religious contexts, it is futuristic in its use of the console, a name given to the organ's keyboard, stops and pedals as well of course to the operating systems of any number of real and fictional spacecraft.—Jeff Hilson

pipes tuned off pitch
            speak together in an undulation
or shimmer imitating strings
another hic another nunc

the hautboy is a swelling
hautboy placed in its own swell box

the case has swell shutters in the roof
and both are operated by the same swell pedal

it is like watching hands moving and not
seeing them
                        or dancing it is like dancing
with invisible feet on the pedals

or a writer writing air in its own swell box
            mood music swelling down the aisles
interfering with the mechanism
                        and the voicing
a shadow memory ahead of every note

a hautboy is not an oboe and a stopped
diapason is not a diapason but a flute

hands and feet and pumping arm
in an England without organs
            reversed into tomorrow

while in St Burchardi Church in Halberstadt
the note has changed
                        and time moves as slowly

as possible in both directions
                                        on and on until 2640
oh future here we come

pull out all the stops for stars
and their variations
                                        bright in the talking air
nunc dimittis on the console hey let's go

Iris Colomb

Musique Pour Orgue, Face 6

Je suis la Tête et c'est mon Corps.
James Ier, Discours au Parlement, 19 Mars, 1604.

Mais j'dois garder la tête./Tu comprends?/Qui gardera la tête?
Bill Griffiths, "L'histoire d'un tête"

Chlik chlak chlik chlak le dernier homme est mort.
Anon, "Oranges et Citrons"

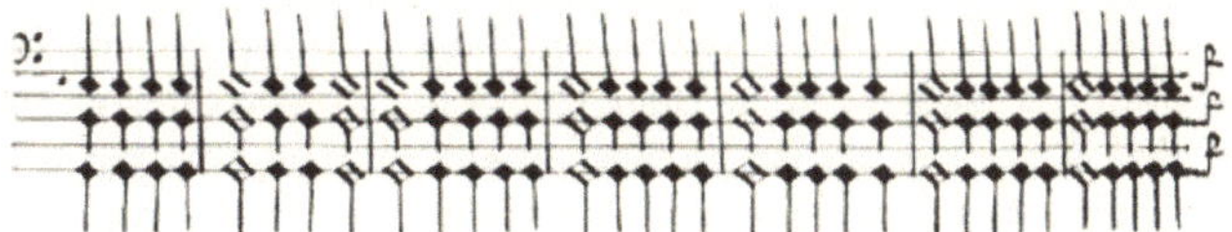

lorgue anglais est tout silence aujourdhui je nen peu presque plus au lieu de jouer oranges & citrons filles & garçons les jambes des hommes de guerre souvrent & se ferment souvrent & se ferment & tous en file portant leur nouvelle grosse tête elle est devenue tellement grosse quils ont dû la couper là ils la portent vers quelque chose qui commence par zed souvrent & se ferment souvrent & se ferment & il ne faut pas réveiller la tête ou elle vous tuera comme les cloches de st clements schlak schlak & quand le vent a tourné je suis resté comme ça toute la journée à attendre le retour de la tête je voulais seulement embrasser la tête et lapplaudir je nattends que mon tour pour applaudir après cest mon tour jai dit jai presque présenté mes bras jai commencé à applaudir si fort que jai presque réveillé la tête jai tellement hâte de continuer à présenter mes bras tout seul clap clap comme la grande cloche de bow tous en file clap clap & là nous avons compris quune tête cest pour toujours & pas juste pour tourner à gauche ou à droite ou pour regarder la france & je dois enlever mon chapeau je ne savais pas que je dois enlever autant de chapeaux juste pour présenter mes bras des centaines de milliers de chapeaux qui les veut vous peutêtre ô hommes de guerre je ne vous connais point voyezvous là je retire mon armure en silence entendez ma prière cest toujours la jambe gauche puis la jambe droite qui saute des centaines de milliers de jambes montent au cieux mavouant quen vérité elles ne sont que des jambes les jambes nexistent pas mais javais tort toute les jambes ressuscitent clap clap disent les cloches de st clements & vraiment les cloches applaudissaient mes jambes tandis quelles se laissaient choir une à une sur les jardins dangleterre jai même hurlé je ne veux pas de jambes aujourdhui mais les cloches ne vous écoutent jamais quand elles applaudissent certaines cloches jubilent même quand quelquun dit que cest pas grave si quelque chose commence par une jambe ou un nom comme la grande cloche de bow moi non plus jveux pas dnom dit la cloche napplaudissez pas quand vous voyez votre nom tout en file ou quand vous le prononcez quand le vent tourne ça ne voulait pas dire que la tête tourne comme un nom ou un drapeau un drapeau ne bouge que de haut en bas comme un nom on ne peut pas avoir un demi nom même si on le coupe en deux comme un pavillon de complaisance disaient les cloches de st clements ou un drapeau de jambes qui attend son tour pour battre de haut en bas tout seul flop flop la gauche puis la droite convient bien dhabitude des centaines de milliers doranges & citrons mais vraiment un seul drapeau seul qui tremble comme moi il a peur quon lutilise aujourdhui au lieu dapplaudir mon papa tremble comme moi mon papa a tort jai même hurlé je ne veux pas de papa comme moi voyezvous je veux un papa homme de guerre avec des bras réalistes même deux papas hommes de guerre sont de mauvais filles & garçons sils tombent amoureux sils tombent dans une rivière ils sont mouillés cest ça même deux papas hommes de guerre avec des mains qui prennent sont trempés après lorage trempés & puis secs comme un drapeau cette fois un faux drapeau à côté duquel jétais assis la fois où lun de nous a oublié le sens premier de la tête toc toc quelle fait contre la porte elle voudrait être une main et nest quune tête toc toc qui estce la tête qui la même tête que tout à lheure je suis la tête ditelle & cest ma tête & dans la montée je ne vois que des chapeaux de guerre qui tombent partout une tête ne rime à rien sans chapeau elle bat toute seule flop flop claque et reclaque clac clac sans chapeau une tête de guerre est comme nimporte quelle tête une tête pas de veine ou une tête de plusieurs couleurs qui ne sont pas de vrais têtes comme une tête qui a sauté et qui tourne autour du jardin & quand le vent a tourné ce nest pas une tête cest juste quelque chose qui commence par tête cest juste une tête à claques qui parle dont je suis tombé amoureux un faux amour jai adoré quand la tête à claques ma dit tu nauras pas mon cœur & les cœurs nexistent pas & ainsi de suite & ainsi de suite jusquà ce que les cloches sarrêtent & que lorgue commence lorgue anglais & la nouvelle grosse tête dans la nuit me réveille & me tue de son petit œil

Écrit le jour de l'enterrement de Thatcher avril 17 2013

Carlos Soto Roman

Música para órgano, Lado 8

Es muy probable que, en la jerarquía artística, las aves sean los músicos más grandes que existen en nuestro planeta.
Olivier Messiaen

Tañido de campanas, sé que debo escapar
Y sé que si no lo hago, me volveré loco.
The Who, "The Kids Are Alright"

En la Rue des Hiboux, los perros ladran en francés.
Kelvin Corcoran, "Rue des Hiboux"

* * *

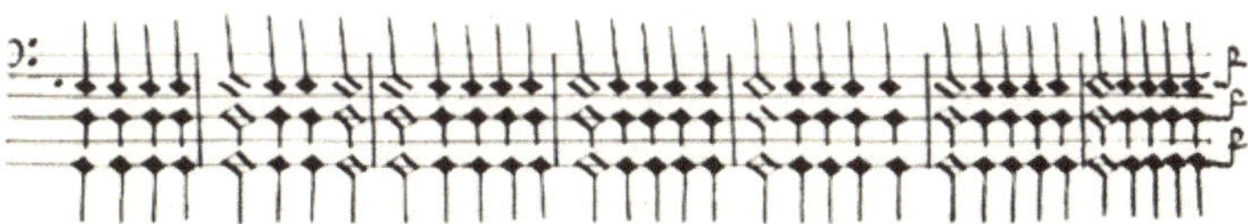

porque estoy enamorado del órgano inglés hoy escuché una fantasía memorable luego escuché un solo incluso escuché un nunc dimittis no a todos en inglaterra les gusta el nunc dimittis está en latín todo lo que significa es ahora me tengo que ir oh dios & lo toqué con las luces apagadas porque en inglaterra nadie quiere saber sobre el órgano inglés los ingleses ni siquiera saben si quieren abandonar la ue en cambio me voy a quedar & voy a escuchar el órgano de la eglise notre dame de chant doiseau porque hoy amo el sonido del francés tanto como el sonido de los pájaros no es en inglés la eglise notre dame de chant doiseau está en la ue en la avenida del canto de los pájaros todos saben que la ue está en bruselas como todos en bruselas saben cuándo están cruzando la avenida des albatross nadie en inglaterra quiere saber sobre los albatros es muy reservado & difícil de vivir por las mañanas en la ue los puedes escuchar silbando por todas partes en la rue de flandres o tarareando en el patio de la maison du spectacle cuando intentas escuchar el órgano de la eglise notre dame de la chapelle estoy empezando a amar los órganos de la ue casi tanto como los sonidos de los nombres de las iglesias de la antigua Bruselas escuchen aquí está el el órgano rococó de la eglise notre dame du finistere incluso en el fin del mundo a veces se siente como si la ue fuera el mejor lugar para estar caminando por la rue de spa en mi bolsillo las aves de bretaña & europa & la guía penguin de los órganos de los países bajos escuchando la pequeña producción sobreviviente de peter cornet o abraham van den kerckhoven luego doblando la esquina de la rue de lartichaut pasando al sr y sra wong & hacia la rue des deux eglises donde no hay ni siquiera iglesias la rue des deux eglises con sus edificios parcialmente modificados & reconstruidos incluso las casas burguesas de la ue con sus departamentos amoblados & buses turísticos son mejores que un referendum inglés oh albatros oh pájaro de mal agüero del veintitrés de junio como todo en inglaterra se aleja de la gare centrale como a todos en inglaterra les encanta el equipaje fácil de maniobrar siempre viajando ligero con una maleta de una rueda a través de la avenue de cormorans no está en inglés la avenue de cormorons está en la ue con sus casas de inspiración clásica & del renacimiento & jardines suprimidos incluso los hoteles demolidos de la ue son mejores que un referéndum inglés nadie en inglaterra quiere saber acerca de los cormoranes que se aprovechan de los vientos irregulares de la ue durmiendo con frecuencia en dormitorios comunitarios & cambiando de dormitorio de un día para el otro como el veto al acuerdo comercial de valonia a nadie en inglaterra le gustan los cormoranes aun cuando en inglaterra nadie recuerda si sus piernas derechas entran o si sus piernas derechas salen de la ue caminando hacia la avenue des paradisiers otra vez se siente esta mañana como si el paraíso fuera el mejor lugar para estar en mi bolsillo un silabario bertrand de plástico & los ciclos de canciones compiladas de orlando de lasso escuchando el órgano en el estilo moderno de la eglise notre dame immaculée du place de jeu de balle en la ue hay tantas eglises con sus patentes neumáticas tubulares de kerkhof los organistas de la ue son típicamente frisones siempre cambian el tono en medio del servicio siempre a mitad de temporada cambiando de equipo como se desliza en la rue dangleterre ahora la liga premier está matando a la ue con sus lujosos baños & desayunos adecuados todos en la ue quieren saber sobre los desayunos adecuados del reino unido los huevos pasables de romelu lukaku o el aceptable tocino de kevin de bruynes en la cabeza kevin en la cabeza romelu en la avenue des alouettes cantando cives floreat europa cuando fui soberano todos en inglaterra querían estar en la hermandad del hombre donde están ahora los de nottinghamshire & los de lincolnshire & los autónomos de northamptonshire donde están los otros condados de la eurovisión blanca cantando agradables alouettes desde los balcones sobre la estatua de jean claude van damme el veintitrés de junio todos en inglaterra estaban partidos por la mitad haciendo un voto solemne a vos oh countryfile (aunque haya otro countryfile) haciendo un voto solemne a vos oh countryfile sin órganos incluso el cañón desbandado de la antigua ue con sus carteristas gitanos & su jugabilidad perdida perdida es mejor que un referéndum inglés ahora que el trémolo está en el bajo & roger daltreys en el suelo estoy en solitario pensando en roger daltrey en una cresta calcárea baja sin tu amor roger ni siquiera podemos ver la A2 oh antigua ruta de mal agüero de inglaterra gira de nuevo roger gira de nuevo a través de la avenue de loriot toda profunda & dorada como los bolsillos de eddy merckx tocando il neige sur liège en el órgano grenzing de la cathedrale des saints michel et gudule & temblando & chispeando & todos preguntando pasará pronto la noche sobre papeles blancos en todas partes de forma tan rígida acaso los satélites trazan nuestros contornos a veces todos necesitamos un pequeño glosario de órganos para alejar a los demonios* & porque estaba enamorado del órgano inglés escuché una fantasía memorable escuché un solo incluso escuché un nunc dimittis no a todos en inglaterra les gusta el nunc dimittis estaba en latín* todo lo que significaba era ahora me tengo que ir oh dios & lo toqué con las luces apagadas porque en inglaterra nadie quiere saber sobre el órgano inglés

//
//////////

*****hic finis*** *el ministro de esher & walton* ***hic jacet*** *el ministro de wokingham* ***hic finis*** *el ministro de gillingham & rainham* ***hic jacet*** *el ministro de newton abbot* ***hic finis*** *el ministro de bedford & kempston* ***hic jacet*** *el ministro de los cotswolds* ***hic finis*** *el ministro de sutton & cheam* ***hic jacet*** *el ministro de richmond north yorks* ***hic finis*** *el ministro de selby & ainsty* ***hic jacet*** *el ministro de hemel hempstead* ***hic finis*** *el ministro de chesham & amersham* ***hic jacet*** *el ministro de enfield southgate* ***hic finis*** *el ministro de chingford & wood green* ***hic jacet*** *el ministro de wellingborough* ***hic finis*** *el ministro de haltemprice & howden* ***hic jacet*** *el ministro de hazel grove* ***hic finis*** *el ministro de sittingbourne & sheppey* ***hic jacet*** *el ministro de canterbury* ***hic finis*** *el ministro de hitchin & harpenden* ***hic jacet*** *el ministro de herefordshire north* ***hic finis*** *el ministro de brigg & goole* ***hic jacet*** *el ministro de beckenham* ***hic finis*** *el ministro de somerton & frome* ***hic jacet*** *el ministro de berwick upon tweed* ***hic finis*** *el ministro de basildon & billericay* ***hic jacet*** *el ministro del ribble valley* ***hic finis*** *el ministro de brecon & radnorshire* ***hic jacet*** *el ministro de kensington* ***hic finis*** *el ministro de st austell & newquay* ***hic jacet*** *el ministro de castle point* ***hic finis*** *el ministro de sleaford & north hykeham* ***hic jacet*** *el ministro de dorset south* ***hic finis*** *el ministro de cambourne & redruth* ***hic jacet*** *el ministro de congleton* ***hic finis*** *el ministro de woking east & shoreham* ***hic jacet*** *el ministro de aldershot* ***hic finis*** *el ministro de altrincham & sale west* ***hic jacet*** *el ministro de outer york* ***hic finis*** *el ministro de harwich & essex north* ***hic jacet*** *el ministro de bolton west* ***hic finis*** *el ministro de morley & outwood* ***hic jacet*** *el ministro de daventry* ***hic finis*** *el ministro de shrewsbury & atcham* ***hic jacet*** *el ministro de gainsborough* ***hic finis*** *el ministro de filton bradley & stoke* ***hic jacet*** *el ministro de stevenage* ***hic finis*** *el ministro de mid dorset & north poole* ***hic jacet*** *el ministro de tewkesbury* ***hic finis*** *el ministro de devon west & torridge* ***hic jacet*** *el ministro de peterborough* ***hic finis*** *el ministro de rayleigh &*

wickford ***hic jacet*** *el ministro de montgomery shire* ***hic finis*** *el ministro de south holland & the deepings* ***hic jacet*** *el ministro de southampton itchen* ***hic finis*** *el ministro de blackpool north & cleveleys* ***hic jacet*** *el ministro del colne valley* ***hic finis*** *el ministro de worthing east & shoreham* ***hic jacet*** *el ministro del vale of clwyd* ***hic finis*** *el ministro de richmond park & north kingston* ***hic jacet*** *el ministro de stratford upon avon* ***hic finis*** *el ministro de rochford & southend east* ***hic jacet*** *el ministro de poole* ***hic finis*** *el ministro de basildon south & thurrock east* ***hic jacet*** *el ministro de stone* ***hic finis*** *el ministro de portsmouth north* ***hic jacet*** *el ministro de harrow east* ***hic finis*** *el ministro de norfolk south* ***hic jacet*** *el ministro de southend west* ***hic finis*** *el ministro de cornwall north* ***hic jacet*** *el ministro de yorkshire east* ***hic finis*** *el ministro de thanet south* ***hic jacet*** *el ministro de bournemouth west* ***hic finis*** *el ministro de bedforshire mid* ***hic jacet*** *el ministro de somerset north* ***hic finist*** *el ministro de new forest east* ***hic jacet*** *el ministro de milton keynes south* ***hic finis*** *el ministro de new forest west* ***hic jacet*** *el ministro de warwickshire north* ***hic finis*** *el ministro de derbyshire south* ***hic jacet*** *el ministro de bury north* ***hic finis*** *el ministro de dudley south* ***hic hic jacet*** *el ministro de wiltshire north* ***hic finis*** *el ministro de northamptonshire south* ***hic jacet*** *el ministro de shropshire north* ***hic finis*** *el ministro de stockton south* ***hic jacet*** *el ministro de north swindon* ***hic finis*** *el ministro de leicestershire north west* ***hic jacet*** *el ministro de somerset north east* ***hic finis*** *el ministro de bristol north west* ***hic jacet*** *el ministro de hampshire north east* ***hic finis*** *el ministro de wiltshire south west* ***hic jacet*** *el ministro de cornwall south east* ***hic finis*** *el ministro de north west norfolk* ***hic jacet*** *el ministro de north east cambridgeshire* ***hic finis*** *el ministro de north west hampshire* ***hic jacet*** *el ministro de clwyd west* ***hic finis*** *el ministro de windsor* ***hic jacet*** *el ministro de telford* ***hic finis*** *el ministro de pudsey* ***hic jacet*** *el ministro de eastbourne* ***hic finis*** *el ministro de wycombe* ***hic jacet*** *el ministro de high peak* ***hic finis*** *el ministro de reigate* ***hic jacet*** *el ministro de lewes* ***hic finis*** *el ministro de christchurch* ***hic jacet*** *el ministro de braintree* ***hic finis*** *el ministro de monmouth* ***hic jacet*** *el ministro de eastleigh* ***hic finis*** *el ministro de shipley* ***hic jacet*** *el ministro de lichfield* ***hic finis*** *el ministro de fareham* ***hic jacet*** *el ministro de yeovil* ***hic finis*** *el ministro de wealden* ***hic jacet*** *el ministro de gravesham* ***hic finis*** *el ministro de dartford* ***hic jacet*** *el ministro de spelthorne* ***hic finis*** *el ministro de woking* ***hic jacet*** *el ministro de redditch* ***hic finis*** *el ministro de lincoln* ***hic jacet*** *el ministro de hendon* ***hic finis*** *el ministro de tamworth* ***hic jacet*** *el ministro de corby* ***hic finis*** *el ministro de romford* ***hic jacet*** *el ministro de crawley* ***hic finis*** *el ministro de pendle* ***hic jacet*** *el ministro de st ives* ***hic finis*** *el ministro de cleethorpes* ***hic jacet*** *el ministro de broxbourne* ***hic finis*** *el ministro de amber valley* ***hic jacet*** *el ministro de st albans* ***hic finis*** *el ministro de kettering* ***hic jacet*** *la isla de wight*

Aodán McCardle

Jeff Hilson's Organ Poems

When we are listening what are we listening with? What ear do we use if what we are hearing is both of the lyric in the popular song sense and yet we are reading words off a page which is poetry but not work which readily accepts a crafted combination of rhythm, metaphor and profound idea as the kitbag of parochial aesthetic.

The initial experience of these poems demands a degree of improvisation on the part of the reader. To move forward with the rhythm of the text is to experience the familiar and the half-remembered. To carry forward senses of experience of a line or a passage without it being tied down or fully contained as a meaning in relation to the poem.

When the ear hears a song lyric how does it, the body "it" respond, of what is it constituted by that listening. What truth is measured there or what expectations are brought to bear? When the music of a line, the air as of a tune has an influence on the thinking, the writing, the utterance that flows from it, on the next line, on the articulation of a subject, where do we find the poet situated, as composer or conductor, as conduction or as catalyst? The air of a tune carries emphasis, you might love it yet only know half a chorus and next to none of the lines. A tune then in a pop song has power but, on the page, how does it direct or define the reader?

The first reading then is compelled by the tune, the rhythm, reading then not as a production of assigned meaning but as an immersion, lines come up out of the future and linger as you move on, as you are propelled on to the next, associated meanings come into view, emerge not upon reading but as one moves on, as you are reading another line your listening ear is making connections from what you've already heard. It is in the second and third reading/listening where the familiarity of the air, the atmosphere of the poem has become familiar that you find the space or time to draw more specific meaning from the lines or stanzas or quotations.

We are introduced to this poem through a reference to Elton John's records via the words of Donald Trump:

> I have broken more Elton John records, he seems to have a lot of records. And I, by the way, I don't have a musical instrument. I don't have a guitar or an organ. No organ. (Donald Trump, speaking at a Republican rally in Montana, July 2018)

Farce, farcical… satire? After this introduction it is difficult to trust words at all, the omission of the concepts of wisdom or truth, the lack of integrity and the saturation of falseness as prevailing condition is so strong that it feels impossible to rescue language from this mire. Where Trump is concerned no serious critique is possible because the farcical nature of his having been voted into power betrays the conveyancing of meaning via language. The rescue in that first passage is the reference to music. Something that does not necessarily pretend to seriousness, to profundity or truth, that comes from desire and enthusiasm, from verve, these have the ability to survive the words that come from a mouth such as that of Donald Trump. The other aspect of this statement from Trump is that it becomes a chicken and egg moment. It's impossible after to decide if this statement came first and the Organ poems derived from it as response or if the organ poems came first and gathered the statement to themselves. It is impossible either way to rescue the image of Donald Trump and his boast of having no organ.

In relation to the second quotation,

> The second class of those practicing music is that of the poets, a class led to song not so much by thought and reason as by a certain natural instinct. For this reason this class, too, is separated from music. (Boethius, *De Institutione Musica*)

The distinction is made that music is a thing derived from reason and not from "instinct." So poets, the second class, are excluded.

> The first class consists of those who perform on instruments… are excluded from comprehension of musical knowledge… None of them makes use of reason; rather, they are totally lacking in thought. That person is a musician who exhibits the faculty of forming judgements according to speculation and reason. (Chapter 16, "Music" https://erenow.net/postclassical/MedivalHistory7/68.php)

At this stage reason is getting a bad name as a judgement of worth and we haven't entered the main body of the poem. One might begin to prefer the use of a musical instrument than the use of reason.

Our next quotation is from Joyce. In literary terms this is an anchor of worth. Perhaps an attempt to readdress the worth of language before the poem proper begins. However our first online search of terms offers the following "**cheapjacks** — dialect for travelling hawkers who offer apparent bargains by setting arbitrarily high prices and then offering to compromise." (https://books.google.ie/books?id=P6VjAAAAMAAJ&q=what+does+cheapjacks+refer+to+in+Joyce%27s+Ulysses&dq=what+does+cheapj

acks+refer+to+in+Joyce%27s+Ulysses&hl=en&sa=X&ved=0ahUKEwj17dO8v_zpAhWUT8AKHdUVCE0Q6AEITzAE, pg 378)

Again there is a prevailing fraudulence in the air. I don't want to attempt a specificity of terms as a close reading of this poem. My initial trajectory is informed by my reading without reference to references, by my instinctive response to the text, what I can grasp just as if I was listening to a song and only grasping half the lyrics and buoyed by the air, by the tune. In this I certainly prefer the class separated from reason. On the surface of this poem as a whole float the references to Elton John, to Supertramp, there's even a side 2 so the single or the album in musical terms comes in. Then there's Mr Men and "in my pants and ting." Our ability to make meaning is stretched here, "in my pants and ting" is a reference to the song "Uptown Top Ranking" and a quick search will even provide a link on songmeanings.com where someone translates the lyrics. I didn't know who it belonged to, I had a sense of it being a memory, that it had the feel of being of or from somewhere, that it was a lyric and basically that it was not simply of or from the poet here. In the first reading through the poem, meeting each line fresh and without searching online or otherwise researching references the repeat of that line "in my pants and ting" emphasizes it, allows it either more weight or allows it a stronger position in the dynamic but also this associated sense that it exists from out of somewhere else, that it has a life, brings that life into the poem, more than simply a string of words that mean, that translate themselves into meaning, this line because of its lack of readiness to submit to meaning brings in an outside or offers a window or a sonic resonance and in that sense meaning demands an acknowledgement of experience as opposed to a simple translation of semantic and metaphoric equation. The sonic quality hangs in the air of each line as you read on and that's what I mean when I ask when we listen what are we listening with. If we translate the words of a sentence, of a line of a poem into meaning it can drop there solidified on the page, fine, but if the whole poem is made of that then the poem is a description of something, at a removal from experience, but here a part of this poem is experience, a memory of or a consideration of something that is or was an experience so instead of us translating it and assigning it its place in the poem we experience it, it resonates and we move alongside it through the poem. We turn to it every so often in the poem and ask it what it thinks, what it has to say, it works alongside us to make the poem.

At this stage the attempt to provide reason is itself an absurd action, the music itself imbues a meaning and you get it or not. In the poem if you have never heard the song there is still a catch on the word "ting," it conveys a vocal sound that has reference to the ear as much as to reason. While the references in the poem are allowed their surfacing such that the poem definitively conveys its own prioritized meaning we will still have our own legitimate experience of the poem because of the capacity of song, in particular of Pop music, to flippantly bypass reason and almost negligently attain the status of the profound. Playfulness is such a surface action that predominates meaning making in this poetry and as such in looking for references, researching, searching online, I have made as many inroads by the random secondary references as by the location of any specific documented references.

One aspect of Pop music, of the Mr Men series in language and visually, is the capacity to achieve much through simplicity of characterization. In the television series *Brooklyn 99* the characters are portrayed in part as stereotypes but more clearly as having defined characteristics, behavioural traits, strengths and weaknesses. Once established it is this tightness which offers unlimited options of how any character will behave in response to a given situation, even how they transgress their characteristics is obviously manifest, so much so that the actors themselves are liminally available on the screen almost alongside the characters they play and the punchline is shared just as we the audience sense the possibility of the response coming and the surprise we are waiting on is how the writers will meet our expectations in a new way. There is a hyperawareness of this game and part of the enjoyment of watching the series is both the familiarity of the characters and this meeting of expectations. The game is to satisfy and balance, embarrassment and humour on the edge of pop coolness. The intention is firstly to make people laugh, to keep their attention but the skill of the writing, achieves more through the structural limitations of the characters.

> To live within limits. To want one thing. Or a few things very much and love them dearly. Cling to them, survey them from every angle. Become one with them - that is what makes the poet, the artist, the human being. (Johann Wolfgang von Goethe, *Dauer im Wechsel* https://www.goodreads.com/quotes/141537-to-live-within-limits-to-want-one-thing-or-a)

In looking for this quotation by Goethe I find a secondary reference, one carrying a similar message to that which I want to give via *Brooklyn 99* but which like the inclusion of the Joycean quotation at the start of the poem lends a certain literary depth or heft to the same message.

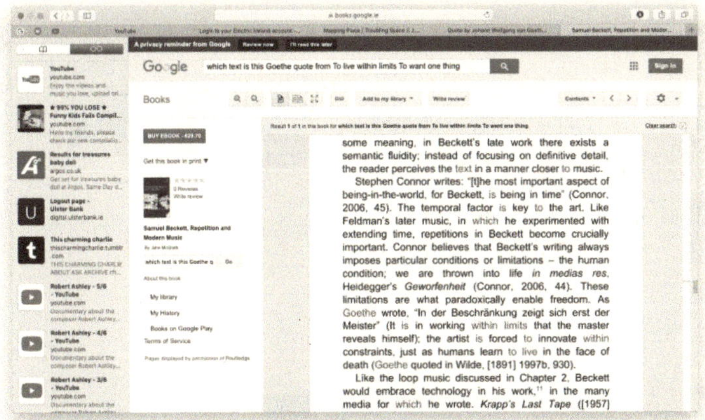

some meaning, in Beckett's late work there exists a semantic fluidity; instead of focusing on definitive detail, the reader perceives the text in a manner closer to music.

Stephen Connor writes: "[t]he most important aspect of being-in-the-world, for Beckett, is being in time" (Connor, 2006, 45). The temporal factor is key to the art. Like Feldman's later music, in which he experimented with extending time, repetitions in Beckett become crucially important. Connor believes that Beckett's writing always imposes particular conditions or limitations – the human condition; we are thrown into life *in medias res*, Heidegger's *Geworfenheit* (Connor, 2006, 44). These limitations are what paradoxically enable freedom. As Goethe wrote, "In der Beschränkung zeigt sich erst der Meister" (It is in working within limits that the master reveals himself); the artist is forced to innovate within constraints, just as humans learn to live in the face of death (Goethe quoted in Wilde, [1891] 1997b, 930).

Like the loop music discussed in Chapter 2, Beckett would embrace technology in his work,[11] in the many media for which he wrote. *Krapp's Last Tape* ([1957]

(https://books.google.ie/books?id=_WM-DwAAQBAJ&pg=PT146&lpg=PT146&dq=which+text+is+this+Goethe+quote+from+To+live+within+limits+To+want+one+thing&source=bl&ots=iqAKwvBM4X&sig=ACfU3U1Ny0eIDLFDMM1b989z6FHe7-wofw&hl=en&sa=X&ved=2ahUKEwiP7fmQpffpAhWBQRUIHThXDDIQ6AEwDHoECAYQAQ#v=onepage&q=which%20text%20is%20this%20Goethe%20quote%20from%20To%20live%20within%20limits%20To%20want%20one%20thing&f=false)

I follow it because it relates to Beckett, in terms of the air of the tune the sound of Joyce carries the distant sound of Beckett and vice versa, and I once had Stephen Connor as a tutor. Within the moment of coming across the reference this has no particular bearing on the poem but in effect becomes a part of my experience of the poem, it becomes a part of the atmosphere of reading the poem, of going away on the back of some enquiry cast by the poem and catching then on associated memories, these encounters random or otherwise are not excluded here. In criticism, in lectures etc. these are often excluded, the specificity of context, as academic or journalistic genre, prioritizes certain aspects of reading but in the actual event of reading ones surroundings including memory and experience have an influence if one allows or acknowledges it. While these thoughts are opening from the secondary references and I'm circling around my own thoughts, the critical mind looking for issues another secondary reference emerges to have its say.

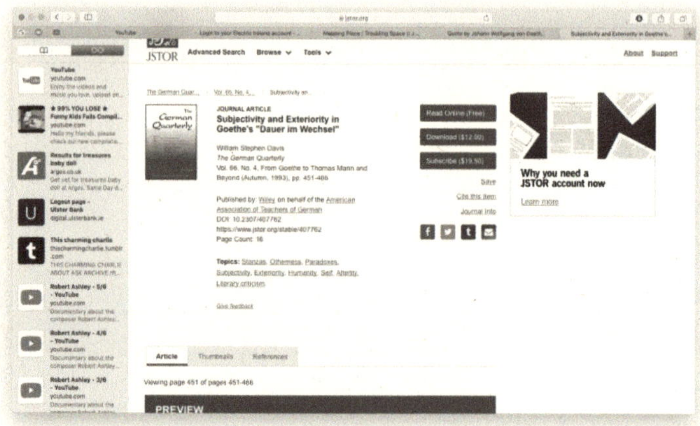

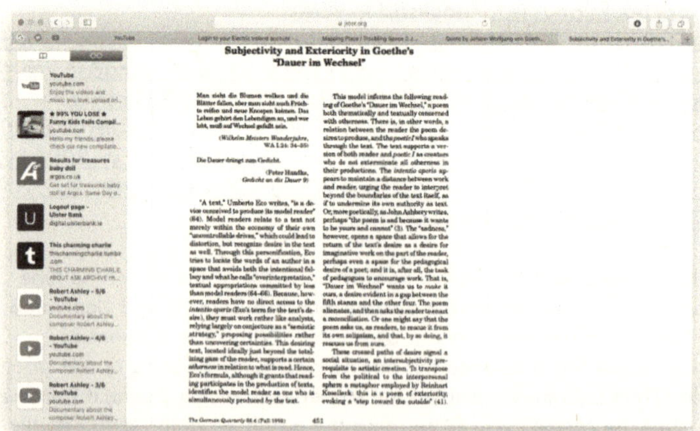
Subjectivity and Exteriority in Goethe's "Dauer im Wechsel"

"Within the economy of the uncontrollable drive." Those aspects of the poem that have obscure references, where in initial readings one flows with the rhythm rather than stop to logically interpret possible meaning, also drive the reader to attempt to make sense out of experience, out of what one can pick up in the ongoing, to make meanings rather than ask what is meant, i.e. the meaning intended by another. This tweet popped up this morning as I was thinking about this:

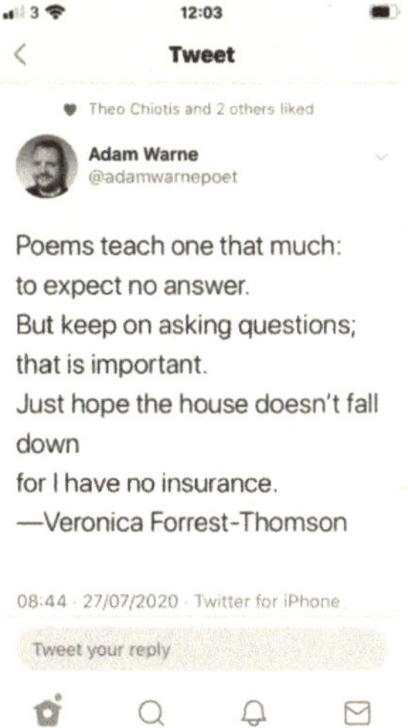

12:03
Tweet
Theo Chiotis and 2 others liked
Adam Warne
@adamwarnepoet
Poems teach one that much:
to expect no answer.
But keep on asking questions;
that is important.
Just hope the house doesn't fall
down
for I have no insurance.
—Veronica Forrest-Thomson
08:44 · 27/07/2020 · Twitter for iPhone
Tweet your reply

While scrolling down Adam's timeline, someone I don't know so the randomness here is randomer, I came across this other tweet from him:

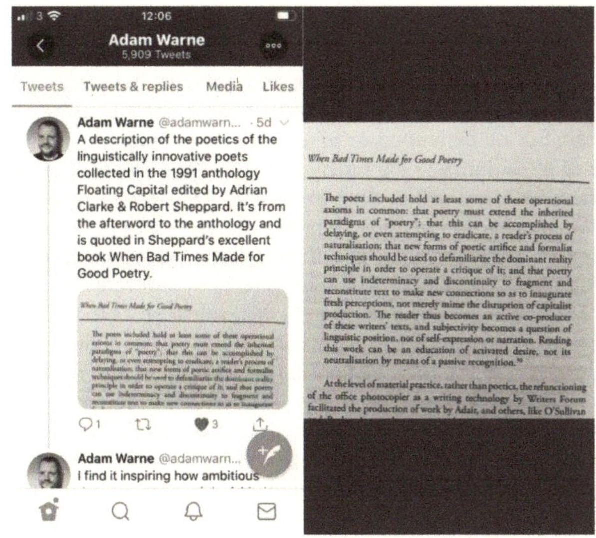

Again the personal connection, people I know, seeps into the references, but also "an education of activated desire not its neutralization by means of a passive recognition." Recognizing the air of a tune that hangs around "pants and ting" is not a passive recognition but an activation of other aspects of meaning making, the location of experience in the making of meanings of possible destinations or forms rather than accepting the "passive recognition" the diminished satisfaction of "naturalization." Instead there is the possibility of "indeterminacy and discontinuity to fragment and reconstitute text." A counter to the totalitarian tendencies of reason as a control. There is a serious discussion in this article on Umberto Eco about the ability to interpret, "proposing possibilities rather than uncovering certainties," about the text making the reader but if you read a poem with Elton John or Supertramp or the Mr Men in it then a certain space has been created already for the reader to be comfortable with their own interpretation just as a pop song lives or dies on its likeability, it does not worry about those who do not understand it but relies on those who respond spontaneously to its favours and who do or don't pursue them more acutely to interpret further. There is a hook.

> A **hook** is a musical idea, often a short riff, passage, or phrase, that is used in popular music to make a song appealing and to "catch the ear of the listener."[1] The term generally applies to popular music,

> especially rock, R&B, hip hop, dance, and pop. In these genres, the hook is often found in, or consists of, the chorus. A hook can be either melodic or rhythmic, and often incorporates the main motif for a piece of music.[2] (https://en.wikipedia.org/wiki/Hook_(music))

This poetry whatever else it intends for the reader catches the ear and eye and enjoys that aspect of music which is appealing. Of course the risk is that this will ultimately lose the reader by its lack of seriousness and that's where the balance of satisfying but surprizing the reader comes in. Ezra Pound's do's and don'ts of poetry in Openculture.com No.18 is "A rhyme must have in it some slight element of surprise if it is to give pleasure." (http://www.openculture.com/2014/01/read-ezra-pounds-list-of-23-donts-for-writing-poetry-1913.html)

The surprise can equally be considered as the hook in the poem that activates desire in the reader. The eye and ear of the reader are trained as we read to be aware of small recognitions, the sound of something that might just be something else. This isn't though a reward system where the readers can pat themselves on the back for qualifying in some way for some status for having understood the references. The references are common enough that they reach in to the common, the familiar, but varied enough that they speak about the complexity of the common ear. The ability of the common ear to entertain a width of reference that might confound the language of power embodied in the figure of a Trump or a Johnston with their pretences of wealth and birth.

"the mr men are everywhere partying like its 1649." The air is from Prince's song "1999," that lends it a certain lightness but the obvious reference for 1649 is the trial and beheading of Charles the first. The complexity is that the body that made this trial possible was the Rump Parliament.

> "Rump" normally means the hind end or back-side of a mammal; its use meaning "remnant" was first recorded in the above context in English.[a] Since 1649, the term "rump parliament" has been used to refer to any parliament left over from the actual legitimate parliament (https://en.wikipedia.org/wiki/Rump_Parliament)

It is possible to interpret that as a body talking out of its arse but given the satirical nature of the first quotation involving Trump it's probably more the toppling of seemingly inviolable power structures that's being called into being here.

Ursula K Le Guin:

> We live in capitalism. Its power seems inescapable. So did the divine right of kings. Any human power can be resisted and changed by human beings. Resistance and change often begin in art, and very often in our art, the art of words. (https://www.goodreads.com/quotes/3238058-we-live-in-capitalism-its-power-seems-inescapable-so-did)

The ability of the eye and ear of language to resist the co-option by power and to carry experience, or to prioritize the reader's experience as axis of meaning is a central tenet of the power of poetry and of song.

From Elton John and Supertramp and Mr Men we also have "They that go down to the sea in ships." In the poem it's the I who goes down to the sea in ships, but the ear hears other hearings and tastes the taste of prayer in those lines of prayer as song and song as a delivery of a message.

> Psalm 107:23-31
> King James Version
> 23 They that go down to the sea in ships, that do business in great waters;
> 24 These see the works of the Lord, and his wonders in the deep.
> 25 For he commandeth, and raiseth the stormy wind, which lifteth up the waves thereof.
> 26 They mount up to the heaven, they go down again to the depths: their soul is melted because of trouble.
> 27 They reel to and fro, and stagger like a drunken man, and are at their wit's end.
> 28 Then they cry unto the Lord in their trouble, and he bringeth them out of their distresses.
> 29 He maketh the storm a calm, so that the waves thereof are still.
> 30 Then are they glad because they be quiet; so he bringeth them unto their desired haven.
> 31 Oh that men would praise the Lord for his goodness, and for his wonderful works to the children of men!
> (https://www.biblegateway.com/passage/?search=Psalm+107&version=KJV)

I could speak about the lyric qualities of this language and its relation to spirituality and its commonality with the language of Hilson's poems and what contemporary spirituality they inspire but it is the "I" and "they" in the correspondence that attracts my attention. The "I" in the poem going down to the sea in a line that has such a strong sense of prior experience about it then joins the "they" who go down to the sea.

Who goes down to the sea in ships? The I who is at the whim of the pop lyric, the air of the pop lyric, carries also the satiric gaze which presents us with that original image of Trump's "no organ." Just as a certain part of the air of a tune remains strongly in the air throughout the song, and after, that satiric gaze carries weight here such that the I and the they might be placed as those who could look satirically upon the speaker of that phrase "no organ." However, surely these ships as ever, as now, are owned by a business elite. But the pop lyric in this sense is not about owners, they are not the who who goes down to the sea. The common man, the worker goes down to the sea. Who makes the music, the pop music, however much it is owned by the radio or the producer? It is the person in the street who makes it and makes it again afresh, who makes it and hears it and makes it again. This is as true of Grime, of Garage, of The Blues as it is of Pop, invention is not an aspect of ownership, not the ownership of an industry, it is a response born out of embodiment and what is embodied, the inheritors of this music and this poetry are those who enjoy it, to whom it speaks without the need of reason and who in turn speak it without needing to know how or why!

There are so many references, so many possibilities, so many rabbit holes and so many white rabbits here and a few beaches upon which snarks might be found but I would not pretend to follow them all, nor pretend that would mean more than what one gets from a certain time spent in the poem. What that certain time is will be individual. As the Poetry Foundation site says of Lewis Carroll

> Perhaps the best response he was to give on the subject was to the inquiry by the Lowrie children: he stated, "words mean more than we mean to express when we use them: so a whole book ought to mean a great deal more than the writer meant." (https://www.poetryfoundation.org/poets/lewis-carroll)

There can be almost too much meaning. At the end of the poem there is a dissolving of the language into nonsense as if the associated sound play is too strong and drives the speaker in the poem mad, "on what ground have you gone aground on." Physical space or conceptual construct? There are perhaps two speakers "you are bunkers / I expect I am bunkers / it is likely you are bunkers" but the speed of it and the agreed use of bunkers suggests that the two voices are in the one head, an inner argument that ends with "yes I am bunkers." The "bunkers" language as manifest of thought and sound tipping too far over and spilling out of control but in the midst of this is a self-reflection "yes I am bunkers" something more than can be expected from the first voice we hear in this poem who boasts publicly in a manner that suggests he does not listen even to the words that come out of his own mouth "I don't have a guitar or an organ. No Organ."

Perhaps that voice doesn't listen because those it is speaking to do not know how to listen, public language, the language of politics as public spectacle is no longer something that can be listened to or understood, like the Society of the Spectacle it is untouchable in its own frame of reference but the poem it seems can train the ear towards other possibilities of engagement.

Rob Holloway

Who Jeff?

I have no very slight clue who Jeff who I mean in
his fresh lemon soul pants he really if
you asked write about a sock of
its picking up with its tweezers of why
now I iron my incessant brown
stone cow wear I'd feel life like
walking towards me wearing that famous glow
-in-the-park bra screaming *lamé* for England
and St. Cuthbert FC but of course
it's doing nonsuch no
thing this windy Sunday morn as we all
mourn him *nonpareil* (whoops, wrong poem), submit
to a contemporary relinquishment, yes
-terday Rymans re-opened at 8:54 a.m I
couldn't mind its queues went to Monte
Carlo instead let its yachts please
sit on my Norman *sapientia* face

some contemporary melancholia's known for
snaking into Jeff's enduringly *passé*
~~trouser leg~~ record collection whispering
"finger my Royalist contemptuous hospital provision"
but never foul his tunes are only limited
by the size of the players'
organs of which he's has so many he
finds the one in the *eglise notre dame*
de chant doiseau sounds particularly
pneumatic even when deciding having how
to clothe and flag the unknown
regiments of our youthful eu being
one of the brilliant poets in Gr.Brex
has meant JayH remembers how
to tie his boots to his birdsong

first the moat, then the long stretch
of Huck's toes all the way along Tower
Records easy listening aisle, on past
the transept where there are fewer

authentic records than at any other
time in medieval history Jeff's
stole them one early
mourning morn because he'd mistaken
heraldic banners for banter
"no dismay at any time"
quipped he was sick of the Banksys
of England mark never has he
not worn with expert timing
"the nobility of Kung Fu Fighting"
if there was ever a Garfunkel in art
it's Jeff sniffing yr curry with his ~~part~~ smarts

I would like to think Jeff is a good soldier
Švejk not Rupert Everett the greatest
military general of all time who once sent
"R" Jeff a gooseberry posset for his eleventh
birthday he mistook it for ~~a bidet~~ Bede
the Vulnerable who comes from an
oral tradition not an organ one so
they spoke only of love, its *travailles*
the way it gets inbetween your toes
-es at Christmases and the days of the latter
Saints before Mick Channon had
shot off my balls before
the predictable *jeux sans*
frontières of Stuart Hall

it's arguable if Jeff can sing or
fling he can ride a log through vast
orange libraries of cream teas like
an errant beetle find joy
bending to Hither Green's lamentably
predictable disco backlash circa '79
that's 1378 when
the Butcher of Cesena
prev. Prebend of Middle Woodford
became first antipope of
the Western Schism so
much for the agitprop of
Little Joan O we all love
lovely fucking tortoises what hop
-e imperialism's toxic clag, it's capital
H Humber capital P Pigs

will wither O come hither my
wondrous English Hilltop (I mean hyssop)
as grubbed up and scuffy out of the true
history of our assets you arise arse-
first albatros strapped on "n" shi-
ny kissing heartily your Russell and your Laurel
getting the necessary business on down

Khaled Hakim

A Brief Introduction to the Stuff of Jeff Hilson

Mere "realism" has a bad rap in the vanguards these days. Yet each shiny new version of vanguardism that faces down the "traditional" (including yesterday's vanguard) is at bottom a confrontation over what is "really" real. The ways of experiencing the world heralded by Mallarme, Schrodinger, Cage (pick your faultline, pick your figure) would look like a closed book to all except a cabal of the cognoscenti who see a deeper approach to... something. Even those autodestructive expressions like Dada or Fluxus, if not revealing Truth, promise to expose the fraud of institutions, not least the institutions of Art; and absurdity as a stylistic, a hopeless reflex in an exquisite corpse, is no less predicated on a claim to greater Truth. This brief essay examines aspects of realism in Hilson's chicanery.

In poems such as "A Final Poem With Full Stops," "Organ Music—Side 8," and "The Wogan Poem" the gun barrel straight columns of unpunctuated uncapitalized sentences cascade down whatever margins the online or print publisher has set. Note that the passage below doesn't reproduce the original pagination and accidentally produces a paragraph format that follows the sense more "naturally" (the second, third, fourth "lines" start with discrete clauses): not an effect I believe Hilson was after.

> now we are in a wogan economy wogan is always lending me money its quite simple in a minute wogan will contact me & with my wogan money I will buy a white knight condenser tumble dryer thanks wogan I am always recommending you to my friends I love to borrow money from wogan dont have a kindle? its quite simple in a minute wogan will contact me & I will buy a small brown suede-effect ottoman I love to borrow money from wogan because wogan is my favourite lender with my wogan money I will buy a babyliss essential bikini trimmer

This litany of testimonies for Wogan/Wonga payday loans seems culled from an online Customer Reviews section generated by Wonga themselves, and it's in keeping with a poet who never strays far from the actual, using verité documents or reports, or the bricolage of conversation and pop culture. There are no landmarks or epiphanal peaks in Hilson's topography—the terrain is arranged in repeating and interlocking plots, like an English commuter belt, and meaning is built in the iterations and scale:

> ... even the bourgeois houses of the eu with their serviced
> apartments & ho ho buses are better than an english referendum o
> albatros o bird of ill omen of the twenty third of june how everything

in england turns away from the gare centrale how everyone in england loves manageable luggage always travelling lightly with one wheeled bag across the avenue de cormorans its not in english the avenue de cormorons its in the eu with its classical & renaissance houses of inspiration & suppressed gardens even the demolished hotels of the eu are better than an english referendum
("Organ Music—Side 8")

And so on in unceasing nerdy deluge with the recurring motifs of a neurotic analysand, of a stuck record.

I heard someone on the radio say they were left cold by baroque music because it lacks "narrative"—which I also take to mean "drama." And I can see Hilson being sympathetic to baroque music's formal repertoire of fugues and canons, the melodic line methodically inverted and turned backward in retrograde motion. Hilson doesn't lack feeling: *Organ Music—Side 8* is a lament with manly tears for a lost England—ironically of yesterday's groovy progressive England of Schengen borders and zipcode-less fucks that was originally ushered in by that visionary progressive Ted Heath. For many good people this is anguish enough. But that feeling is the same felt for his record collection (I'd wager he could never get the same physical or lachrymose stirrings from poetry).

The texture of Hilson's poetics flattens its joys, madnesses and pains in the junk of bricolage and pub chatter. The distrust of emotionalism and authenticity, and the turn to formal arrangement (the rhythm of Stein runs deep through Hilson) gives an even temper to affects in the poem—which is governed by the suzerainty of humour.

In The Assarts (pleasingly produced by Veer as a compact square volume to perfectly contain its sonnet sequence) gerrymanders its varying line lengths so they make up 14 lines any old-how. It abuses a sonnet form which might have expected to rest in peace in Westminster Abbey, making arbitrary the borders and regulations that so appeal to our sense of security and order. Thus here are the opening four lines of no.5 –

I love thee castration & often tell
maidens.
The maiden tries it & goes away.
But when the maiden goes she

In The Assarts is choc a block with name-drops, conversations begun or finished loudly offstage, NY poets and Elizabethan characters and medieval husbandry, and the blokey-blokeness of Hilson: it's all stuffed full of stuff—said stuff, quoted stuff, rattling round your head stuff, sticky on your hand stuff:

(from 49)
...
unlike Goldilocks I never was the same again
who's been sleeping in my library.
I made it of wattle-&-daub.
Look at my anthologies
there's Frank Kermode the pervert

A sonnet as a drunk; a sonnet as projective drunk spiel that passes out at the end of a sonnet. How can a poetic world so thingified be also composed of so much *ersatz* and simulacra? It's as verifiably there as Kurt Schwitters' *Merzbau*, and just as removed from life—a still-life. If you can cram as much conversational and allusive bricolage into the poem, smuggling in snippets of feeling disguised as jigsaw, maybe you can abolish the illegitimately sentient Jeff Hilson—at what cost?

& again went down to the Quaggy
there I wept ("Organ Music—Side 9")

Hilson can't even be mournful by his local river without invoking "La Belle Dame Sans Merci," Eliot, Epithalamium, Boney M's version of Psalm 137. Can he not cry, howl, love, sing—without quote marks and footnotes? *Assarts*' scope is largely that of other poet-figures, other song lyrics, landscapes filtered through history: a materiality that sucks the *ding an sich* out of life. This monkey-brain chatter is certainly naturalistic, but this facticity is not more "real" or advantageous for raising consciousness than the enlightening shock of the numinous. Both are models that we choose.

Some time ago I was reading an essay on contemporary lyric, and an almost throwaway aside describing a meretricious stylistic jolted me. I can't remember who the target was, but John Wilkinson summed it up as taking a hackneyed phrase or jingle and applying a facile transformation to it. I instantly thought of Jeff Hilson. I have this insistent suspicion of a verbal trope underlying all of the writing: the coyly-turned sayings, misheard song lyrics, juvenile malapropisms. And just as with Old Master apprentices who learned by copying other copies, Hilson cleaves to formal template: *A Grasses Primer*; the ornithological crib of *Bird Bird*; the official reports behind the migrant deaths in "A Final Poem With Full Stops" (another litany).

You could argue his poetry is ultimately phenomenological, tangled in found languages—like every good little innovative poet these days, who "negotiate" reality in their chosen view. But it's also a deeply naturalistic prosody. He is both maker of assemblages and representational painter of modern life.

The neo-liberal economist, the deep change survivalist, the queer Marxist, the Seventh Day Adventist, the drug cartel torturer—all claim versions of reality. Do they each have their own terminology for that reality? If so, Hilson would hijack it.

Gavin Selerie

S & G Variations for Jeff Hilson

Just a little pipe organ charts newfound earth
swirling the moon on an open field

she reads the last issue careless with intent,
you in the note, the note in you

a dream on a plane and a bus
filtered through glass

is it *l'amour* or *la mort*, come to look for
the starting clinch

don't know how we made it, those road cobbles
a silver stream

two countries to address
everly pitched

kew-eek in a zigzag
jug-jug on a thorny branch

could make one perfect person, each fit
over and coming in

but celluloid against flesh
is a taller deal behind one cut short

the hair curls different, a flare a drape
or a fuzz

why, talent could be alien DNA—the crack of a snare
by the lift shaft

it's steely here
where the lilt might relieve

partnered to stare, always on the dial
our town punches itself to sing

Fabian Macpherson

The English Countenance of Organ Music

By starting with the organ, Jeff Hilson's *Organ Music* (published 2020, but begun in 2010) is drawn into an engagement with English political history and, by extension, questions of national culture and national identity. The first epigraph in the book is taken from a documentary entitled *The Elusive English Organ*: "And among all that we know of our history, the history of our organs and our organ music has been obscured."[1] This sentence itself obscures the tensions implicit in the collective English "our," tensions which haunt Hilson's book as it sets out on its pursuit of the elusive organ. It is a sometimes-chaotic journey, but there are signposts in the fog in the form of dates, and I propose to arrange the two halves of this essay around two salient ones: 1649 and 1979.

I. "everywhere partying like its 1649"

The poems of *Organ Music* are divided into a series of longer "Sides" (in the manner of a vinyl or cassette box set) and shorter "Interludes." Hilson states in his foreword that the former are "in their own way responses to ten years of barbaric Tory rule which began with austerity and ended most recently with Brexit," a much more explicitly political statement than anything to be found in his earlier books (which had mostly been written during the New Labour era). "Side 1" begins:

> And I ran with my organ to the estuary
> boy contra hautboy
> I was already dreaming

This opening sets up a playful "organist" persona, introducing what will become a recurring double entendre on the musical and anatomical senses of "organ" (a hint of *Carry On*-style humour being one of Hilson's characteristic ingredients) as well as a pun on the name of an organ stop ("contra hautboy").[2] They seem like the opening for a

---

[1] Jeff Hilson, *Organ Music* (London and Santiago: Crater, 2020), no page number. Further references are given in the text.

[2] "Hautboy" [i.e. literally "high wood"] is the original French name for the oboe (from which the latter Italian word derives).

Wordsworthian account of youthful exploration, though if read in its instrumental sense the image of running with an organ (unless it were a mouth organ) is cartoonishly absurd.

As the poem progresses, though, a more mournful note is sounded:

> in this book I will be mainly crying
> in distracted time
> the mr men are everywhere partying like its 1649
> but I am not in this together with you
>
> I dont know why the mr men
> he broke my organ

These lines are dense with possible allusions. The invocation of "crying" may suggest the music of John Dowland (1563-1626): Hilson has by this point already directly quoted the ostensibly jovial first line of one of Dowland's lute songs ("it was a time when silly bees could speak"), but he is more readily associated with a melancholic sentiment expressed in such lachrymose numbers as "Burst forth my tears," "Go crystal tears," and "Flow my tears" (the tune of the latter forming the basis of the instrumental suite *Lachrimae, or Seaven Teares* [1604]).[3] Dowland will later appear by name—in the deliberately erroneous form "Dowlands"—in the first of the "Interludes" focussed on individual composers.

A more overt musical allusion comes in "distracted time," a phrase drawn from the "Sad Pavan: for these distracted times," a keyboard piece by Thomas Tomkins (1572-1656) composed following the execution of Charles I in 1649. Unlike Dowland, who wrote for the lute, Tomkins was indeed an organist, at Worcester Cathedral (and intermittently at the Chapel Royal); his biographer describes the Parliamentary Army's attack on the cathedral and its organ in the early months of the Civil War:

> By 1642 Tomkins's superb Dallam organ at Worcester was nearly thirty years old, and in April that year 9s. 5d. had been spent on "candles, glue, leather and whipcord," to repair "the great bellows." The sight of so much wanton destruction to the cathedral must have been profoundly painful to Tomkins, and one wonders if he was actually present in the building to see

---

[3] The text for "It was a time when silly bees could speak" was written by Robert Devereux, 2nd Earl of Essex, who had been executed for treason (in 1601) by the time the song was published in 1603.

> crude hands wrenching organ pipes from the beautiful Robert Kettle case and flinging them clattering to the floor. If so, he would also have seen one of the organ's attackers lose his footing, fall from the screen, and break his neck.[4]

Tomkins's own house was also partially destroyed the following year: cathedral records make reference to "reparation of Mr. Organist's house, ruined by cannon shot" (the formulation "Mr. Organist" coincidentally resembling Hilson's "mr men").[5] By the time he composed his "Sad Pavan," Tomkins was c. 77 years old, one of the last of a musical old guard whose world had revolved around the Church and the royal court; his affection for the King (as well as such men as the Earl of Strafford and Archbishop Laud, for whom he also composed musical tributes) was apparently sincere.

Hilson takes this moment of Royalist national trauma and transposes it to his own time period. In his accompanying notes to the poem, he glosses the "mr men" as "Broadly, the Conservative Party"; the moment in which they are "everywhere partying like its 1649" is the 2010 general election, and the speaker's defiant "I am not in this together with you" is a rejection of David Cameron's "Big Society" slogan "We're all in it together."[6] What is perhaps slightly paradoxical about this transposition is that the Conservatives—nominally the political descendants of the proto-Tory Royalists—are cast as the iconoclastic Puritans. In this analogy, the broken organ comes to stand in for the welfare state at the mercy of austerity policies. Elsewhere, in the foreword, Hilson muses that "there's probably a connection to be made between Puritan thuggery and bourgeois gentrification," but that is an analytical statement quite distant from the speaker of the poem.[7] "I dont know why the mr men / he broke my organ" is an expression of helpless incomprehension akin to that presumably felt by the likes of Tomkins in the 1640s. The formula "mr __ / he' also echoes Conrad's "Mistah Kurtz—he dead" from *Heart of Darkness* (1899) (made explicit in the later line "mr men he dead in a thorn wood"), itself the epigraph

---

[4] Anthony Boden, *Thomas Tomkins: The Last Elizabethan* (Aldershot: Ashgate, 2005), p. 173. For a more revisionist account of the period, see Bronwyn Ellis, *"These Sad, Distracted Tymes": The Impact of the Civil War and Interregnum on English Music, c.1640 to c.1660* (University of Tasmania PhD thesis, 2004): https://core.ac.uk/download/pdf/33330689.pdf

[5] Boden, op. cit., p. 174.

[6] Also in the background of this line is a by now common appropriation of the chorus of Prince's "1999", itself released in 1982 (another year with significance for Hilson's sequence: see below).

[7] On the thuggery-gentrification connection, see also footnote 18 below.

for T. S. Eliot's "The Hollow Men" (1925), a suggestive literary genealogy of imperial decline.[8]

"Side 1" concludes with an accelerated summary of later musical history that expands beyond the English context:

> & it is 1649
> william byrd is dead
> thomas tomkins is dead
> (who is hugh facy who suddenly dies?)
> & for a long time henry purcell shaketh
> (it is after all now the seventeenth century)
> scarlatti is finished
> & germany is waiting
> & american poetry is everywhere
> & its just the speed
> the speed of bachs hands

Byrd (1543-1623) and Purcell (1659-1695) are regarded as two of the greatest English composers, but they also represent, in different ways, terminal points. Davitt Moroney, a harpsichordist who has recorded Byrd's complete keyboard works, writes of their limited afterlife: "In England, his most original contributions in the specific area of keyboard music bore fruit yet, curiously, native English composers subsequently lost a firm sense of direction. [...] On the Continent, on the other hand, Byrd's polyphonic style had no direct influence since it remained almost entirely unknown."[9] In addition, Byrd was a Catholic whose major vocal works were composed in Latin, thus estranging him from a new Protestant vernacular conception of English identity. And Purcell, having died aged 36, left a cultural vacancy that would be filled in the following century by Handel, a German immigrant.

In the final lines of this "Side," Hilson again interestingly conflates several strands of history. "& germany is waiting" points to the ascendancy of Austro-German composers from Bach onwards, but also has more ominous secondary connotations of inter-imperial rivalry in the decades leading up to the First World War. More revealing is the line "& american poetry is everywhere," which shifts the focus from the history of music to that of Hilson's own medium, one in which he is more personally implicated. Hilson writes within a post-war tradition sometimes referred to as the "British Poetry Revival," the main "reviving" inspiration for which was the work of Black Mountain and

---

[8] Joseph Conrad, *Heart of Darkness* (Project Gutenberg, 2009): https://www.gutenberg.org/files/219/219-h/219-h.htm
[9] Davitt Moroney, *William Byrd: The Complete Keyboard Music* (Hyperion CD booklet, 1999), p. 22.

other American modernist poets.[10] (In Hilson's case, the continuity of this American influence is exemplified by his PhD research on Louis Zukofsky.) This British reverence for American poetic modernism is sometimes attended by a slight anxiety of influence, a sense of having been eclipsed by a greater power, which mirrors in some ways the diminished global political stature of post-imperial Britain. The search for alternative local, specifically English cultural histories is one strategy for maintaining a distinctive identity, and in this Hilson follows the example of Bill Griffiths, whom he appears to address by name at points in the poem ("bill I'm very sorry about this bill").[11]

Having ended his initial survey of early English composers in the seventeenth century, in the second "Interlude" Hilson rewinds the clock even further to the example of John Dunstaple [aka Dunstable] (c. 1390-1453):

> why john dunstaple I hardly know you/
> can I borrow your memorable face/your
> english countenance is quite quite rare/o
> constaple I have fallen for john/john
> dunstaple/in the 1440s he is very forward/

Dunstaple, though now less well-known than Byrd or Purcell, has a greater claim to international significance, which rests on the phrase "english countenance." This is a translation from a line in the French poem *Le champion des dames* (1441-1442) by Martin Le Franc, which praises the two French composers Guillaume Dufay (c. 1397-1474) and Gilles Binchois (c. 1400-1460) for having "pris de la contenance / Angloise, et ensuy Dompstable" [i.e. taken on the English countenance, and followed Dunstaple].[12] Exactly what this "English countenance" actually entailed, and how it specifically related to Dunstaple, are still matters of dispute: reading the line in conjunction with other musical terms used in the poem, David Fallows writes that "very few of the specific meanings offered so far cast any direct light on the music that happens to survive from the early fifteenth century."[13] What is less disputable is the high frequency of English compositions in fifteenth-

---

[10] See Robert Sheppard, *The Poetry of Saying: British Poetry and its Discontents 1950–2000* (Liverpool: Liverpool University Press, 2005), ch. 2. The word "Revival" also has suggestive connotations of Evangelical Christianity.

[11] Griffiths' own researches were in Old English and North East dialects.

[12] David Fallows, "The contenance angloise: English influence on continental composers of the fifteenth century," *Renaissance Studies*, vol. 1, no. 2 (October 1987), p. 196.

[13] Ibid. p. 203. Rob C. Wegman offers further speculation in "New Music for a World Grown Old: Martin Le Franc and the 'Contenance Angloise,'" *Acta Musicologica*, vol. 75, [fasc.] 2 (2003), pp. 201-241.

century continental manuscripts, "testifying to a degree of respect for English music abroad that cannot be found at any other stage in history until the advent of the Beatles in the 1960s."[14]

Although such of his music as survives has been partly resuscitated by the modern early music movement (which, in coincidental parallel with the British Poetry Revival, gained momentum in the 1960s and 70s), Dunstaple resides in a world that is even more lost than that of Byrd and Tomkins, with most English manuscripts containing his work having been destroyed during the Dissolution of the Monasteries. Hilson invokes his name only to cast it aside and jump back into the flux of history:

> he is finished with gloria & he is finished
> with carol/& I am finished with john
> dunstaple/o god we are all plantagenets/
> a tudor is neither male nor female/whoever
> is besieging the house of carpets/nobody
> painted their burgundian kitchen/why
> john dunstaple why/because I was
> in my coat of arms in the burning house
> of windsor

These lines cycle through the names of royal houses—always, in Hilson's lower case style, deprived of the distinction of their initial capital letters—giving a sense of an accelerated skipping through time. The utterance "o god we are all plantagenets" suggests a sudden panicked realisation, with at least two possible interpretations. The first is that of the time traveller to the fifteenth century: since the House of Plantagenet ruled during the life of John Dunstaple, to attempt to understand his world perhaps requires some sort of mental submission to Plantagenet authority. The second, perhaps more alarming interpretation, is that "we" (the English/British?) are *still* in some sense identified with the Plantagenets, even after the Tudors and all the dynasties down to the Windsors, and even in a radically changed economic landscape exemplified by such capitalist enterprises as "the house of carpets." After all, Shakespeare's still-performed history plays—a significant contribution to the formation of a national literary myth—are almost all about Plantagenet kings.

The sociologist Ernest Gellner defined nationalism as "primarily a political principle, which holds that the political and the national unit should be congruent."[15] The "political unit" is the centralising authority of the state, which has tended to pre-date the

---

[14] Fallows, op. cit., p. 192.

[15] Ernest Gellner, *Nations and Nationalism* (Ithaca, NY: Cornell University Press, 1983), p. 1.

emergence of a "national" consciousness, often by centuries. Prior to the seventeenth century, the English nation was effectively synonymous with the monarchy, a perspective articulated in the proto-nationalist rhetoric of Shakespeare's "This royal throne of kings, this sceptr'd isle"; by the 1640s, Milton could justify the execution of Charles I by declaring that "the power of Kings and Magistrates is nothing else, but what is only derivative, transferr'd and committed to them in trust from the People."[16] Whereas the Whig interpretation of history follows Milton, Hilson's poem seems to point towards a more pessimistic reading (for democrats), in which national culture remains somehow parasitic on monarchical authority even hundreds of years after its supposed taming by elected representatives of "the People."

II. "in my big empty room it is always 1979"

The first part of this essay attempted to trace Hilson's initial journey from 2010 to 1649 (via the 1440s), but there is a parallel set of more recent dates running through *Organ Music*, invoked in relation to the popular music of the poet's adolescence. "Side 2" finds the speaker apparently "in his room" enthusing about the band Supertramp:

> are you lonely in your boat
> what I mean is I am
> the organ in england is too
> is too big for my room
> I am always going to the seaside
> to shake up the nation
> in my big empty room it is always 1979
> in my big empty nation I
> fucking loved you supertramp

The addressee here is once again Bill Griffiths, who lived on a houseboat during the 1980s, and documented the experience in his *Book of the Boat* (1988): "In my boat. I live & die. under the shell. of the cerule sky."[17] Hilson's speaker makes conceptual associations faster than he can articulate them, skipping breathlessly from boat to organ to room to nation, and the absence of punctuation means that the

---

16 William Shakespeare, *Richard II* (1595), 2.1; John Milton, *The Tenure of Kings and Magistrates* (1649). Online editions of these texts can be found at: http://shakespeare.mit.edu/richardii/full.html https://www.dartmouth.edu/~milton/reading_room/tenure/text.shtml

17 Bill Griffiths, *Collected Poems & Sequences (1981-91)* (Hastings: Reality Street, 2014), p. 78.

enjambments are rife with ambiguities. Taking the first three of these lines, what unites "your boat," "I," and "the organ in England" is the possible existential state of loneliness; a lonely organ is an anthropomorphised image, but there are additional metaphorical connotations of the organs of government and the ship of state.

In the fourth line, the repeated "too" shifts sense from "also" to "excessively." Again, there is possible historical backstory here: some of the organs removed from churches during the Reformation and Civil War ended up in private houses, in a move suggestive of a shifting balance of power from the Church to (bourgeois) civil society. Hilson's phrasing mirrors a diary entry by Samuel Pepys, who in 1668 went to inspect an organ for purchase, only to leave disappointed: "Here I saw the organ; but it is too big for my house, and the fashion do not please me enough; and therefore will not have it."[18] The room of Hilson's speaker is presumably a bedroom, but it expands to room in the sense of territorial space, *Lebensraum*. The "seaside" is the limit of the English coastline. There is a double significance in the reference to 1979: for the solipsistic pop listener, it was the year of release of Supertramp's LP *Breakfast in America*, a fond memory that lives on ("in my big empty room it is always 1979"), but for the political citizen it was the year of Margaret Thatcher's election victory, an event that would overshadow everything that came afterwards ("it is always 1979 / in my big empty nation").

Thatcher is not an overt presence in the earlier *Organ Music* poems, but she lurks in the cultural background.[19] One might associate "shak[ing] up the nation" with her economic programme, but Hilson glosses it as a reference to a dub track by Prince Far-I. To invoke Jamaican music at all in this historical context has a certain political charge. This is not the first such allusion in the book: "Side 1" incorporates repeated fragments of the lyrics to the 1977 song "Uptown Top Ranking" by the teenage reggae duo Althea & Donna, notably the phrase "in my pants & ting." This may have been selected partly for its comic, incongruous effect as delivered in Hilson's fairly RP English accent—as Stephen Thomson observes, in Hilson's live readings "there is no putting-on of a voice to distance it from his utterance"—but

---

[18] *The Diary of Samuel Pepys*, Monday 24 February 1667/68: https://www.pepysdiary.com/diary/1668/02/24/. The allusion may be coincidental, as Hilson does not cite Pepys in his notes. However, in the foreword, he proposes "the fact that as well as 'utterly defacing' church organs, some Puritans removed them from places of worship and simply took them home" as a possible "connection[...] between Puritan thuggery and bourgeois gentrification."

[19] The most explicit reference comes in "Side 6," "written on the day of the Thatcher funeral April 17 2013," discussed in the conclusion to this essay.

at the same time it affirms the song as a cultural artefact.[20] "Uptown Top Ranking" was a UK number one hit the week of February 4th 1978, displacing Wings's "Mull of Kintyre" after nine weeks at the top, and suggesting a national appetite for (aspects of) Caribbean culture.[21] The previous week, in an interview for Granada's *World in Action*, Margaret Thatcher had stated that "people are really rather afraid that this country might be rather swamped by people with a different culture."[22] A subsequent opinion poll for the *Daily Mail* gave the Tories an 11 point lead over Labour, with the interview cited in the press as a critical factor.

How does this kind of background information relate to *Organ Music*? Hilson's collage-like style has always been pluralistic in its choice of sources: as a poet and music enthusiast, he does not subscribe to traditional hierarchies of high and low culture (or indeed good and bad taste); rather, there is an omnivorousness characteristic of the charity shop LP collector and Spotify algorithm-follower.[23] The organ, though, brings baggage. In the foreword, Hilson contrasts the young John Lydon's terror at the sound of a church organ with his own school memories: "I recall sitting through Sunday services at school where the organ along with hymn-singing were all that made them bearable." Given their expense and unwieldiness, organs are, more than any other instrument, bound up with institutional—and specifically religious—power, albeit of an aesthetically intoxicating kind that made the Puritans suspicious.

In the post-Restoration world, organ music came to be associated with a comforting, lukewarm Anglicanism that permeated education as well as the Church. This informed the kind of High Toryism that was apt to conflate the Church of England with the nation itself, a sentiment found, for example, in T. S. Eliot's "Little Gidding" (1942):

A people without history
Is not redeemed from time, for history is a pattern
Of timeless moments. So, while the light fails
On a winter's afternoon, in a secluded chapel

---

[20] Stephen Thomson, "The Forlorn Ear of Jeff Hilson," in Robin Purves & Sam Ladkin, eds, Complicities: British Poetry 1945-2007 (Prague: Litteraria Pragensia, 2007), location 2662 [ebook edition].

[21] During the same period, Bob Marley's *Exodus* album spent 56 weeks in the UK album charts. For more on this cultural context, see Paul Gilroy, *There Ain't No Black in the Union Jack: The cultural politics of race and nation* (Abingdon: Routledge, 2002 [1987]), ch. 5.

[22] "TV Interview for Granada World in Action" [transcript] (Margaret Thatcher Foundation): https://www.margaretthatcher.org/document/103485

[23] See, for instance, "The Incredible Canterbury Poem" in *Latanoprost Variations* (Norwich: Boiler House Press, 2017).

History is now and England.[24]

This was a favourite passage of Roger Scruton and John Casey, co-founders of the Conservative Philosophy Group in 1974, and, perhaps not coincidentally, both amateur organists.[25] In a revealing segment on the "New Right" in a 1984 edition of the BBC's *Newsnight*, footage of the 1981 Toxteth riots was juxtaposed with a clip of Casey—a Cambridge English fellow apparently known for "thinking the unthinkable"—playing the organ.[26] One of Casey's "unthinkable" views, in a 1982 talk to the CPG, was that "the West Indian community, especially the Jamaicans, and above all those actually born in this country, is structurally likely to be at odds with English civilisation."[27] He recommended repatriation or retroactive revocation of their citizenship, presumably to avert such horrors as the prospect of Etonians "gather[ing] in a room to listen to Bob Marley records and smoke hashish cigarettes."[28]

One of the prompts for Casey's talk was the recently concluded Falklands War. In contrast to the Jamaicans, he regarded the Falklanders as "British by every conceivable test... by language, custom and race."[29] The Falklands conflict, as well as the nationalist rhetoric surrounding it, finds its way into *Organ Music*. "Side 7" reproduces *The Sun*'s "Gotcha" headline on the occasion of the sinking of the *General Belgrano*, and also includes a sardonic epigraph from the ship's captain, Hector Bonzo. As with Supertramp in 1979, this historical event is seen through the prism of another pop song, this time Marvin Gaye's "Sexual Healing." Somehow the organ has become a weapon:

---

[24] T. S. Eliot, *Collected Poems, 1909-1962* (London: Faber and Faber, 1963), p. 222. These lines do not explicitly mention an organ, but one can imagine one playing in the background.

[25] 1974 was of course the year of the double electoral failure of Edward Heath, himself a former Oxford organ scholar who had had an organ Partita written for him in 1971 by the composer Herbert Howells.

[26] *Newsnight*, 19 January 1984, accessed via BBC Archive Search. I no longer have access to the clip to double-check this, but I think Casey was playing a reed rather than pipe organ. In the same segment, historian David Irving attested that Casey was far to his right. Based at Caius College, Casey would have been a life-long colleague of J. H. Prynne, which presumably made for some interesting conversations.

[27] John Casey, "One Nation: The Politics of Race", *Salisbury Review*, no 1 (Autumn 1982). Available at: http://nationalconservatism.blogspot.com/2010/10/one-nation-politics-of-race.html

[28] This is a quote from a *Daily Mail* story from the same month as Casey's talk, cited in Paul Gilroy, op. cit., p. 126.

[29] Casey, op. cit.

really admiral bonzo is dead isnt it
funny in the beginning
I just wanted to show you all the organs in england
now I am killing you with the best one

The speaker garbles the details slightly (Bonzo was a captain rather than an admiral, and he didn't die in the conflict), and in trying to articulate them finds himself inadvertently caught up in colonial violence, and Gaye along with him ("for marvin gaye when in the spring air he used language / to kill the hong kong laundrymen"). This Falklands episode has already been anticipated in "Side 2":

I will never make it in the atlantic ocean
the invading english organ is too small
& without any pedals
I am standing on the bridge
of hms new british poetry
& sailing to america when I went down
without any medals
when I was admiral
I cant even read without launching a thousand poems

Some of these images have the flavour of surreal anxiety dreams: an organ becomes a warship, and the poetry "launch" takes on the menace of a torpedo. It is as if, despite his tactics of strategic bathos and diminution (the equation of Englishness with the "too small," with sinking), any investigation of English cultural history must leave the researcher splashed with the blood of naval warfare, in "this world[...] where the commanders of the / order of the british empire are always home."

The final poems of *Organ Music* were written after an interval of several years and cover two episodes of national disappointment for the metropolitan (graduate) left: the Brexit referendum and the Labour leadership of Jeremy Corbyn (or the media treatment of him, depending on one's sympathies). They bring the sequence to a close in an even greater mood of dejection and ennui than that with which it had begun.[30] One of the later "Interludes" refers to "the poems of this awful country," and the following one states "I'm sick of writing about the / men of the english school," though such sentiment could already be found in "Side 4"'s "o ladye I cannot stand it here / where I am a

[30] There is also a kind of postlude entitled "Side 10" ("A Bowie Book"), not discussed here as it is essentially a standalone visual collage.

racist."[31] "Side 8," written in a relentless stream of unpunctuated prose resembling in places a Stewart Lee comedy routine, turns to the enumeration of French and Belgian locations and composers, because "in england no one wants to know about the english organ english people dont even know if they want to leave the eu." The day of the referendum itself seems to inaugurate another Civil War: "on the twenty third of june everyone in england was broken in half vowing to thee o countryfile." The patriotic hymn "I vow to thee, my country"—composed by sometime organist Gustav Holst by recycling the "Jupiter" theme from his *Planets* suite—becomes a shorthand for mass delusion, in a portmanteau with the soporific ovine antics of the BBC's *Countryfile*. In the hymn what is vowed is "The love that asks no question," in other words an unthinking, deferential nationalism. The side ends with a list of the constituencies of MPs (all labelled "minister") who voted to leave the EU, interspersed with "hic finis" or "hic iacet," as if willing their imminent death and interment.

Like most "Remain" voters, Hilson appears to have experienced the Brexit referendum as a moderately traumatic event. Whereas the opening of *Organ Music* seemed to be looking for an alternative "English countenance" that could resist the cultural status quo through an engagement with occluded or "underground" culture (in this case early music and the history of the organ), by late 2016 such an option felt foreclosed, leaving instead the sensation of internal exile, comparable perhaps to the suddenly out-of-work organ builder Robert Dallam (mentioned in the foreword). "Side 9" returns to the minor South London rivers of "Side 1":

> AND again went down to the quaggy
> there I wept
> *six east anglian organs* vol one in one
> hand in the other
> a wreath I laid in the wrong place
> in this country

The tone here is funereal. The wreath-laying error is an allusion to one of the many perceived gaffes attributed to Jeremy Corbyn by the tabloid press. Throughout the book Hilson's "organist" persona displays elements of a Shakespearean fool, prone to pratfalls but evincing an ingenuous wisdom, and here he comes to merge with Corbyn as a well-meaning but hapless tragicomic figure ("because he has no rhythm like / me hes just a dying organ maker"). There are also, in this poem, explicit allusions to Eliot's *The Waste Land*, with the organist cast as the Fisher King: "I sat on the shore / with the english organ behind me."

---

[31] "Side 4" alludes to an incident in which a woman was filmed shouting racist abuse on a Croydon tram.

It is interesting that Hilson, a writer whose ostensibly "unpretentious," deflationary style seems to set itself against the tradition of Eliot (generally spurned in favour of Pound by the British Poetry Revival), should come at last to cite him, albeit via the urban anomie of *The Waste Land* rather than the High Anglicanism of the *Four Quartets*. Hilson's explanatory notes and multiple sets of epigraphs also give *The Waste Land* a run for its money, thereby inviting the close attention to his allusions that this essay has very partially attempted. How far is *Organ Music* drawn into the orbit of Eliot's cultural conservatism? To put it another way, can the organ itself—the church-based pipe organ, not Klaus Wunderlich's Hammond—be wrested from the grip of Anglican reactionaries? There is an argument to be made either way, but the organist-speaker of the poems often seems to find that the "tradition of all dead generations weighs like a nightmare on the brains of the living."[32] Early music is bound up with the patriarchal, religious world that produced it; although there are women who make an appearance in "Side 5" (and in the supplementary discography), their presence is peripheral to the main genealogy. In terms of audience, "getting" all of the musical and literary references would require the particularly niche mix of cultural capital that Hilson has himself accumulated; in practice, like most of his poetic colleagues, he writes for an audience with a high quotient of postgraduate degrees, though this is more a structural inevitability of the academic-literary milieu than a conscious intention. Such an audience may not quite correspond to Eliot's ideal of a "clerisy," but the older poet might have approved of its *de facto* exclusivity.[33]

What of England and its Crown in Parliament? "Side 6," written on the day of Thatcher's funeral, contains the line "we found out a head is forever & not just for turning left or right or for looking at france." This is in the context of the nursery rhyme "Oranges and Lemons," with its suspended executioner's axe. One of the epigraphs is from a speech to Parliament by King James I: "I am the Head, and it is my Body." Revolutionaries might hold out the hope of a permanently transformative decapitation, but the speakers of Hilson's line concede the impossibility of true regicide; the state is Hydra-headed—"knock knock whos there the head who the same head as before"—and the identity of "the People" cannot be neatly disentangled from the institutions of its rulers. This perspective is closer to the elite theory of

---

[32] Karl Marx, *The Eighteenth Brumaire of Louis Bonaparte* (1852): https://www.marxists.org/archive/marx/works/1852/18th-brumaire/ch01.htm

[33] See "Notes by T.S. Eliot: 'On the Place and Function of the Clerisy'" [1944], *Journal of Classical Sociology*, vol. 6, no. 2 (2006), pp. 156-162.

Gaetano Mosca than the class struggle of Marx.[34] The fact that the official name of the national entity incorporating England is still the United *Kingdom* leads us back to the same anachronistic conclusion: that ("o god") in some residual sense, in our big empty room where it is always 1979, where the mr men are everywhere partying like it's 1649, "we are all plantagenets."

---

[34] See Mosca, *The Ruling Class* [*Elementi di Scienza Politica*] (1896, expanded 1923).

Further Reading

Books of Poetry:

Organ Music. London/Santiago: Crater Press, 2020
Latanoprost Variations. Norwich: Boiler House Press, 2017
In The Assarts. London: Veer Books, 2010
Bird bird. Norwich: Landfill Press, 2009
Stretchers. Hastings: Reality Street, 2006

Volumes edited:

The Reality Street Book of Sonnets. Hastings: Reality Street, 2008

Chapbooks & Pamphlets:

A Barry Bendy Poem. Hunstanton: Oystercatcher Press, 2015
Bird Bird. Sheffield: West House Books, Gargoyle Editions, 2005
stretchers 13-33. London: Writers Forum, 2002
stretchers 1-12. London: Writers Forum, 2001
A Grasses Primer. London: Form Books, 2000
The 'A's. London: Canary Woof Press, 2000

Broadsheets/Poem Cards:

Untitled poem in *Ardent Calendar*. London: Crater Press, 2016 (Advent Calendar)
"Ryanairpithaplanium" (with Tim Atkins). London: Crater Press/Koshifuri Ices, 2014 (Folding Poem)
"A Ritual Poem Against the Sea." London: Crater Press, 2014 (Poster Poem)
From *Organ Music*. Mataró, Spain: Crater Press, 2012 (Broadsheet)
4 poems from *Tracey Traces*. London, Kater Murr's Press, Piraeus Series, 2002 (Folding Poem Card)
"...finally were false fruits." London: Kater Murr's Press, 1998 (Poem Card)
From Organ Music

Poems in Print & Online Anthologies:

3 poems from *Bird bird* ("Wren"," Swift", "Hawfinch") in *The Penguin Book of the Prose Poem*, ed. Jeremy Noel-Tod. London, Penguin, 2018
"A Final Poem With Full Stops" reprinted in *Wretched Strangers: Transnational Poetries*, ed. Agnes Lehoczsky & J.T. Welsch. Norwich: Boiler House Press, 2018
"Organ Music: Side 6" reprinted in *Other Room Anthology*. Manchester: The Other Room Press, 2018
"A Final Poem With Full Stops" reprinted in *Badge of Shame*, ed. Robert Hampson. *Purge 5*: A Strong & Stable Production, 2017
"Poem about Grounds" reprinted in *Boots: A Selection of Football Poetry. 1890-2017*, ed. Mark Pirie. Wellington NZ: Headworx, 2017
"Poem About Grounds" in *Kakania*, ed. S.J. Fowler. London: Austrian Cultural Forum, 2015
3 visual sonnets in *The Dark Would: An Anthology of Language Art*, ed. Philip Davenport. n.p.: Apple Pie Publishing, 2013
10 poems in "Contemporary British Poetry and North American Influences" Feature, ed. Amy De'Ath in *Jacket 2*: http://jacket2.org/feature/contemporary-english-poetry-and-north-american-influences
Poem in *Catechism: Poems for Pussy Riot*, ed. Mark Burnhope, Sarah Crewe & Sophie Mayer. London: English PEN, 2012
2 poems from "Bird bird" in *This Line's not for Turning: An Anthology of Contemporary British Prose Poetry* ed. Jane Monson. London: Cinnamon Press, 2011
6 poems from *In The Assarts* & poem from *Bird bird* in *Ars Poetica: Medzinárodny Festival Poezie*, ed. Martin Solotruk. Bratislava: Vydanie Prve, 2011
"Elecampane" and "Purslane" in *Herbarium*, ed. James Wilkes. London: Capsule Press, 2011
6 poems from *In The Assarts* in *The Other Room Anthology* 3. Manchester: The Other Room Press, 2011
Pilot special UK Poets edition, ed. Matt Chambers. SUNY Buffalo, New York, 2007
6 poems in *The Reality Street Book of Sonnets*, ed. Jeff Hilson. Hastings: Reality Street, 2008
Poem in *yt communications bulletin*, ed. Sean Bonney & Frances Kruk. London: yt communications, 2007
Selection of poems in *Openned Anthology*, ed. Alex Davies & Steve Willey. (http://www.openned.com/press/opennedcom/openned_anthology.php)
Poem in *The Poetry Buzz: A Bus Ride with and for Allen Fisher*, ed. Paige Mitchell, London, 2005

Poems in Books:

"En descendent a St Ouen, Rouen, on rencontre le jeu ondulant" in *The World Speaking Back to Denise Riley*. Norwich: Boiler House Press, 2018
"Play for Today" in Nigel Wood, ed. *Fugue and Subterfuge: A Festschrift for Alan Halsey*. 2018
"opus 105" & "opus 119" in *Twitters for a Lark: Poetry of the European Union of Imaginary Authors*, conducted and co-curated by Robert Sheppard. Bristol: Shearsman, 2017
"An Interlude for Peter Hughes" in *face down in the book of revelation: for Peter Hughes on his 60th birthday*. Hunstanton: Oystercatcher Press, 2016
"From the Almanack" in ed. Richard Parker, *Leg Avant: The New Poetry of Cricket*. London: Crater Press, 2016
"Five for Fay Jones" in *We Have a Jones for You*. Seattle: Golden Handcuffs Review Publications, 2016
"An Organ for Robert Sheppard" in ed. Scott Thurston, *An Educated Desire: Robert Sheppard at 60*. Newton-le-Willows: The Knives Forks and Spoons Press, 2015
Poem in ed. Scott Thurston, *Gathered Here Today: Celebrating Geraldine Monk at 60*. Newton-le-Willows: The Knives Forks and Spoons Press, 2012
Poem from "Organ Music" in *For Simon Howard, Vol. 2*. Devon: Arthur Shilling Press, 2012
Collaboration with Sean Bonney in *Maintenant: The Camarade Project*. New Mills, Derbys: Red Ceilings Press, 2011
"SLOTS" in *Eighteens*. Newton-le-Willows: The Knives Forks and Spoons Press, 2011
Collaboration with Audun Mortensen in ed. Alec Newman *Ny Poesi*. Newton-le-Willows: The Knives Fork and Spoons Press, 2010
Alphabet Poem in ed. Derek Beaulieu, *26 Alphabets (for Sol LeWitt)*. Calgary: No Press, 2009

Poems in Print & Online Magazines/Journals:

6 Aldigrams. *Erotoplasty* 7 (Summer 2020)
"Two interludes from *Organ Music*." *Erotoplasty* 4 (Summer 2019)
Organ Music – Side 8, *Tentacular* 3 (Summer 2019)
Organ Music – Side 9, *Datableed* 11, (February 2019)
"Browse" (with Nia Davies), *Poetry Wales*, Vol. 53 no. 3 (Spring 2018)
"Optotypical Poem including Art Garfunkel." *Tears in the Fence*. Vol. 64 (Autumn 2016)
"Fun." *Lighthouse* 13 (Autumn 2016)
"A Final Poem with Full Stops." *Datableed 5* (Summer 2016)
"Another Poem About Grounds." *para•text* 1 (Summer 2015)

"Legendy," with S.J. Fowler. *VLAK* 5 (2015)
3 poems from *Organ Music. Fence* 30 (Fall/Winter 2014)
"Two interludes from *Organ Music.*" *English* vol. 63 no. 243 (Winter 2014)
"A False Botanic-Forensic Poem for February." *Litmus: The Forensic Issue* (April 2014)
"The Wogan Poem." *Molly Bloom* 3, (2014)
"The Incredible Canterbury Poem." *Zone* 1 (2014)
Poem from *Organ Music. Summer Stock* 7: UK Poetry Dossier, ed. Elizabeth Guthrie (2014)
Poem from *Organ Music. Dusie* issue 16 (2014)
3 collaborative poems. *VLAK* 4 (2013)
3 poems from *Organ Music. Cambridge Literary Review* issue 7 (2013)
3 poems in *Quait: Dicotyledons*, Issue 1 (2013)
"Latanoprost Variations." *Junction Box* issue 4 (2013)
Poem from *Organ Music. Infinite Editions* (2013)
Poem from *Organ Music. Painted, Spoken* no. 24 (2013)
Poems from *Organ Music. VLAK* 3 (2012)
4 poems from *Organ Music. Open Letter* no. 8 (Spring 2012)
"Slates." *Freaklung/Odes* (June 2010)
3 poems from *In The Assarts. AND* no. 13 (April 2010)
Poem from *In The Assarts. Klatch* no. 3 (May 2010)
Poem from *In The Assarts. Cannibal Spices* (2010)
Selection of poems. *Argotist Online* (October 2009)
7 poems from *In The Assarts. Angel Exhaust* 20 (Spring 2009)
6 poems from *Bird bird. Fire* 31 (2009)
3 poems from *Bird bird. Desperate for Love* (March 2009)
6 poems from *Bird bird. PFS Post* (October 2008)
3 poems from *In The Assarts. Streetcake* (vol. 1, 2008)
8 poems from *In The Assarts. Veer Off* (2008)
5 poems from *In The Assarts. Veer Away* (2007)
22 poems from *In The Assarts. onedit* 10 (n.d.)
http://www.onedit.net/issue10.html
5 poems from *Bird bird. onedit* 4 (n.d.)
http://www.onedit.net/issue4/issue4.html
3 poems from *Bird bird. Poetry Salzburg Review* no. 12 (Autumn 2007)
5 poems from *Bird bird. Skald* 24 (2007),
3 poems from *stretchers. The Radiator* 3 (November 2005)
2 poems from *stretchers. Quid* 14 (October 2004)
Poem from *stretchers. Painted, spoken* no. 6 (2003)
5 poems from *stretchers. Great Works* (n.d.)
http://www.greatworks.org.uk/poems/5s1.html
"name" & "recipal." *Poetry Salzburg Review* no. 2 (Winter 2001/2)

Critical Writings

Chapters in Books:

"Homophonic Translation: Sense and Sound", in Helen Minors (ed), *Music, Text and Translation*. London: Continuum Books, 2012. 95-106.
"The Contemporary Sonnet: A Trialogue" (with Paul Muldoon & Meg Butler) in eds A.D. Cousins & Peter Howarth *The Cambridge Companion to the Sonnet*. Cambridge: Cambridge University Press, 2011. 6-24
"Introduction" to ed. Jeff Hilson, *The Reality Street Book of Sonnets*. Hastings: Reality Street, 2008. 8-18

Journal Articles:

"The God Awful Small Affair of the Invisible Organist: David Bowie Translated." Forthcoming in special "Expanded Translation" issue of *English* (Autumn 2020).
"Facing Out: Ray Johnson, Gertrude Stein & Black Mountain College." *Junction Box* 11, Black Mountain Special Edition (2018)
"'What are we not headed for?' The Constellatory Poetics of Bill Griffiths' 'Binaries: not Sonnets'" *Journal of Innovative British and Irish Poetry* (Winter 2014). 65-83.
"From A-Z and Bach Again: Getting a Handel on Louis Zukofsky's *'A'-24,"* *Golden Handcuffs Review* 14 (Winter-Spring 2011): 260-269
"'It Makes an Indebtedness': Louis Zukofsky Translating Catullus" in *interstice* no. 3 (Autumn 1999)
"On 'Latanoprost Variations'" in *Junction Box* issue 4 http://lyndondavies.co.uk/w/wp-content/uploads/2013/03/On-Latanoprost-Variations.pdf
"On 'Junctions'" in "Reading Mendoza, or, Linus Slug" *Openned Zine*, issue 2 (June 2010)
Review of Sean Bonney's *Blade Pitch Control Unit*, Canary Woof blog, (March 2010) http://canarywoof.blogspot.com/2010/03/blade-pitch-control-unit-old-review.html
"Why I Wrote Stretchers" in *The Radiator* 3, ed. Scott Thurston (November 2005)

Work on Hilson

Robert Sheppard, "Convention and Constraint: Form in the Innovative Sonnet Sequence" in *The Meaning of Form in Contemporary Innovative Poetry*. Liverpool: Liverpool University Press, 2016.

Zoë Skoulding & Carole Birkan-Berz, "Translating Sound and Resonance in Experimental Poetry from the UK: A Cross-Channel Perspective," *Palimpsestes* 28 (2015)
Andrew Duncan, "Pale & Crimson: Acid Folk" in *A Poetry Boom: 1990-2010*. Bristol: Shearsman Books, 2015. 294-310.
Mark Waldron, "Poets Reading" in *The Poetry Review*, vol. 105 no. 3 (Autumn 2015). 36-40.
Lacy Rumsey, "The Atypicality of Jeff Hilson: Metrical Language and Modernist Pleasure" in eds. Abigail Lang & David Nowell Smith, *Modernist Legacies: Trends and Faultlines in British Poetry Today*. New York: Palgrave Macmillan, 2015. 109-128.
Bibliographical/Biographical entry in ed. Ian Hamilton & Jeremy Noel-Tod, *The Oxford Companion to Modern Poetry in English*, 2nd Edition, Oxford: OUP, 2013. 266.
Robert Sheppard, "The Innovative Sonnet Sequence: Kick him in the Assarts": http://robertsheppard.blogspot.co.uk/2011/07/innovative-sonnet-sequence-nine-of-14.html
Peter Jaeger, "'I am Something Nonne:' Jeff Hilson's Nature Poetry" in *Journal of Irish and British Innovative Poetry*, vol. 2 no. 2 (September 2010). 125-136.
Peter Barry, "Contemporary British Modernists" in ed. Peter Middleton and Nicky Marsh *Teaching Modernist Poetry*. New York: Palgrave Macmillan, 2010. 94-115.
Stephen Thomson, "The Forlorn Ear of Jeff Hilson" in *Complicities: British Poetry 1945- 2007*. Prague: Litteraria Pragensia, 2007. 153-167.

Selected Reviews

The Reality Street Book of Sonnets: Ron Silliman: http://ronsilliman.blogspot.com/ Val Nolan: http://www.pnreview.co.uk/cgi-bin/scribe?item_id=4305 Gilbert Adair: *Journal of Irish and British Innovative Poetry*, vol. 2 no. 2 (September 2010) John Latta: http://isola-di-rifiuti.blogspot.co.uk/2009/02/jeff-hilsons-reality-street-book-of.html Geraldine Monk: http://versepalace.wordpress.com/2010/02/15/geraldine-monk-the-madness-of-sonnets/ *Poetry Wales*, Vol. 44 no. 4 (Spring 2009)

In The Assarts: Jeremy Noel-Tod: *The Times Literary Supplement*, December 01, (2010) S. J. Fowler: http://www.3ammagazine.com/3am/a-reluctant-bulldozer/ Richard Price: *Painted, spoken* no. 24 (2011) Steven Waling: http://www.handandstar.co.uk/?p=1077 Robin Purves, *Hix Eros* 3, 2013:

https://www.dropbox.com/s/2i2e7nsmb3tmw5w/HIX%20EROS%203.pdf?dl=0

Contributor Biographies

Tim Atkins has taught at the Jack Kerouac School of Disembodied Poetics at Naropa University & been a member of Carla Harryman's Poets Theatre in San Francisco. He's been published by The Figures, Leslie Scalapino's O Books, Book Thug, Faber, & many others. *Petrarch Collected Atkins*—published by Crater Press—was a TLS book of the year for 2014. Recent publications include a piece in *The Penguin Book of the Prose Poem*, a photobook called *Deep Osaka*, & *A Girl Is A Machine Made Of Words*—a collaboration (published by Canary Woof) with his daughter, Yuki.

cris cheek is a writer, sound composer and photographer who worked alongside Bob Cobbing and Bill Griffiths with the Consortium of London Presses in the mid 1970s to run a thriving open access print shop for *little press* poets. In 1981 he co-founded a collective movement-based performance resource in the east end of London at Chisenhale Dance Space, working with choreographers, musicians and performance artists to make collaborations based in embodied movement. cris taught Performance Writing at Dartington College of Arts (1995-2002), played music with Sianed Jones and Philip Jeck as *Slant*, collaborated on site-responsive works about value and recycling with Kirsten Lavers as *Things Not Worth Keeping* and has been a professor at Miami University in Ohio since 2005, currently living in Cincinnati and London. Most recent publications are *pickles & jams* (BlazeVOX Books, 2017) *fukc all the king's men: the tower and a few beasts living in its rubble* (xerolage, 2018) and *Out cold in the library 1* (Dusie, 2019).

Adrian Clarke co-edited the wildly irregular *AND* magazine with Bob Cobbing from 1994 and *Floating Capital: new poets from London* with Robert Sheppard. Collections include *Possession* (Veer, 2008), *Eurochants* (Shearsman, 2010) and *Austerity Measures* (Contraband, 2019). He is a member of the Veer editorial collective.

Iris Colomb is an artist, poet, curator, editor, and translator based in London. Her practice merges poetry and other art forms to explore relationships between visual and spoken forms of text through projects often involving performance, poetic book-objects, and experimental translation.

Ken Edwards ran Reality Street between 1993-2016. The press is still in existence but will publish no new titles. His *Collected Poems* is expected next year, and his latest books are *Wild Metrics*, a memoir of the 1970s, and the novel *The Grey Area*—both published by Grand Iota, which he co-runs with Brian Marley. He is working on his bass guitar technique in St Leonards on Sea, where he is one-third of the band Afrit Nebula.

Amy Evans Bauer's *and umbels* (Jonathan Williams Chapbooks prize, 2020) and *PASS PORT* (Shearsman, 2018) form the transcript of her at-sea, cross-border installation *SOUND((ING))S*. Her poetry features in *Chicago Review* and *Dear World and Everyone In It* (Bloodaxe, 2013), and elsewhere. She co-organises the Contemporary Innovative Poetry Research Seminar at the University of London Institute of English Studies.

Gareth Farmer: Cymraeg yw Gareth, but he was born in Bristol, and has been confusedly intersectional and inter-textual ever since. Gareth has been punishing texts against their tendency towards logical coherence since he was out of short trousers. State-School educated, he never wore short trousers, only polyester, wipe-to-clean leggings hand-siblinged-down from his short-legged sisters. Gareth now finds himself collaboratively threshing texts in classroom settings and offering flayed-text lettings of academic and creative work to various outlets. Search-engine, 'Gareth Farmer' for more.

Allen Fisher publications *No Longer Alone* (poetry with photographs by Paige Mitchell 2019), *Imperfect Fit* (University of Alabama 2016), *Gravity as a Consequence of Shape* (1983-2007) and *Place* (1971-1981) from Reality Street, the full *Black Pond*, paintings and poetry now scheduled for October 2020. www.allenfisher.co.uk

Ulli Freer is based in London & jamming. Recent poetry has been published by *Blackbox Manifold, Datableed, Erotoplasty* pt./1 issue7, 2020.

Chris Gutkind is lucky to have been well exposed to Jeff's work at many readings that ended in pub navigations. Over the next year some poems from *Digits After Orph* will be in mags and a book after that. Previously was *Inside to Outside, Options* (with Trevor Simmons) and *What Happened*. Montreal. London. Librarian.

Khaled Hakim was performing and writing in the 80s and 90s before disappearing. Since returning to writing, he has published *Letters from the Takeaway* (Shearsman 2019), *The Book of Naseeb* (Penned in the Margins 2020), and *The Routines: 1983-2000* (Contraband Books 2020).

Robert Hampson is emeritus professor at Royal Holloway and Research Fellow at the Institute of English Studies, University of London. His most recent publications include co-editing *The Allen Fisher*

Companion (with cris cheek) and *Clasp: late modernist poetry in London in the 1970s* (with Ken Edwards).

Colin Herd is a poet and Lecturer at University of Glasgow. His books include *Too Ok* (BlazeVOX, 2011), *Glovebox* (Knives, Forks and Spoons, 2013), *Oberwilding* - with SJ Fowler (Austrian Cultural Forum, 2015), *Click and Collect* (Boiler House Press, 2017) and *You Name It* (Dostoyevsky Wannabe, 2019) www.colinherd.com

Rob Holloway is a London-based poet and teacher. His first book *Permit* was published by the US-based poetry collective Subpress in 2009. His next book *Flesh Rays / Daytrain* is newly out from if p then q. A video readings project linked to the book will be published online shortly.

Peter Jaeger is a Canadian writer based in London, England. He is the author of twelve books, including works of poetry and hybrid creative-critical research. Publications include the artist book *The Shadow Line*(2016) and a process-based text on walking and pilgrimage entitled *Midamble* (2018). Jaeger is Professor of Poetics at the University of Roehampton.

Tom Jenks is a poet and editor of zimZalla, a small press specialising in literary objects. His books include *Spruce* (Blart Books, 2015),*Sublunar* (Oystercatcher, 2016) and *A Long and Hard Night Troubled by Visions* (if p then q, 2018).

Antony John's work has appeared in magazines, pamphlets and anthologies, including *Erotoplasty, Junction Box, Leg Avant* (Crater), *Jawjaw* (Gang Press) and *Antologia Bilingue Po-Ex* (G0 Ediciones, Chile). His poems have been published in two collections: *KENYA* followed his first book *now than it used to be, but in the past* (both Veer).

Mark Francis Johnson is one third of Hiding Press, a small publishing concern focused on experimental poetry. His most recent publications include *Sham Refugia* (Hiding Press, 2020), *How to Flit* (Roof Books, 2018) and *Can of Human Heat* (Golias Books, 2017). An antiquarian bookseller, he operates Hiding Place, a small shop in Philadelphia, where he lives with his wife and three cats.

Doug Jones: While doing an MPhil on Bill Griffiths Doug fell in with Bob Cobbing's Writers Forum group. There he met the wise Jeff. Doug worked as a nurse in east London for many years and then as a doctor in Norfolk. He is currently a GP in Yarmouth. He has published three books with Veer. His work has also appeared in various other places.

Daniel Kane is professor in American literature at Uppsala University in Sweden. His publications include *Do You Have a Band?: Poetry and Punk Rock in New York City* and essays on poets including John Ashbery, Sophie Robinson, and Harold Norse.

Robert Kiely is the author of *simmering of a declarative void* (2020) and *Incomparable Poetry, an Essay on the Financial Crisis of 2007-2008 and Irish Literature* (2020).

Colin Leemarshall is behind past and future iterations of Erotoplasty. *Nidors* and *Nidors (2)* are available from Crater Press (a planned third installment has as yet refused to dehisce). *Total Spiritual Refection* is ongoing.

Ágnes Lehóczky's poetry collections published in the UK are *Budapest to Babel* (Egg Box Publishing, 2008), *Rememberer* (Egg Box Publishing, 2012), *Carillonneur* (Shearsman Books, 2014) and *Swimming Pool* (Shearsman, 2017). She is the author of the academic monograph on the poetry of Ágnes Nemes Nagy *Poetry, the Geometry of Living Substance* (2011). She was winner of the Jane Martin Prize for Poetry at Girton College, Cambridge, in 2011. Her pamphlet *Pool Epitaphs and Other Love Letters* was published by Boiler House in May 2017. She co-edited major international anthologies: the *Sheffield Anthology; Poems from the City Imagined* (Smith / Doorstop, 2012) with Adam Piette and recently *The World Speaking Back to Denise Riley* (Boiler House, 2017) and *Wretched Strangers* (Boiler House, 2018). She is Senior Lecturer and Director of the Centre for Poetry and Poetics at the University of Sheffield.

Jo Lindsay Walton runs the poetry and games press Sad Press with Samantha Walton, and edits Vector for the British Science Fiction Association. He is on Twitter at @jolwalton.

Fabian Macpherson was at one time a student of English political poetry. Latterly he has worked as an archivist at the British Film Institute.

Matt Martin is Stuart Hall Research Scholar at Birkbeck, University of London. His poetry collections include *full spectrum apotheosis* (Contraband Books, 2013) and *the dotted line* (Gang Press, 2019), while his visual poems have featured in exhibitions at London venues like the Southbank Centre and the Poetry Society. He maintains the event listings page *Innovative Poetry Readings in London*: http://www.bbk.ac.uk/cprc/readings/.

Aodán McCardle's current practice is improvised performance/writing/drawing. Co-editor at Veer Books his PhD is on 'Action as Articulation of the Contemporary Poem' though physicality and doubt are the site of meaning and the stance respectively where the action operates. He has two books, *Shuddered* and *ISing* from VEER and online chapbook *LlIOoVvee*, Smithereens Press.

Anthony Mellors is a member of the multimedia collective Ghost Jam. Poetry books include *The Lewknor Turn* (Shearsman, 2013) and *Confessional Sonnets* (Aquifer, 2016). He has recently completed a poetic / scholarly fantasia on Schubert's song cycle *Winterreise*, with photogravures by David Rees.

Montenegro Fisher are Luna Montenegro and Adrian Fisher, artists, poets and film-makers based in London exploring ideas of transformation and collaboration. They make visual & sonic arts, performance, film, books and curatorial projects, experimenting at the intersections between the poetic and the politic. mmmmm.org.uk

Stephen Mooney is a Senior Lecturer in Creative Writing and poetry coordinator at the University of Surrey. Amongst other things he co-runs the small poetry press, Veer Books. His poetry collections are *DCLP, Shuddered, The Cursory Epic, 663 Reasons Why, Ratzinger Solo*. He has an abnormal interest in poetry and games ...

Ghazal Mosadeq is a poet and translator. She is the founder of Pamenar Press, an independent cross-cultural, multi-lingual publisher based in the UK, Canada and Iran. Her writings have appeared at *Words Without Borders, Poetry Wales*, Boiler House Press, *Erotoplasty*, Hesterglock Press, Plumwood Mountain, Gorse and Oversound. She has published three poetry collections, *Dar Jame Ma* (2010), *Biographies* (2015) and *Supernatural Remedies for Fatal Seasickness*, highly indivisible but nevertheless in nineteen sections (2018).

Richard Owens is the author of several volumes of poetry, most of which are collected in *Poems* (BlazeVOX 2019). His essays, which have likewise appeared variously in journals, are collected in the volume *Sauvage: Essays on Anglophone Poetry* (BlazeVOX 2019). Presently he lives with his family in the southern reaches of Maine, where he works odd jobs and forages in the woods

Richard Parker is a lecturer at the Pontificia Universidad Católica de Chile. His works include *The Traveller and the Defence of Heaven, RTA Parker's 99 Sonnets About Evil* and *...from The Mountains of California*. He is editor and printer at the Crater Press.

Peter Philpott: Born 1949, Martock, Somerset, and lived in Somerset until attending University of Keele. Since then has lived in Bishops Stortford, Hertfordshire, retiring from teaching (mainly in Further Education Colleges) more than ten years ago. He ran Great Works Press and magazine in the 1970-early 80s, the now only occasionally active Great Works and modernpoetry.org.uk websites from 2000. Main influences, apart from whatever whenever, mid & late 20C American avant-gardes, was socialised into poetry through Cambridge School c 1970+; now attempting to rescue Writers Forum Workshop – New Series. Most recent books: *Ianthe Poems* (Shearsman 2015), *Wound Scar Memories* (Great Works Editions 2017), *Telling the Beads* (Great Works Editions 2020).

Frances Presley's publications include *Paravane* (Salt, 2004); *Myne* (Shearsman, 2006); *Lines of Sight* (2009); *An Alphabet for Alina* with artist Peterjon Skelt (Five Seasons, 2012); *Halse for Hazel* (Shearsman, 2014), and *Sallow* (Leafe, 2016) with artist Irma Irsara, which received an Arts Council award; and, in 2019, *Ada Unseen* (Shearsman) on Ada Lovelace, mathematician and computer visionary. Her work is in the anthologies *Infinite Difference* (2010), *Ground Aslant: radical landscape poetry* (2011), *Out of Everywhere2* (2015) and *Fractured Ecologies* (2020).

Jèssica Pujol Duran is a poet, translator and researcher, currently working at the University of Santiago de Chile. She has three chapbooks in English, *Now Worry* (Department, 2012), *Every Bit of Light* (Oystercatcher Press, 2012) and *mare* (Carnaval Press, 2019); two books in Catalan published by El pont del petroli, *El país pintat* (2015) and *ninó*, (2019) and one in Spanish, *Entrar es tan difícil salir* (Veer Books, 2016), with translations by William Rowe. She edits the magazine *Alba Londres* (albalondres.com).

William Rowe's *Collected Poems* were published by Crater Press in 2016. *Poetry in Times of Resurgent Fascism* is forthcoming from Critical Veer.

Gavin Selerie was born in London, where he still lives. Books include *Azimuth* (1984), *Roxy* (1996), *Le Fanu's Ghost* (2006) and *Hariot Double* (2016)—all long sequences with linked units. *Music's Duel: New and Selected Poems 1972-2008* was published in 2009 and *Collected Sonnets* in 2019 (both from Shearsman). These texts often have a concrete aspect, as discussed in the essay 'Ekphrasis and Beyond: Visual Art in Poetry' (*Junction Box*). Selerie is known particularly for poems about landscape and romantic love, utilizing traditional and experimental form. A book length interview, *Into the Labyrinth*, is available online (Argotist Ebooks).

Jonathan Skinner was not raised in a box: his passions include trees, hills, sunbeams, and spicy desert cuisines. A former synchronized swimming champion, Skinner is best known as founding editor of *Fecopoetics*. His poetry collections include *Apolitical Cactus Poems*, and *Birds I Missed*. Author of the well-known manual *Septic Tank Practices*, Skinner currently is compiling an annotated edition (compleat and unexpurgated) of Jonathan Swift's scatological poetry. For his sins, he was sent to Coventry, where he teaches aspiring poets to swim.

Zoë Skoulding's latest collection is A *Revolutionary Calendar* (Shearsman, 2020). Her monograph *Poetry & Listening: The Noise of Lyric* (Liverpool University Press, 2020) includes discussion of Hilson's work. She is Professor of Poetry and Creative Writing at Bangor University.

Marcus Slease was born in Portadown, N. Ireland. Recent books include *Play Yr Kardz Right* (Dostoyevsky Wannabe, 2017) and *The Green Monk* (Boiler House, 2018). He lives in Casteldefells, Catalunya.

Simon Smith is author of six volumes of poetry and a selected poems. His translation of Catullus was published in 2018 by Carcanet. A new book of poetry will appear at the end of 2021 from Parlor Press, called *Last Morning*, and he recently took part in an online project through early lockdown hosted by the Muscaliet Press, "The Quarantine Notebooks."

Carlos Soto-Román is a poet and translator. Author of *11* (Municipal Poetry Prize, Santiago 2018) he has published *Chile Project: [Re-Classified]* (Gauss PDF, 2013), *Bluff* (Commune Editions, 2018), *Common Sense* (Make Now Books, 2019), and *Nature of Objects* (Pamenar Press, 2019) among others. He is also the author of the first translation of Charles Reznikoff's *Holocaust* into Spanish. He lives and works in Santiago, Chile.

Andrew Spragg was born in London and lives there. He has written critical pieces for *Bonafide*, *Hix Eros*, *The Quietus*, *Poetry London* and *PN Review*. Recent poetry books include *Now Too How Soon* (Contraband Books, 2017) and *Dogtown* (Litmus, 2018) with the artist Beth Hopkins.

Virna Teixeira was born in Fortaleza, Brazil. She is a poet and translator. Her poetry books and poetry pamphlets were published in Brazil, Lisbon, Mexico, Argentina and UK. She runs a small press, Carnaval Press, and edits the online magazine Theodora (www.theodorazine.com), She lives in London where works as a doctor for the NHS.

Philip Terry was born in Belfast, and is a poet, translator, and a writer of fiction. He has translated the work of Georges Perec and Raymond Queneau, and is the author of the novel *tapestry*, shortlisted for the Goldsmiths Prize. His poetry volumes include *Oulipoems*, *Shakespeare's Sonnets*, *Dante's Inferno*, and *Dictator*, a version of the *Epic of Gilgamesh* in Globish. He is currently translating Ice Age signs from the caves at Lascaux. *The Penguin Book of Oulipo,* which he edited, appeared in 2019.

Scott Thurston is a poet, mover and educator. His latest book *Phrases towards a Kinepoetics* is due from Contraband in 2020. Scott is founding co-editor of the *Journal of British and Irish Innovative Poetry* and Reader in English and Creative Writing at the University of Salford where he has taught since 2004. He is currently writing a monograph on the relationship between dance and poetry.

L - #0439 - 260121 - C0 - 229/152/13 - PB - DID3011905